Preaching the Gospel of Luke

Preaching the Gospel of Luke

Proclaiming God's Royal Rule

Keith F. Nickle

Westminster John Knox Press
Louisville, Kentucky

Book design by Sharon Adams
Cover design by Kevin Darst & Jennifer K. Cox

First edition
Published by Westminster John Knox Press
Louisville, Kentucky

This book is printed on acid-free paper that meets the American National Standards Institute Z39.48 standard. ♾

PRINTED IN THE UNITED STATES OF AMERICA
00 01 02 03 04 05 06 07 08 09 — 10 9 8 7 6 5 4 3 2 1

Library of Congress Cataloging-in-Publication Data

Nickle, Keith F., 1933–
    Preaching the Gospel of Luke : proclaiming God's royal rule / Keith F. Nickle.
        p. cm.
    Includes bibliographical references.
    ISBN 0-664-22239-0 (alk. paper)
    1. Bible. N.T. Luke—Homiletical use.   2. Bible. N.T. Luke— Commentaries.   I. Title.

BS2595.5 .N53 2000
226.4′06—dc21
                                                                99-053854

*To all the saints
in congregation, college, and community
at Mossy Creek (Jefferson City), Tennessee*

CONTENTS

Introduction

As far as we can tell from the literature, Luke was the most prolific writer in the New Testament church. Taking both volumes of his work into consideration, the Gospel and the Acts of the Apostles, the Third Evangelist is responsible for the largest portion of the literature of the New Testament of any of its authors—more even than the Apostle Paul. His Gospel is the longest of the four Gospels in the Christian Bible.

Who, precisely, was the Third Evangelist? The answer is uncertain. Each of the two volumes he wrote is anonymous. The association of the name "Luke" with the Third Gospel can be established no earlier than toward the end of the second century, C.E., about one hundred years after its composition. Later Christians were surely mistaken when they equated the Third Evangelist with the physician who was Paul's companion and "fellow-worker" during segments of his missionary travels (Philem. 24; cf. also Col. 4:14; 2 Tim. 4:11). There simply are too many disparities between Acts' observations about Paul and information Paul provides about himself for that identification to remain credible.

However, for the sake of convenience, I will refer to the author as "Luke" throughout. As he indicated in the initial statement to his Gospel (Luke 1:1–3), Luke knew himself to belong to the third stage of transmission, at the earliest, of those handing on Christian traditions about Jesus and the early church. Luke 21:20–24 (cf. also 13:34–35; 19:41–44) leads us to believe that the author had specific information about the Roman siege of Jerusalem and the destruction of its Temple in 70 C.E., so the Gospel had to have been written after that event. Most scholars date its composition somewhere around the early to middle eighties.

If we cannot identify Luke by his association with Paul, do we have other clues in his writings about his identity? The results are disappointing. We do not have enough evidence to decide whether he was a Jewish Christian or a Gentile Christian. On the one hand, Luke was thoroughly

1

immersed in the Jewish scriptures and believed that Jesus' life, teachings, and fate culminated, fulfilled, and confirmed Jewish religious aspirations concerning the Messiah of God. On the other hand, it seems clear that he had little interest in the religious language of Judaism and in technical aspects of its contemporary cultic practice, nor did he have accurate information about the physical geography of Palestine. Perhaps he was a Gentile who had become a proselyte convert to Judaism before he became a Christian. Perhaps he was a highly educated Hellenistic Jewish Christian. We simply cannot say.

Nor are we any better informed when we try to describe Luke's primary audience(s). The "Theophilus" that Luke addressed at the start of both volumes (Luke 1:3; Acts 1:1) is shadowy and ambiguous. Perhaps "Theophilus" was a well-born Roman patrician who had recently responded positively to the proclamation of the Easter message and, as a new convert, needed confirming in the faith, but who also offered the potential for considerably improving the general situation of the Christian community in the area. Maybe "Theophilus" was a regional ruler appointed by Imperial Rome to govern, who exercised considerable political authority. Or, "Theophilus" may be a symbol standing for Roman authority and control overall which Luke was anxious to persuade was not at all the focus of Christian insurrectionist plots when Christians spoke openly and persuasively about obedience to the royal rule of God.

Moreover, it is not possible to locate geographically Luke's primary audience, or to determine if the Evangelist was living and worshiping together with them as he wrote. Luke expected the recipients of his two-volume project to listen attentively and discriminately, and to follow themes, make connections, and perceive enlightening cross-references all the way through that extended work — a demand that we who are visually oriented and who have not been raised in an oral culture must find equally daunting, even unimaginable.

The best we can do, then, is to draft a general, theoretical characterization of those early Christians whom he addressed. They must have been a religious community with, already, a rich local heritage and a strong sense of identity as the community of faith. They surely saw themselves as called by God to announce through worship, teaching, and living example the renewing power of the royal rule of God revealed in Jesus, the Christ, and reiterated in their life together when they were at their Christian best. This is not at all unlike the Spirit-inspired self-identity many Christian congregations strive today to incarnate in their corporate life together under the direction of Jesus, the Lord of the church.

Our usual view of Luke as the reverent chronicler of the ministry of

Jesus and of the emerging church gets sorely taxed from time to time by those who delight in and flaunt factual inaccuracies discovered in his text from time to time. "Well," they condescendingly assure us, "first-century historians were not all that interested in factual accuracy anyway." First-century historians *were* interested in recording information accurately, but they were often impeded in that effort because of undependable resources and lack of access to research facilities.

However, like present-day historians, first-century historians understood that their work was not done well until they had organized available information into a comprehensible arrangement and also indicated the meaning undergirding those events.

Luke is a theological historian. His final interest in the Jesus narrative is not limited to reporting with accuracy details about what really happened during the public ministry of Jesus. Luke is far more interested, and wants us to be, too, in what the Jesus narrative discloses about the plans and purposes of God. He is convinced that it is through human events and affairs that God accomplishes God's will to judge and to save. In the final analysis, Luke understood the truth claims of his narrative to be ratified by the extent to which he perceived the career of Jesus to fulfill and confirm the will of God, already disclosed in the Jewish scriptures.

Luke was a consummate literary artist. His narrative style compares very favorably with each of the other Gospel writers. One observes in awe the artful skill with which he wove the infancy narratives about John the Baptist and Jesus in literary counterpoint (chapters 1–2). He sometimes adopted a manner of expression that reflected the tone of "Bible language." (One campus where I taught had a sign that said, "Thou shalt not park here." That is a style of expression which hopes to borrow authority from the reverence in which people hold scripture. I regret to report that it did not work very well. Another sign that had the silhouette of a car being hauled by a tow truck was much more effective.) The moving intimacy in the telling of some of the stories—for instance the Mary and Martha episode (10:38–42), or the story of the sinful woman (7:36–50)— is striking. Luke's literary style is the most sophisticated of them all.

Luke did not begin to write just off the top of his head. He had sources that supplied him with stories about Jesus. He could pick and rearrange those stories that promised to serve his literary and theological goals. Down through the years, scholars have debated the list of sources Luke used and in what form he had access to them.

I am persuaded that the Third Evangelist used an early version of the Gospel of Mark as one source for his portrait of Jesus. I think it likely that Luke's own Christian community knew Mark's Gospel well and had both benefited from it and, at times, been confused by it. When Luke revised and expanded Mark's earlier narrative account of the public ministry and the passion of Jesus, he fully intended for his revision to supplant Mark's version as a resource for his church's evangelizing, teaching, preaching, and worship.

I also concur with those Lukan scholars who maintain that Luke shared with the First Evangelist, Matthew, another written source we have come to call "Q," which contained additional stories about Jesus and his teachings that Mark had not included in his Gospel. Luke also drew on other Jesus stories circulating around in early Christianity, some of which may have been in written form, though certainly he derived others from oral traditions being passed on from one Christian to another. My discussion of Luke's narrative in this book presumes this understanding of the sources he used, although I devote little space to making actual comparisons.

Contrasting Luke's Gospel with Mark's narration discloses that Luke constructed his Gospel by using material from his various sources in large segments, which he then joined together. So, his Gospel begins with a collection of stories about the conception and birth of John the Baptist and Jesus which came from his special source. (Luke is the only one of the four Gospels in the New Testament that contains precisely those stories.) To these stories Luke then joined a block of material from Mark, and so on.

Luke also extended the end of Mark's Gospel by including several post-resurrection appearance stories as well as a charge and commissioning of the disciples by Jesus, which Mark did not have. (Of course, the most extensive lengthening he made to Mark's story was by continuing the narrative into a second volume, Acts, which related stories out of the early decades in the life of the post-Easter church.)

The greatest internal expansion Luke imposed on Mark's narrative was the extensive enlargement of Mark's "travel narrative," which described the course of Jesus' journey from Galilee to Jerusalem. Whereas Mark portrayed Jesus as making his way from the region where he accomplished the early portion of his ministry to Jerusalem where he was to be executed in about one and a half chapters (Mark 10:1–11:10), Luke stretched that trip out to extend over almost *ten* chapters (Luke 9:51–19:40). That provided Luke with a great deal of additional space within which he could integrate additional stories not found in Mark into his narrative account. The list of Luke's special stories includes:

three additional healing miracle stories
> Healing of the sick woman (13:10–17)
> Healing of the man with dropsy (14:1–6)
> Healing of the ten lepers (17:11–19)

thirteen additional parables
> The good Samaritan (10:29–37)
> The friend at midnight (11:5–8)
> The rich fool (12:13–21)
> The barren fig tree (13:6–9)
> On building a tower (14:28–30)
> On going to war (14:31–32)
> The lost coin (15:8–10)
> The prodigal son (15:11–32)
> The unjust steward (16:1–12)
> The rich man and Lazarus (16:19–31)
> The servant's duties (17:7–10)
> The unjust judge (18:1–8)
> The Pharisee and the publican (18:9–14)

This list of additional stories—to which we could add the narrative accounts of the Samaritan villages rejecting Jesus (9:51–56) and the Zacchaeus story (19:1–10)—make us realize how much more abundant our fund of stories about Jesus is because of Luke's literary efforts, and how impoverished the church's teaching and preaching would have been down through the centuries without them.

A particularly prominent emphasis in Luke's narrative is his conviction that God feels strong compassion for the poor. Jesus is God's agent for forgiveness to all kinds of unlikely people, including the economically oppressed, the "sinners," and others who have been excluded from participation in the community of the people of God by the religiously arrogant. He brokers belonging to the household of God over which God rules. God expects those in the community of the Easter faith also to reflect and embody that concern.

Other special emphases in the Third Gospel that have been widely and appreciatively recognized include: sympathetic interest in the role of the women associated with Jesus' ministry, the importance of prayer both for Jesus and for his disciples, the need for prudent and compassionate use of material goods in the service of God, a more sustained focus on Jesus' ministry in Judea, and the prominent role of Samaritan motifs. The reader will want to be alert to these themes when reading Luke's Gospel.

Above all, the activity of the Spirit of God in the ministry of Jesus, and in the ministry of the disciples, was crucial for Luke's understanding of who we are and what we are to be about in this interim before the end of time. Luke considered that the interval between the resurrection/ascension of Jesus and his return at the end of the ages was the unique time of the church to be blessed with a crucial role in the advancement of God's saving purposes throughout the inhabited world. The church's empowering by the Spirit enables it to withstand persecution and to persevere in the faithful prosecution of its dominically defined mission.

Finally, I would like to make a practical suggestion concerning the appropriate use of this book. It stands, at best, third in line. Above all, read Luke's Gospel. Then turn to the more detailed analytical commentaries produced in abundance by the community of scholarship to aid our comprehension of Luke's literature. (I have listed several in the bibliography at the back of this book.) This volume will then serve as a provocative and evocative companion as you move from listening carefully to the text and strive to bridge the interpretive arch so the claim of God announced through the text and the consecrated devotion of the called community of faith converge. Then we, too, can know more clearly who we are and what we are to do for the greater glory of God in the service of Jesus Christ our Lord.

The Prologue

Prologues invite neglect. Frequently they are little more than pream-
bled formalities, a kind of "a running start." One senses that more often
than not they serve the author rather than the reader. A good prologue
generates momentum, which encourages the author to address the substantial material in the body of the document that follows.

To many, Luke's first words seem to offer little more than that. After all,
Jesus is not even mentioned. And the text has the flavor of an initial paren-
thesis. It just does not "preach." This view is especially understandable given
the pedestrian renderings of most English translations. It does not matter if
they reproduce all four verses as one sentence (mimicking Luke's Greek) or
break them into several short sentences (more manageable in English). The
verses rarely sing. Even the Common Lectionary ignores them.

We would pass by these verses with scarcely a glance except that New
Testament commentators on the Gospel of Luke plead with and even
require us to pause, take notice, and reflect.

(*a*) *Literary style of the passage.* Those commentators observe in the
Greek what we fail to see in most English translations. The first sentence
of Luke's Gospel exhibits remarkable literary skill and beauty. This four-
verse sentence is artful Greek, carefully crafted in the best formal Hellenistic literary style. It is an exemplar of rhetorical balance and structure.
The sentence is dichotomous, with each half having three components
related to three in the other half: "many have undertaken" and "I too";
"set down an orderly account" and "write an orderly account"; certitude
of the "eyewitness" tradition and "you may know the truth."

Although the prologue has the Gospel narrative of the life and ministry
of Jesus in immediate purview, it also encompasses the second volume of
his work, the Acts of the Apostles. Together with the prologue of Acts, it
assures us that Luke intended for the two "books" to be read as two parts
of the same work.

7

(*b*) *Luke's purpose is to persuade.* Luke is not interested simply in accumulating and presenting accurate data. His goal is not primarily to inform but to persuade. He wants Theophilus (and all other readers/hearers) to "know the truth" about the Christian faith. "Truth" is more than "information about." Luke perceives historical events against the backdrop of faith. History and theology are interwoven. Through his narrative he expects to discern clearly the claim of the gospel on his life. We are required to do the same.

Although Luke does not name Jesus yet, he does register what for him is a crucial theme. The phrase "the events that have been fulfilled among us" (v.1) contains terms Luke will use repeatedly to refer to the will of God already disclosed in the Jewish scriptural traditions. This rhythm of promise and fulfillment is central to how he interprets the meaning of the Jesus story.

(*c*) *Luke's place in the handing on of the traditions about Jesus.* Luke locates himself and his literary work in the ongoing process by which the Christian community collected and selectively reflected on the traditions about Jesus. We might flesh out the progression: 1) actual events, 2) reports of eyewitnesses and servants of the word, 3) versions of the extended oral tradition, 4) others' written versions, 5) Luke's version, and 6) Theophilus's strengthened conviction. Luke is thereby not so much claiming superiority through greater accuracy as he is acknowledging his own participation and contribution to the process of effectively articulating the gospel message.

Preaching options suggested by the prologue include:

1. A summons to superior discipleship. Luke's careful crafting of his literary style may serve as a model for the Christian believer's glad offering of quality discipleship. Spiritual formation schools us in the devout honing of personal skills so that we offer only our very best in the service of the gospel. That is not a challenge to perfectionism but a very helpful corrective to shoddiness.

2. Lessons on the nature of the church. Luke has a vivid sense of his place in the larger community. His awareness encourages us to moderate any preoccupation we may have with individualistic religion by recovering our sense of solidarity with, dependence on, and investment in the broader community of faith. A poignant recognition is that many of the "eyewitnesses and ministers" Luke mentioned have long been anonymous and forgotten. Yet they were faithful. They played their part. Luke appreciatively built on their work. Without them he could not have done what he did.

3. Christian nurture is cumulative and transforming. This theme might be lifted up on Christian Education Sunday, Rally Day, or when church schoolteachers are recognized. Luke adds his labors to those who have already instructed Theophilus. He expects Theophilus not just to comprehend more about the truth, but also to be known by the truth. He expects Theophilus's life to change. Luke's version of Jesus' life and ministry and the ministry of the early church is designed to provide undergirding, confirmation, support, and assistance for fellow Christians. It is intended to help shape and inform their teaching and proclamation as well as their own faith.

Birth and Infancy Stories

Before we consider each of these stories in sequence, some general remarks about the rest of chapters 1 and 2 are in order.

(*a*) *Gospel overture.* The stories in this section serve as a prelude to Luke's narrative portrait of the life and ministry of Jesus. Themes and motifs are inlaid in the stories, to which he will return in the course of his narration. One might well think of the analogy of an operatic overture in which melodic and harmonic statements are first introduced that are important to the musical development of the opera. Apparently the use of such a prelude is typical of Luke's writing style, for the first two chapters in Acts function in a similar way.

(*b*) *"Biblical" flavor to Luke's style.* The literary tone of these stories differs greatly from the prologue. In contrast to the elegant Greek of that preface, Luke now writes with a strongly Semitised flavor. He adopts the vocabulary and style of the translation Greek used in the Septuagint, the Greek version of the Jewish scriptures. His purpose in using "Bible language" was to declare, even by the way he told the stories, that the events they described had been anticipated in First (Old) Testament events. As the Jewish scriptures testified, God was fulfilling purposes God had disclosed and promises God had made.

(*c*) *Nativity hymns are added.* The nativity hymns are spectacularly conspicuous components of the birth narratives. These include the Magnificat (1:46–55), the Benedictus (1:67–79), the Gloria in Excelsis (2:13–14), and the Nunc Dimittis (2:28–32). (All of these titles come from the Latin versions of the hymns.) Luke probably did not compose these hymns but rather adapted them from very early Christian tradition. They obtrude upon the narrative. The stories flow smoothly without them. Luke included them to emphasize further the awesome religious character of the events being described and to introduce some of the important themes he wanted to draw on later in his narrative.

(*d*) *Comparison of the portrayals of John the Baptist and of Jesus.* As Luke alternated infancy stories about John and about Jesus, he nurtured a parallelism between the two through similar story structure, similar sequence of events within the stories, and even similar terminology. He presented both John and Jesus as exceptional agents through whom God is working to reestablish God's saving rule over creation.

The correspondence is artfully counterbalanced by Luke's clear portrayal of Jesus as superior to John. Although John came prior to Jesus in time, he ranks below Jesus in importance. The Bible frequently depicts significant figures in salvation-history in pairs, but rarely does the second surpass the first. When it does happen (Ishmael-Isaac, Esau-Jacob, Saul-David), it indicates God's extraordinary intervention in human events. Although John is greater than any prophet, he serves as a precursor to Jesus, the Messiah.

THE ANNOUNCEMENT TO
ZECHARIAH ABOUT JOHN (1:5–25)

This first story relating the divine promise of John's birth falls into four sections: (a) Zechariah and Elizabeth are introduced, (b) Gabriel's announcement to Zechariah, (c) Zechariah's muteness, and (d) the conception of John the Baptist.

This story depicts John's role as forerunner of the Messiah. He will be the prophet par excellence, filled with the Holy Spirit, mighty in word and deed. His task is "to make ready a people prepared for the Lord" (v. 17).

Luke underscores John's roots in the priestly tradition as it centered on the Temple in Jerusalem. Since his father was a priest and his mother belonged to a priestly line, theoretically John also would be eligible for priestly service in the Temple. Furthermore, his birth was foretold in the Temple during the execution of priestly duties. John functions as a transitional figure who embodies the shift in focus from the presence of God in the Temple to the presence of God in Jesus.

(*a*) *Zechariah and Elizabeth are introduced (vv. 5–7).* The anecdote begins with an historical reference to King Herod (the Great, son of Antipater). That permits us to locate the story sometime prior to 4 B.C.E., the year of Herod's death.

A child born by the touch of divine grace to aged, barren parents is a familiar Old Testament theme, recalling Isaac (Gen. 17:17; 18:11), Samson (Judg. 13:2–7), and especially Samuel (1 Sam. 1:3–18). That they were righteous and blameless before God means that the lack of a child was not the consequence of divine judgment.

(*b*) *Gabriel's announcement to Zechariah (vv. 8–20).* The cultic burning of incense in the Temple is the setting for the beginning of this longest section to the story. It recalls the expectation in popular Jewish piety of God's coming to Mount Zion, the Temple mount, to establish God's royal rule on the Day of the Lord (Mal. 3:1).

As Zechariah prayed to God to accept the people's sacrifice, the prayers on behalf of Israel by the people outside were also lifted up. Those prayers were answered in two ways: 1) the sudden appearance of Gabriel to Zechariah, and 2) the promise of a son. Zechariah was prepared for neither. The first evoked fear, the second confusion.

Gabriel's appearance announced a new intervention of God's presence in Israel. A son is promised long after Zechariah had given up asking. Zechariah is the first to know that the gospel ("good news," v. 19) of God's salvation will be heralded by his son.

Gabriel's message underscored repeatedly the promised child's special greatness. God preempts the father's right to name the son. John will evoke ecstatic, religious joy. He will always be under a special vow to God that binds him to an exceptional discipline (the Nazirite vow, see Num. 6:1–8). That he is continually filled with the Holy Spirit marks him as an end-time agent of God, the forerunner of the Messiah. The allusion to Elijah corresponds to a messianic expectation of many. (Luke avoids identifying John with Elijah, although Mark had done so; see Mark 9:13.) John will fulfill Malachi 4:6 by turning "the hearts of parents to their children."

Zechariah is flabbergasted. He responds with incredulity. His limited grasp of the scope of divine freedom drives him to require a sign for confirmation. The sign given (he is struck dumb) confirms the announcement. It also disciplines his unbelief and lack of trust.

(*c*) *Zechariah's muteness (vv. 21–23).* Zechariah emerges from the Temple and stands before the people speechless. His cultic role required him now to speak a priestly blessing upon them. The message of blessing with which he has been entrusted far surpasses anything they might have expected to hear—only he cannot tell.

Zechariah's long delay in the Temple and his muteness were both indications to the perceptive people that he had seen a vision. Theologically, the section introduces the motif that God's presence and activity with the Jewish people is not limited to the Temple and its cult. Literarily, it serves to heighten the tension for what is to follow.

(*d*) *Conception of John the Baptist (vv. 24–25).* Gabriel's forecast is realized and Elizabeth conceives a child. The reproach, which thereby is removed by the Lord, consisted of the implication that it was God's judgment that had left her childless. Elizabeth's five-month interval of seclusion will serve as a sign to Mary (vv. 26, 36). The section concludes the story of the announcement about John's birth and anticipates the subsequent merging of the two stories (vv. 39ff.).

Options for preaching include:

1. *Compare the announcement of John's birth with the announcement of the birth of Jesus.* The parallels between the two stories are so striking that they throw the differences into even sharper contrast. The parallelism promotes a progressive intensification of meaning. As great as John the Baptist is to be, his most significant function will be to serve as precursor to Jesus Messiah. His life has meaning only in relation to Jesus, as is true for every Christian believer. The interpreter might do well during Advent to consider this story and the next in tandem to note both the parallels and the contrasts.

2. *The contrasting responses of Zechariah and of Mary.* Zechariah and Elizabeth, his wife, are devout, pious, religious people—the type of folks we would expect to be especially sensitive and responsive to divine saving interventions. It takes more than pious devotion to be alert to God's transforming intrusions into the human story. As much as they had prayed for God's presence, they did not really expect an intervention to happen, certainly not in such an immediate and personal way.

Zechariah's first reaction to the indication of divine presence was one of fear (vv. 1:12–13)—so was Mary's (1:29–30), and so was the shepherds' (2:9–10). We do not really expect God to intervene in concrete and specific ways into our lives. When God does we are aghast and flabbergasted. At a deeper level we become profoundly apprehensive, for we are exposed and vulnerable before perfect righteousness. God meets our anxiety with the words of grace, "Be not afraid."

Not only are we paralyzed by the divine presence intersecting our lives, we are wholly unprepared to hear what God has to say to us. So when God speaks, we equivocate by posing questions, raising objections, and requiring demonstrable proof. We betray the fraudulent side of our piety, for God's word is inherently true and the test of our faith is whether we can discern and acclaim that authentic veracity. Zechariah did not believe (v. 20) and was struck dumb. Because he did not believe, he really had nothing to say. Mary believed (1:38, 45) and is "blessed." This story and a lot of others also were written "that *you may know the truth*" (v. 4).

3. *Compare the precursor roles of John and the church.* One could bring the story of the announcement of John the Baptist's birth into conversation with the first two chapters in Luke's second volume, Acts. As John was the precursor of Jesus' first Advent, so the church is precursor of his second Advent. The church is filled with end-of-the-ages, ultimate joy, and it should evoke similar joy from others (v. 14). The church knows the profounder

inebriation of the spirit-filled life (cf. the "filled with new wine" charge in Acts 2:13). The church's task is to summon people to prepare themselves for the coming of the Lord.

THE ANNOUNCEMENT TO
MARY ABOUT JESUS (1:26–38)

The correspondence between the two announcement stories of the conceptions of John and of Jesus is obvious. A detailed comparison of the two stories may be found in Raymond E. Brown, *The Birth of the Messiah*, (Garden City, N.Y.: Doubleday, 1977), pp. 292ff.

(*a*) *The two announcement stories.* Luke orchestrates a progression from the lesser to the greater that displays the superiority of Jesus over John. John's conception is a marvelous event by which God fulfills the long-abandoned human longing of Zechariah and Elizabeth. Jesus' conception is even more miraculous, for God takes an initiative that transcends human expectation. John was to be filled with the Holy Spirit from his mother's womb; Jesus was conceived by the Holy Spirit. John was to summon the people to prepare themselves for the coming of God; the entire life and ministry of Jesus was the promised visitation of God.

As we saw when we considered the prior story, God's presence is no longer focused primarily on the Temple location. From now on God's presence is most clearly encountered in the person of the Son, Jesus Christ. The relation between John and Jesus personified an interest that was cardinal for Luke. The continuity between John and Jesus corresponded to the continuity between Israel and the church in salvation-history.

(*b*) *Angelic annunciations.* The standard pattern in Semitic literature for angelic annunciations contains the following elements: the appearance of the angel, the response of fear, the message, objections raised, and the sign of confirmation. These elements are present both in this and in the previous announcement story. Especially noteworthy in this story are those features of Luke's narration added to the standard pattern. These include descriptions of what Jesus is to accomplish, the miraculous conception, and the portrayal of Mary.

(*c*) *Jesus' mission revealed.* Luke presented the mission of Jesus in the two-stage exchange between Gabriel and Mary. In the first stage (vv. 28–33), he describes Jesus as the extraordinary agent of God who will function as Davidic-messianic ruler forever. In the second stage (vv. 34–38), Jesus is Son of God with whom God inaugurates a new creation. It is striking to note that in both stages there is neither reference nor allusion to Jesus' suffering, humiliation, and execution.

(*d*) *The conception miracle is new creation.* Luke's Gospel shared Matthew's interest in the miraculous conception of Jesus. The teaching is missing in the earliest writings of the infant church (for example, Paul and Mark), which encourages us to conclude that the concept was not very important for the earliest Christians. Apparently they had different opinions about when Jesus became Son of God. One view held that it was through the resurrection that God elevated Jesus to that status (see Rom. 1:3; Acts 13:33 shows that Luke knew of that view). Other solutions focused on the transfiguration (Luke 9:34) or on Jesus' baptism (Luke 3:22). For Luke, Jesus was Son of God from his conception. (There is no evidence that Luke knew of a view that affirmed preexistence which became incarnate as the Son of God, as we find in the Gospel of John.)

Since Luke never referred subsequently to the virgin birth either in his Gospel or in Acts, we may view his interest in it not for its own sake but for what it said about Jesus. The miraculous conception affirms direct creative intervention of God in fulfillment of the ancient promise of redemption. Virginal conception signifies new creation. Jesus is Son of God as the progenitor of a new order of creation just as Adam was Son of God as the progenitor of the prior order of creation (3:38).

The Holy Spirit is that creative, active power of God through which the new creation is born in Jesus, as the causal "therefore" of verse 35 requires us to conclude. The language Luke used in this verse—"come upon you," "overshadow you"—recalls the same Holy Spirit of God brooding over the waters of primordial chaos in the Genesis account of creation. (It is interesting that Luke portrayed the resurrected Jesus using the same language for the promise of Pentecost in Acts 1:8.)

(*e*) *Luke describes Mary.* Particularly winsome is Luke's portrait of Mary. Luke lays the foundation here for a presentation of Mary that consistently depicts her as faithful adherent and follower of Jesus. By the world's standards, she would hardly command notice. Zechariah at least was a man, a priest, actively engaged in the cultic worship of God in the Temple. Mary was young, a girl, in an insignificant village—certainly the epitome of "the lowly" (v. 52). Yet she far surpasses Zechariah for, even when she is troubled and uncertain, she is still open to the creative power of God working in her and through her to accomplish divine purposes.

Luke offers Mary as the first and therefore model believer in his Gospel narrative. Subsequent references to her are consistent with this pattern (Luke 1:45ff.; 8:19–21; 11:27–28; Acts 1:14). Her humble acquiescence to the will and workings of God (v. 38) commends itself to every believer. ("Servant" [v. 48] is the feminine equivalent to the term Paul used when he described himself as a "slave of Christ.") Luke presents Mary to his community as a "type" of the church, the community of faith.

There are several options for sermon development:

    1. *The miracle points to the mystery.* The interpreter would do well to be guided by the reserve with which the Evangelist reports the virgin birth. The miraculous conception in and of itself attracts no major interest. As elsewhere throughout the Bible, miracle more often than not points to mystery. The miracle of the virgin birth confronts us with the mystery of God's new creation inaugurated in Jesus and offered to us to embrace by faith. The Spirit of God overshadowing Mary announces that God has intervened salvifically in human history, coming into human life in Jesus Christ for our salvation.

    2. *The mixed consequences of "finding favor with God."* For Mary such favor did not mean finding a life of peaceful tranquility insulated from turmoil, privation, and pain. Being visited by God exposed her to the threat of social criticism, the dangers of a difficult journey under adverse circumstances, and birthing under unsettling, unsanitary, isolated, and traumatic conditions.

    Mary found the son who was the fruit of such divine favor to be confusing and at times impenetrable. She experienced the hostility he evoked from friends, neighbors, and even family members. She endured watching him launch on a collision course with the religious authorities. She bore his arrest, public trial, and condemnation. She suffered his humiliating execution and burial. Only retrospectively do we grasp that all of that was included in Gabriel's admonition, "Do not be afraid, Mary, for you have found favor with God" (v. 30)."

    In the person of Jesus and through the church's preaching, God still admonishes the community of faith like that. As did Mary, we find that message both comforting and discomforting. It humbles and consoles us; it also challenges us to acquiesce as God makes known God's will and purposes for us, and to serve God obediently no matter what. We need to hear Gabriel's word also—"Do not be afraid!"—even though at any moment in our faith pilgrimage what that message of courage and comfort embraces is not at all clear or certain. The church, modeling Mary, must offer itself as the slave of the Lord. Because Mary was willing to "let it be" with her according to God's word, it has been according to God's word (v. 38) for millions after her.

    3. *Encountering God's presence.* A more adventurous initiative might be to explore this passage during Lent or in the season of Pentecost during the dog days of August, instead of restricting it to the end of the year. The study could explore Mary's experience as a pattern for spiritual formation in religious encounter with the presence of God:

1) The troubled disturbance and fear evoked (v. 29) when we must come to terms with the reality of God and all that reality implies about who we are and what we are about, gives way to
2) confusion and perplexity (v. 34), and maybe even not a little anxiety and resentment, as we grasp that we are being addressed directly, personally by God, who seems to have some unlikely and even impossible things in mind for us to become and to do.
3) Penetrating through our misgivings comes the ringing assurance (v. 37) of God's faithfulness, dependability, and sufficiency. Then when we take God on God's terms, knowing that God has taken us, our terms notwithstanding, come
4) complete acquiescence and total surrender to God's purposes (v. 38).

MARY'S VISIT TO ELIZABETH (1:39–56)

This story serves as a transition panel, connecting the two announcement stories that precede it with the two birth stories that follow. Luke anticipated this encounter between the two pregnant women by describing Elizabeth as having gone into an extended interval of seclusion after she conceived (v. 24). Consequently Mary could not have known of Elizabeth's condition until God chose to disclose it to her during her own annunciation experience (v. 36), where it served as the supernatural sign corroborating the angel's message to her.

(*a*) *Witness of the fetal John.* The account begins by portraying Mary acting with single-minded obedience on the angel's revelation concerning Elizabeth. At her greeting to Elizabeth upon entering the house, John began to serve his prophetic role by leaping in his mother's womb, thereby becoming the agent for God's revelation to Elizabeth of Mary's condition and the identity of her unborn child. (Later Luke will include another tradition [7:18–19] which describes John the Baptist, toward the end of his own career, as being extremely uncertain about Jesus' identity.) His fetal testimony to his mother was inspired by the Spirit and fulfilled the angel's prediction (v. 15). Elizabeth is thus filled with the Holy Spirit, and her greeting of Mary is supernaturally inspired.

(*b*) *Elizabeth's greeting.* The first words of Elizabeth's greeting (v. 42) combined with the words with which the angel greeted Mary (v. 28) supply the scriptural words which are a part of the traditional Ave Maria. Elizabeth's blessing of Mary has two focal points. Mary was blessed because her baby was acknowledged by Elizabeth to be "my Lord." Then she blessed Mary because of her resolute trust in God and her faithful response to God's word.

Luke is again able to present Mary as a model for faithful believers. When God made God's will known to Mary, she received that word and surrendered herself to it completely. "Blessed is she who believed . . ." (v. 45) is a beatitude that stands at the center of the Second (New) Testament message and expands to embrace *all* who believe.

(*c*) *The Magnificat.* Mary's reply to Elizabeth's greeting constitutes the first of the four major nativity hymns in the beginning two chapters of Luke's Gospel. Many scholars believe that Luke borrowed these hymns from very early Christian tradition and accommodated them to advance and enhance his narrative. Whatever its prior history, the Magnificat serves here as a vehicle through which Mary celebrated her experience of the startlingly unexpected grace of God as a paradigm for what God intended to accomplish for the entire creation.

The Magnificat has a strong resemblance to the Song of Hannah in 1 Samuel 2:1–10 and apparently was based on it. It reflects on the goodness of God and God's redemptive deeds, manifesting justice and mercy throughout human history. Mary began her song by praising God for deeds of mercy toward her. Taking the initiative, God has visited her in her "lowliness" and exalted her by using her for God's redemptive purposes.

With verse 51 a dramatic shift in the focus of the hymn occurs. Mary's experience is an archetype for what God projects to accomplish throughout creation. The verbs in past tense are prophetic—describing future acts of God perceived as already having been accomplished. What God says God will do is considered the act itself, because God's word is powerfully efficacious. In its latter section, the hymn projects nothing less than political and economic revolution. God will bring about a radical reversal in the social order.

Sermonic directions suggested by this passage include:

1. The potential of the gospel for effecting social transformation. Many of the motifs in the hymn would be at home in a liberation theology sermon. The proud, the rich, and the royal represent the established power structures who oppose God. The poor, the hungry, and the humble are those who have learned because of their vulnerability to rely on God for compassion and righteous vindication. They are "kingdom people."

Charles H. Talbert (*Reading Luke* [New York: Crossroad, 1982], pp. 22ff.) helpfully explores the implication for social revolution suggested by the Magnificat. God did not empower Mary to produce a child worthy to be God's son—God intervened in Mary's life. God does not empower humanity to bring about perfection in the world—God intervenes, breaking into human history to accomplish "social revolution through eschatological reversal."

Jesus' role—and the church's—is not to form one more power block that will confront existing exploitive power structures on their own terms and transform or destroy them. Only God can accomplish the establishment of a just society and that is an end-of-time expectation. Jesus and the community of faith, by the example of the quality of their life together and by the compassion of their ministry, are to witness the efficacious mercy of God at work in the world.

2. *Individual and communal dimensions to encounters with God.* Eduard Schweizer (*The Good News According to Luke* [Atlanta: John Knox Press, 1984], p. 33) directs attention to the shifts in personal reference in the hymn. Mary extols her personal experience with God in the first person singular (vv. 46–49), then the universal experience of God in the third person (vv. 50–53), and finally the experience of God in Israel's history in the first person plural (vv. 54–55).

BIRTH OF JOHN THE BAPTIST (1:57–80)

Luke has made artful preparation, and now he cashes in by weaving this story securely into the fabric of his narrative. The story has two major focal points: (a) the naming of the newborn baby, and (b) Zechariah's hymn, the Benedictus.

(a) **The naming of the baby.** Luke uses the naming of the baby as an opportunity to underscore the faithful piety of Zechariah and Elizabeth. Their trust in God was so firm that they withstood the pressure of relatives and friends to choose for the baby the name the neighbors considered appropriate.

As the story unfolds, Elizabeth appears to have arrived at the name "John" independent of any communication from Zechariah. Having been filled with the Holy Spirit (v. 41), she was inspired by divine guidance to settle on this name. Her insistence emphasized her fidelity to the will of God. After the company appealed to Zechariah for a more reasonable choice, they were astounded when he confirmed Elizabeth's choice. At this point, Luke portrays Zechariah not only as mute but also deaf (v. 62) as a consequence of his former lack of trust in God's ability to accomplish the impossible. The Greek term is ambiguous and allows for either or both meanings. Luke used the same word in 7:22 where it clearly means "deaf." Thus, since Zechariah was deaf, he could not have known the name she had announced for the baby.

Preaching possibilities for this first part include:

1. *The idea of joy as a sign of God's activity in human life.* In verse 14, the angel predicted that John the Baptist would be a source of great joy to many. He had certainly already given great joy to his parents, Zechariah

and Elizabeth. Mary also had shared their joy. Now the circle of those rejoicing expands to include relatives and neighbors, who celebrate with the parents this irrefutable evidence of divine grace and approval. John's birth refutes any gossipy criticism her former childlessness may have stimulated, because now it is clear that God has mercifully vindicated Elizabeth. The response for all, even the child in the womb (v. 44), is joy.

2. *The sense of wonder, mystery, epiphany, and miracle surrounding God's activity in human life.* Luke intensifies the narrative by heaping miracle upon miracle. First, barren Elizabeth, who had nonetheless conceived, had given birth to a son. Then she and Zechariah had, without collusion, agreed on his name. Now Zechariah, who had been silent for nine months, begins to speak. (Luke told us he would in verse 20 after "these things occur.") The abundance of wonders in this passage (anticipating the later prophetic role of the adult John the Baptist) compels the church to ask, "Where do we look for God?" and "What do we expect to call the place, or person, or event that discloses God's presence?" Instead of surrendering to our strong inclination to decide those things in advance, usually long before the epiphany actually occurs, we need to develop the discipline of watchful, expectant, but also unconditioned waiting.

We are to train ourselves to be alert for where, and when, and in whom the self-revelation of God occurs. It may be through the testimony of other Christians. It may be in the context of the church's corporate worship. It may be elsewhere in the life of the community of faith. It also may very well be through new and unexpected epiphanies for which our preconceptions have not at all prepared us. If we are not flexible and open to innovative divine intervention, just look at what we may be missing!

3. *To discern the action of God in human life opens up the possibility of response in witness and obedience.* Responding obediently to the prompting of the Holy Spirit, Elizabeth and Zechariah insisted on the name John, in spite of their neighbors' protest. Moreover, when they were confronted with incontrovertible evidence of divine influence and guidance, the neighbors themselves responded as they should—with godly awe and fear—and they related their astonishing experiences far and wide. Thus, Luke prepares us for the multitudes who will later respond obediently to the preaching of this obviously singular and holy child when, as a man, he enters into his public activity at the appointed time (3:1ff.).

(*b*) *The Benedictus.* Luke described those who heard the news of these marvelous happenings as questioning "What then will this child become?" (v. 66). This provides a transition to the Benedictus, an answer to the question. Zechariah did not recover his voice solely as a release from divine judgment on his lack of trust. God had something for

Zechariah to say, and God empowered him with the Holy Spirit. This indwelling of Zechariah by the Spirit made it unanimous for the entire family (vvs. 15, 41, 67).

The Benedictus extols the ethical transformation that will occur because of the saving work of Jesus for whose coming John's ministry will prepare. It emphasizes the continuity between what God has accomplished in past dealings with Israel and what God will accomplish through the work of the savior.

The hymn has two main sections. In the first section (vv. 68–75), God is praised for past faithfulness, for keeping the promises made to David and to Abraham. Israel's history, finding climactic fulfillment in the coming of the Messiah, constitutes the unfolding of the divine plan to liberate God's people and to restore creation. God is unswervingly faithful to this plan for renewal and restoration.

The hymn's second main section (vv. 76–79) describes John's role in the unfolding of the divine design for redemption. It is an expansion of the angel's prediction in verses 16f. John is God's prophet, assigned the task of preparing a repentant people to receive the coming Messiah.

The last verse in the section (v. 80) provides a conclusion to the episode and also allowed Luke to prepare for the beginning of John's public activity in 3:1ff. John's sojourn in the wilderness does more than just have him waiting in the wings to do his thing when Jesus is ready to begin his public ministry. It is a familiar biblical theme to Luke and his community. An interval spent in the wilderness is a time of preparation in anticipation of a new advance in the divine plan of redemption. Moses went through such a time of testing and formation; so did the people of Israel. Jesus will. It is the obvious thing for one to do who has been designated by God to play a significant role as an agent through whom God advances salvation-history.

Preaching possibilities on this part of the passage include:

1. This is basically a story of three events— God acts, people perceive, people respond in faith. Eduard Schweizer (*The Good News According to Luke* [Atlanta: John Knox Press, 1984], p. 39) offers a sentence that could well serve as a three-point outline for a sermon: "'The hand of God,' guiding providence, is revealed in this section in the concrete fulfillment of God's promise through the birth of a child, in the ability of others to see in this birth something of the greatness of God's mercy, and in the way those directly concerned learn to accept God's gift and witness to it before others through their obedience."

2. Zechariah moves from faithless to wonder to praise. Think about what spiritual growth has occurred in the life of this priest of God in the last

nine months! It happened because, through the visitation of divine judgment for his lack of trust, Zechariah reflected with single-minded intensity
on the religious meaning of the impending birth of his son and the coming of the Messiah.

3. *Counting everyone's blessings.* "Count your blessings," the song
requires of us, "name them one by one." That is what Zechariah was doing
in the Benedictus, offering his hymn of praise to God once his ability to
speak (and hear) had been restored. Notice the scope of his vision—no
exclusively individualistic religious perspective and awareness here.
Zechariah's hymn looked beyond his personal joy and focused on the gift
of John as an integral component of the gift of messianic salvation to the
entire nation, and through the entire nation to the whole world. The baby
with which God had graced the lives of Zechariah and Elizabeth would
be the instrument of God's mercy, light, and peace for an entire nation,
in which everyone would have a part. When Zechariah "counts his blessings," they are primarily nationwide—better, worldwide. He sees all of
holy history focused in the gift of his son, John, and the role that son will
play vis-à-vis the Messiah.

BIRTH OF JESUS (2:1–20)

Luke's version of the birth of Jesus is marked by great simplicity and
reserve. As he composed it he interwove multiple allusions to themes and
motifs from the Jewish scriptures. It is striking that Luke could relate the
birth of Jesus with such restraint. It is more striking to reflect on the extrav-
agances that have been inflicted on Luke's unpretentious account. Taken
by itself, the story does not sanction all the sentimental accretions that
popular piety has imposed on it down through the years.

The narrative has three subsections: (a) setting and birth, (b) announcement to the shepherds, and (c) various reactions.

(*a*) *Setting and birth.* Luke began his account of the birth of Jesus with
reference to a registration conducted under the command of Imperial
Rome, which offers us tantalizing promise of an anchor point for the exact
dating of the birth. The discrepancies involved in sorting out the details
are notoriously complex.

The problems raised by a census associated with Caesar Augustus and
Governor Quirinius and King Herod simply defy resolution. Luke apparently was working with scanty data and may have conflated details from
two different attempts to register inhabitants. Since Augustus was
acclaimed as the restorer and maintainer of peace in the Empire, Luke,
perhaps, wanted to exploit the contrast between the extravagance associ-

ated with Caesar's person and rule and the humble, little-noted origins of the real bringer of peace.

In any event Augustus Caesar served as an unknowing instrument through whom God was accomplishing God's saving purposes just as other political powers of this world, such as Cyrus, had done before him. Luke was not concerned about giving detailed information of how Rome arranged state fiscal procedures, anyway. He wanted this story to announce clearly and without ambiguity a divine intervention into human history. Functionally the registration is a literary device Luke employed to provide "transportation" to get Mary and Joseph to Bethlehem, the "city of David," where the Davidic messiah Jesus was to be born.

The setting for the birth as Luke described it also has been distorted by popular pious imagination. The (absent from the story) innkeeper has been the object of a bad "rap," often being described as callous, greedy, unfeeling, cruel, and insensitive. A caravansary in the Near East, usually consisting of one large room where transients together with their livestock gathered to spend the night, provided little opportunity for the isolation a birthing would require. Even if, as some commentators suggest, Joseph and Mary sought shelter with some relatives, the problem of seclusion would have been similarly difficult. Verse 7 suggests humble, rustic surroundings that were chosen as the best setting for privacy.

The manger in which Mary laid the baby deserves special notice. Christmas pageants often accentuate the rude, common setting by having animals (cow, donkey, sheep, and so forth) gazing wonderingly at the small bundle that has displaced their evening fodder. Certainly the manger underscores the humble nature of the scene where earth-transforming events have occurred.

Luke intended for the manger to convey much more. He mentioned the manger three times—verses 7, 12, and 16. In verse 12 it is designated as a "sign" by the angel to the shepherds. (The cloths with which Mary wrapped the child were commonly used in the care of a newborn infant and carry no special significance.) Luke found in the symbol of the manger allusion to Isaiah 1:3:

> The ox knows its owner,
>   and the donkey its master's crib;
> but Israel does not know,
>   my people do not understand.

With the birth of Jesus that ancient, pessimistic prophecy was to be tested in a new way, which tells us something of the importance that Luke placed in the faithful response of the shepherds. Their worship (v. 20) announced the beginning of the time when the spiritually open and perceptive in Israel were beginning to know "the manger of its Lord."

(*b*) *Announcement to the shepherds.* Luke's narrative emphasis falls not on the birth itself but rather on the angelic announcement of that birth to the shepherds and their response to it. Luke bound the sections together through repeated references to "the city of David" (vv. 4, 11), "bands of cloth" (vv. 7, 12), and "manger" (vv. 7, 12, 16). The story reaches its climax with the praise that the shepherds offered to God for the experience of seeing the baby, which confirmed the angel's message in the vision (v. 20).

The angelic announcement to the shepherds (vv. 8–14) begins on an equally humble note. The shepherds were guarding their livestock. They were plain folk shepherding their sheep in the area around Bethlehem, the city of King David, who also had been a shepherd. In sharp contrast to the simplicity of the account Luke had given of the birth itself, the shepherds experience an angel vision, an extraordinary message, the chorusing of the angelic legion!

(*c*) *Various reactions.* At this manifestation the shepherds' *initial* reaction was one of fear and holy awe (consistent with Luke's portrayal of simple, pious people and their reactions to other manifestations of supernatural presence and power, cf. 1:12, 29, 65). It is the *second* reaction, their response to the content of what the angel had to say, that was crucial. For those with faithful and attentive ears the angel's message would supplant their great fear with great joy.

Although the "good news" of the Davidic messiah who brings salvation was announced first to the shepherds, it had universal import. Nevertheless they were the first beyond the family itself (or the extended family, taking Elizabeth into account) who had the opportunity to experience the great joy God intended for all people ultimately to know. Behind the angel's announcement are echoes of Isaiah 9:6, "For a child has been born for us, a son given to us." The "sign" of the manger cradling the infant was commended to the shepherds.

The sudden appearance of the heavenly host lauding God's saving initiative in the birth of the messiah was an invitation to the shepherds to become the first of humanity to join with them in cosmological acclamation. The "Gloria in Excelsis" of the angels (v. 14) ascribed glory to God and announced peace on earth. This peace is the "shalom" of God which Zechariah celebrated by anticipation in the Benedictus (1:79), and into which Simeon was to enter upon seeing the infant Jesus, thereby completing his duty as watchman (2:29).

The heavenly vision opened for the shepherds the option of also sharing in this shalom of God depending on how they responded to the angel's announcement. If their response is faithful, they are included among those upon whom God's favor rests, and therefore belong to the elect of God. It is very significant that Luke, alone among the evangelists, allowed the content of the canticle of the angelic host to shape the acclamation the disciples of Jesus offered to him upon his triumphal entry into Jerusalem just prior to his passion (19:38).

Sermon possibilities for this passage include:

1. The response of faithful obedience is to proclaim. The shepherds' response to the angelic epiphany is crucial. They resolved to experience the "sign" revealed to them by the angel, and did so "with haste"—an indication of faithful obedience (as with Mary earlier, 1:39). They saw the sign that confirmed to them the "good news" of the angel's message. They then did what every community of faith that has been brought into being by encounter with the gospel must do: They told others of the good news and joined together with the heavenly host in offering praise and glory to God. As such, they become a prototype for the community of faith gathered around Jesus during his ministry and continuing to praise and proclaim with fidelity following his resurrection and ascension.

2. Capitalizing on the story's overexposure. For the interpreter who seeks to effect convergence between this story and the faith needs of her community, a problem lurks in an overfamiliarity that renders the account banal or, worse, sentimental. Overfamiliarity can be a blessing. Few biblical stories have been so carefully plowed or so frequently reaped as this one. The accumulated riches of the church's reflections on the story of the birth of Jesus means that the proclaimer has ready access to a wealth of resources to stimulate the imagination for homiletical appropriation.

As complicated as the discrepancies in historical detail are, they in no way detract from the impact of Luke's artful narrative setting. What stands out is the contrast between the two realms of lordly authority. One's perspective controls which of the two appears to be the most spectacular and majestic. Either it is that Augustus Caesar sent forth a decree and Mary and Joseph took an awkwardly inconvenient trip, or it is that God sent forth the Spirit and new creation was inaugurated in the person of God's Son.

The world has ever since been confused and double-minded about which is the more important and praiseworthy. We long for angel choruses to decide the issue for us, while being too frequently unimpressed with the confirmation and vindication of Jesus' identity and work the resurrection places before us. Yet how much more beyond the shepherds' experience ought we to find that persuasive.

3. The birth of Jesus as new creation. Luke stressed the conception and birth of Jesus as initiating a new creation. "To you is born *this day . . .*"

might well be called the "eighth day of creation." The glory the angels ascribed to God finally will be complete with his passion. That was why Luke had the disciples rephrase the angels' hymn as their greeting upon Jesus' triumphal entry into Jerusalem at the beginning of Passion Week. Behind the cradle looms the cross-event (execution and resurrection), both completing and interpreting what was begun in Bethlehem.

The "peace on earth" bestowed by God did not signal the banishment of human hostility from the earth. It is the "shalom" of God which is life experienced in all its fullness, richness, and completeness in accord with the will of God. The realization of that peace began with Jesus himself "whom (God) favors." Through the cross-event God's shalom extends to embrace all who believe in him, and who thereby become people upon whom God's favor rests.

Another feature that stands out in Luke's story is the incongruous manner by which divine presence manifested itself within human history. This is expressed in the content of the good news the angel announced to the shepherds—the coming of "the Savior, Christ the Lord"—and the sign that confirmed it—the baby wound in cloth strips "lying in a manger." It is the epitome of the extraordinary manifested in the ordinary. And the ordinary shepherds, after all they had heard and seen, returned to the ordinary, only it had become extraordinary because their faithful obedience to the word of God made them extraordinary, too.

4. Response options to the incarnation. Luke recounted three reactions to the event and the message announcing it that might be profitably explored:

1) The shepherds "come and see"—they not only hear the good news of the birth of the messiah, they experience it; they "go and tell"—announcing and proclaiming to others the truth they had experienced; they "praise and glorify God"—adding their voices on earth to the hymn of the angelic chorus.

2) Those to whom the shepherds told of their experience wondered and were astonished. Was that all? No confirmation now? No passing on of the good news to others? No follow-up later, when Jesus entered into his public ministry?

3) Mary treasured and "pondered"—an indication of an extended period of sustained reflection, trying to make sense and plumb the depths of all that she had experienced (in clear and intentional contrast to the shepherds' spontaneous reaction), which, when done faithfully, led her to become the type of all those "blessed" who "hear the word of God and obey it" (11:28).

PRESENTATION IN THE TEMPLE (2:21–40)

The account of the circumcision and naming of Jesus in verse 21 is a transitional section that can be linked equally well either with what comes before or after. It parallels, though in much more abbreviated form, the circumcision and naming account of John the Baptist, with which Luke had concluded the John the Baptist infancy cycle. But it also displays the faithful adherence of the parents of Jesus to the requirements of Mosaic law. That theme becomes prominent in the remainder of chapter 2.

(a) *Faithful to the Mosaic law.* Luke was very interested in underscoring the continuity between the Jewish religious heritage, as represented by the law of Moses and the Temple cult, and the impending accomplishment of salvation through the person and ministry of Jesus, even though that would extend far beyond the defining limits of Israel. The reference to the circumcision, with its implication of fidelity to the law, is accompanied by the naming of the baby conforming to the angel's instructions (see 1:31). Mary and Joseph showed themselves faithful to the word of God both as it had been enshrined in religious tradition and as it had been announced to them directly by the angel.

That Luke was absorbed with the theme of faithful observance of the law is confirmed in the story that follows. In five instance, Luke refers to actions dictated by provisions of the Torah (vv. 22, 23, 24, 27, 39). Also he stressed in this and the next accounts the motif of Temple piety, which supported his insistent emphasis on continuity between Israel's expectations and Jesus' accomplishments.

Luke betrayed his confusion about the specifics of Jewish ritual law by combining separate provisions concerning postpartum purification and the "redeeming" of the first male child. Given Luke's prior appreciative dependence on the Hannah-Samuel story (1 Sam. 1–2), he may have intentionally omitted reference to the payment of the five "holy shekels of the sanctuary," which was the redemption price for a firstborn male. Consequently Jesus continued to be dedicated to God (as did Samuel) and remained God's property. Such an implication then received concrete application in the final story of chapter 2 where, like Samuel, Jesus considered himself "at home" in the Temple, for it was his "Father's house."

(b) *Conformance to Jewish piety.* The occasion for purification and presentation of the firstborn serves the literary function of shifting the scene from Bethlehem back to the Temple in Jerusalem. The requirements of Mosaic law (Torah piety) caused them to come to the Temple (Temple cult piety) to be encountered by the Spirit-endowed Simeon and the prophetess Anna (prophetic charism piety). Luke described this convergence as carefully choreographed by God. Through God's Spirit, Simeon had been put on alert—set to keep the watch, so to speak. The same Spirit directed him to the Temple at the opportune time. Both Simeon and Anna focused their devotional anticipation on the restoration by God of the religious fortunes of Israel ("the consolation of Israel"—v. 25, "the redemption of Jerusalem"—v. 38). That conformed to a hope around which an increasing segment of pious Jews centered their messianic expectations.

(*c*) *The* **Nunc Dimittis.** Luke did not identify Simeon as a priest, nor did he specifically say he was old (vv. 26, 29 permit the suspicion that Luke thought of him as elderly). Simeon was devout, righteous, and pious, and endowed with God's Spirit (mentioned three times in vv. 25–27). Luke's repeated use of "see" ("see death," "seen the Lord's Messiah"— v. 26) lends intensification to Simeon's glad affirmation, "my eyes have seen your salvation" (v. 30).

The pattern of celebration before God of the greatness of God's agent, followed by descriptions of the divinely designated functions that agent was to fulfill, had been well established in the other hymns and oracles that Luke had included in his infancy narratives up until now. With Simeon's utterances in the Spirit, the joy of the celebration (vv. 29–32) stands in stark contrast to the somber prophetic warning of the described function (vv. 34–35).

The *Nunc Dimittis* (vv. 29–32) is not a request or a prayer but a statement of fact. Simeon was not asking God to let him die in the full experience of God's shalom. He was affirming and celebrating God's fidelity to the promise to Israel and the nations that, through his Holy Spirit, had been given specific promissory focus for Simeon. Simeon was the Lord's watchman, ever alert for the coming Messiah. With the presentation of Jesus, his assignment had been completed, his hope fulfilled. He was ready to be dismissed from duty (in other words, to die). The hymn goes beyond the scope of his hope. Simeon looked for the "consolation of *Israel*"; God's salvation embodied in the infant was *universal* in compass.

(*d*) *Simeon warns Mary.* Simeon next addressed an oracle of prophetic warning to Mary (vv. 34–35). The child's allotted task will be to provoke division in Israel. He will launch a process of self-judgment in which people choose the nature of their accountability before God by the way in which they respond—either with faith or with rejection and hostility to the presence of the Lord's Christ. The parenthetic comment to Mary (v. 35b) may mean Mary herself would have to undergo the testing of how she was to come to regard Jesus, not as son but as Son and Messiah. A less likely reference might be to the suffering she would have to endure as she watched him moving toward his destiny.

(e) *Anna praises God.* The accompanying narrative concerning the prophetess Anna served to moderate the sober note on which Simeon's oracle concluded. Whereas Simeon ceremoniously acknowledged the divine identity and destiny of the child, Anna would "speak about the child," spreading the word to others who were watching alertly "for the redemption of Israel." Simeon joined the chorus of praise, which included the angels and the shepherds. Anna, like the shepherds, told others and praised God. Verse 39 terminated the Temple scene (again reiterating the fidelity to law motif) and provided transportation to get the family back to Nazareth. Verse 40 resembles the way Luke concluded the infancy story of John the Baptist (1:80), both of them having been modeled by Luke on a similar feature in the Samuel story (1 Sam. 2:26).

Sermon possibilities for this section include:

1. *Personal religious experiences and the Christian community.* Explore this story in conversation with the next story (the boy Jesus in the Temple), both of which focus on a pivotal issue for Luke. There was no discontinuity between God's presence for people in God's word (the law of Moses) and in the Temple cult, and God's presence for people in God's Son. The parents of Jesus were guided to go to the Temple in Jerusalem by their devotion to keep the requirements of the law. In the next section, Jesus himself, reflecting his parents' law and Temple piety, went to the Temple in obedience to the law, where he displayed unusual interest, perception, and competence for discerning the will of God as it was revealed in the teachings of Moses.

Yet in modern times each generation thinks its religious experiences and discoveries are unique and therefore both incomprehensible and even necessarily critical of prior religious values and practices of the community of faith. In the Christian pilgrimage as elsewhere, true disciples need to embrace their past with discriminating appreciation.

Where we have come from shapes our understanding of who we are and what it is God intends for us to be in the future. Until we can harmoniously locate our own individual religious experiences and convictions within the larger view of what God is working to accomplish in the creation from the beginning, but supremely in the person of Jesus, God's Son, and, by extension, within the life of the church, we are ill prepared to assume the role God intends for us in that ongoing enterprise of redemption.

2. *Simeon models spiritual devotion.* Examine the figure of Simeon as a model of Spirit-animated devotion. With reference to the past, he was "righteous": He honored the will of God disclosed in the law, he relied on the forgiveness of God when he transgressed, and he lived in confident

assurance of his covenantal acceptance by God. With reference to the present, he was "devout": He was single-mindedly devoted to the worship and the service of God, and daily he celebrated and renewed his sense of dependence on God. With reference to the future, he was "looking for the consolation of Israel": Although he was probably elderly, he was not depressed or full of regret or despairing; he was buoyed by the conviction that the most important moment and experience of his life was still ahead, and his life was still molded and shaped by vivid expectation of the coming of God's salvation through "the Lord's Messiah."

The Spirit kindled and sustained within Simeon that hope, and it gave him assurance of the accuracy of his conviction. The Spirit brought him into the place of God's presence at the opportune moment, disclosed to him the true nature and identity of the baby whom he held, and stimulated him to pour forth praise, blessing, and adoration to God. He was among the first in Israel to "rise" and not "fall" because of the child.

THE BOY JESUS IN THE TEMPLE (2:41–52)

Luke now relates a story about Jesus as a twelve-year-old boy going to the Jerusalem Temple. To call the occasion his "Bar Mitzvah" intrudes too many distorting modern images onto the first-century story. But he does make a preparatory visit to the Temple just prior to the time when he would become a "son of the Commandment," and assume the responsibilities and obligations of belonging to God's covenant people as well as enjoying the privileges his circumcision had affirmed and celebrated. The impact is even stronger as he identifies himself as the Son of the One who gave the Commandment.

Up until now only others have testified to his messianic sonship. Now Jesus himself confirms what other "men and angels" have been saying about him. His testimony was given prior to any of those other occasions—baptism, transfiguration, resurrection—where other Christian traditions had located the inauguration of his divine sonship. So the story supported Luke's own persuasion that Jesus had been Son of God from conception.

(a) *The multiple functions of Luke's story.* Luke accomplished several things with this story:

1) As a transitional account, it provides one narrative about Jesus between his infancy and the beginning of his public ministry.
2) It illustrates the growth, nurture, and development of Jesus prior to his baptism, as Luke had just summarized it (v. 40).

3) It is an additional example of Temple piety and obedience to Mosaic law.

4) It provides a neat *inclusio,* ending the infancy narratives as Luke had begun them, with a story located in the Temple at Jerusalem (which is also where he will end his Gospel — 24:53).

5) It depicts Jesus giving significant testimony about his own identity as Son of God.

(b) Jesus with the teachers of the law. Luke's story portrays Jesus sitting with the teachers of the law and participating in their discussions. One of the duties of the religious leaders was to support and supplement the family education of the children in matters of the faith. Jesus' participation disclosed a spiritual precocity which demonstrated that he was "filled with wisdom."

The interpreter will want to avoid using this story to perpetuate a popular misunderstanding that, at the age of twelve, Jesus was so divinely omniscient that he "taught the teachers." An illustration appears periodically in Sunday school "take-home" papers that shows Jesus standing and instructing awestruck rabbis, astoundingly holding his own while arguing or disputing with them. That is to read considerably more into the story than Luke intended to communicate.

The amazement that Jesus' astuteness evoked from the teachers of Torah that day anticipated the wonder and astonishment people were to experience later at the authority with which he taught the word of God during his public teaching ministry (4:15, 22, 32; 5:1, etc.). This is a consistent motif in Luke's portrait of Jesus, which reaches climactic expression as the resurrected Jesus "opened (the disciples') minds to understand the scriptures (24:45)" that would inform their witness (24:48).

(c) Mary reacts to Jesus' behavior. Luke crafted an artful tension between Jesus and Mary in the story. "All who heard him were amazed" — she was provoked. They were astonished when they saw him — she scolded him. His understanding went beyond reasonable expectation — she did not understand when he spoke divine revelation. She expected familial obedience to "your father and (me)" — he affirmed allegiance to his "Father."

Verse 51a continues to hold the two loyalties in tension. The adolescent Jesus fulfilled the Mosaic requirement of holding his parents in honor. That tension was to be resolved only later as the mature Jesus redefined "family" in terms of those who shared his allegiance to the higher obedience. Mary's rebuke and her pondering were personal, experiential instances of the "rising and falling" Jesus was sent to provoke (v. 34).

There is profound irony as Luke described Mary and Joseph finding Jesus in the Temple, where he had already "found himself," or, better, "been found," and so, knew himself to be at home. Luke intensified the irony with the play around the term "father." The divergence between what Mary meant by that term and what Jesus meant by his reference to "my Father's house" suggested that the parents and not the boy were closer to being "lost." Mary's anxious rebuke and the observation that they did not understand Jesus' saying about his Father's house augment that impression. Thus the story becomes an instance when Mary already has been painfully and confusedly pierced with the sword of discernment and discrimination (v. 35).

The concluding sentence to the anecdote (v. 52) is a variation of Luke's repeated adaptations of 1 Samuel 2:26 (cf. v. 40 and 1:80).

Possibilities for sermon development include:

1. The differing views of Jesus and Mary on the idea of lost and found. A presentation might be developed under the rubric of "Lost and Found." Jesus' parents traveled from their home to the city for the observance of a significant religious festival. In a very profound sense for Jesus it was a homecoming. The Jerusalem Temple was the traditional site where, according to Jewish piety, one was most intimately exposed to the presence of God.

Although his parents considered him lost, Jesus knew exactly where he was. And he knew exactly with whom he was dealing. Jesus listened and questioned the teachers as they explored dimensions and aspects of scriptural tradition. His attentiveness was more than schoolboy eagerness at finding the exercise intellectually stimulating. Through scripture, God made the divine will known. *That* was what fascinated Jesus and captivated his attention.

2. Zeal for the responsibilities of belonging to God. Reflect on what transpired for Jesus at this stage in his life. Apparently Luke's reference to his age was to present him as being taken by his parents to the Temple in Jerusalem in preparation for the time soon to arrive when he would formally become a "son of the Commandment." To take on the religious responsibilities of obedience to the Mosaic law could mean offering clarifications of obscurities and corrections of distortion coming from unexpected and, to all outward appearances, unlikely quarters.

Obedience to the will of God disclosed in the Torah involves far more than submission to its restrictions and regulations. It means aggressively assuming the role of advocate and broker for the will of God contained and revealed in the law. Knowing the will of God presupposes a disposition to obey that will. First one must will with singleness of heart to be obedient to the plan of God, then discern what the specifics of the divine will for one's life are, and do it.

Preparation For Public Ministry

Luke 3:1–4:13

Luke had discontinued his narrative concerning John the Baptist in 1:80, where he had concluded the story of his circumcision and naming with a typical summary statement about John's nurture and growth, and with a vague allusion to John's sojourn in the wilderness "until the day he appeared publically to Israel." Luke resumed his account of John with the beginning of this section.

Once again the stories of John and Jesus are interwoven. The prominence Luke gave to John up to and including this section aided him in depicting the story of Jesus as the pivotal component in the larger story of salvation-history. John served to link Jesus to the story of what God had been doing throughout the course of Israel's history as related in the Jewish scriptures. Jesus was both continuation and culmination of that holy history. Just as God's saving acts precede Jesus, so they extend beyond his earthly career, as Luke related in the second volume of his work, the book of Acts.

As important as the infancy stories were for Luke as an opening overture, this section is the beginning of the Gospel story proper. Statements Luke wrote later indicate that he thought of it as such (see Acts 1:22; 10:37).

PREACHING OF JOHN (3:1–20)

Luke began this section with a long, complicated sentence that, in the Greek, extends through the first six verses. Its complexity recalls the involved sentence he used for his prologue (1:1–4), though the literary style here is not so elegant. The recitation of the names of political and religious leaders was for effect, not for documentation. The details, pressed too hard, disclose insurmountable discrepancies. Their cumulative effect promoted recognition of the historical framework of salvation-

33

history. The saving presence of God intervened at a specific moment in human history.

(a) *The prophetic role of John the Baptist.* The call that activated John's ministry as precursor and preparer for the coming of the Messiah—a ministry for which he was divinely designated even before his birth—found him in the wilderness where Luke had last let us see him in 1:80. His "baptism of repentance for the forgiveness of sins" (v. 3:3) was an act of prophetic symbolism pointing to the reality of God's forgiveness. It was a purificatory rite whose efficacy depended on religious reform and conversion, and, when that was really present, communicated what it symbolized. So Luke portrayed John's ministry as a proleptic anticipation of the effects of Jesus' life, ministry, and passion.

Luke both corrected and extended Mark's prophetic citation. He dropped the first part since that actually came from Malachi and not Isaiah. He then extended the part from Isaiah 40:3 to include 40:4–5 because it characterized God's salvation as extending beyond the limits of Israel to embrace "all people/all flesh." By his use of the quotation, Luke alerted his readers that the activity of John he was about to describe was to be understood as the fulfillment of that prophecy.

(b) *Illustrations of John's preaching.* In verses 7–17, Luke gave three examples of John's preaching, followed by a general summary in verse 18.

The first (vv. 7–9) is a prophetic oracle of eschatological (end-time) judgment. Especially striking is John's sharp indictment of arrogant Jewish pride and reliance on national privilege. Through transgressions they had forfeited automatic, ethnic inclusion in the people of God. They were in the same situation before the righteous God as was the rest of humanity. Trees were to be evaluated not by their roots, but by their fruits. So John gave a ringing summons for moral reformation. The renewal of heart symbolized by John's baptism had its verification in specific changes in ethical conduct.

The second example of John's preaching (vv. 10–14) offered specific applications of John's call for moral amendment. Neither tax collectors nor soldiers would have been included in the definition by Jewish Pharisaic orthodoxy of the true children of Abraham. They were all the more apt as examples precisely because they represented an extreme on the far edge of Jewish piety. It is remarkable that neither of the first two examples of John's preaching that Luke included make any specific reference to the coming Messiah.

The third example (vv. 15–17) did represent John's messianic alert and was called forth in response to the expectations of the coming Messiah so prominent in Jewish piety. John renounced the role of Messiah for him-

self, describing the differences between them as extreme. Th
to be the personification of the impending end-time wrath, th
"the falling and the rising" of many in Israel (v. 2:34). In that
baptizing "with the Holy Spirit and with fire" corresponded to ᴸsion
of eschatological judgment. For Luke and his community, however, that
was surely heard as recast in the light of the experience of Pentecost.

It is remarkable that in this third example there is no indication that
John had Jesus specifically in mind. Possibly Luke felt that John had
underestimated the scope and function of his own role (cf. 7:18 ff., and the
comments on that section below). Luke concluded this account with an
abbreviated reference to John's arrest and imprisonment. He thereby
effectively removed him from the scene before the onset of Jesus' public
ministry.

A suggested direction for preaching:

Focus on the continuity that exists between the preaching of John and
the ministry and work of Jesus. We tend to think of Jesus primarily in
terms of his special uniqueness. Taken to the extreme, that can result in a
"Jesus piety" that is regarded as radically distinctive and essentially
divorced from what God was about throughout the holy history of Israel.
It also can encourage the false assumption that the Christian hope and the
"consolation of Israel" were not only different but even exclusive of each
other.

Throughout the rest of his Gospel, Luke portrayed Jesus as personify-
ing through his authoritative teaching and his acts of supernatural power
that which John announced through his preaching. God's wrath is God's
grace; God's judgment is salvation. There is no redemption without
repentance; there is no forgiveness without moral reformation. The Messiah who is coming is the embodiment of God's radical claim for the right
to rule the human will. Affirmative response to that radical claim
inevitably results in a new ethical posture vis-à-vis others.

THE IDENTITY OF JESUS:
ANOINTING AND GENEALOGY (3:21–38)

(a) *Luke altered Mark's version.* Luke ordinarily followed the narrative
order of one of his source documents, the Gospel of Mark. When he
altered that order, as he does right at the beginning, we may assume it was
for a significant purpose. Mark told of John's preaching, then related the
baptism of Jesus and followed that with an abbreviated version of Jesus'
temptation in the wilderness (Mark 1:1–13). Luke followed John's preaching with Jesus' baptism (actually, his anointing), then inserted Jesus'

genealogy before proceeding to narrate an expanded version of the temptation tradition.

Mark's account of the baptism of Jesus stressed his empowerment by the Holy Spirit for the prosecution of his ministry, which was then immediately given its initial test with the temptation experience. Luke was interested in the empowering aspect of the story, too, but by inserting the genealogy he gave equally strong emphasis to the disclosure of Jesus' true identity.

Luke's two-verse version (vv. 21–22) relegated mention of Jesus' baptism to a dependent clause, almost as an aside. John was not specifically listed as the agent of Jesus' baptism, probably because Luke had just removed him from the scene by describing his arrest. John had summoned all Israel to a repentance whereby they would fit themselves for the coming salvation-judgment. By being baptized as he approached the inauguration of his public ministry, Jesus claimed solidarity with them.

(*b*) *The Holy Spirit anointed Jesus.* The primary focus of the passage is on the descent of the Holy Spirit and the heavenly voice, all of which occurred, according to Luke, *after* the baptism, while Jesus was praying. Throughout his two-volume narrative, Luke showed particular interest in the posture of prayer assumed by Jesus and others of the community of faith.

Luke stressed the Spirit's descent "in bodily form" to avoid the suggestion that it was fantasy or hallucination. Jesus was thereby anointed and empowered for ministry. The heavenly voice that accompanied this visual manifestation confirmed both who he was and of what his ministry would consist. He stood in the singular relation of sonship to God (Ps. 2:7), whose expression during the course of his ministry would take the shape of self-spending service characteristic of the faithful servant of God (Is. 42:1). So Jesus was portrayed already prior to the inception of his ministry as the paradigm for all with whom God is well pleased (2:14).

(*c*) *The genealogy of Jesus.* Luke intruded a genealogy into Mark's narrative structure that is pocked with obscure details. Thirty-six of the names in his list are unknown in the documents of the Old Testament. Comparison with Matthew's genealogy (Matt. 1:1–17) defies harmonization. What theological interests led Luke to include it? The parenthetic correction "as was thought" to the assertion that Jesus was the son of Joseph (v. 23) conformed to Luke's prior portrayal of the virginal conception. Verse 31 confirmed Davidic ancestry, and verse 34 established linear descent from the foundational patriarch, Abraham.

Especially important for Luke's purposes was the last series of names in the genealogy (vv. 34–38), which went all the way back to Adam, "son of God"! Jesus who had just been identified by the heavenly voice as the

Son of God was descended from a line that went back to Adam and so ultimately to God. Adam's divine sonship, flawed because of disobedience, now comes to perfection in the person of Jesus, and through him, all humanity is to be related to God in a new way.

Luke's inclusion of the genealogy contributed to his interest in stressing continuity between the person and work of Jesus and the historical and religious heritage of Israel. It also advances his conviction that the effects of what God accomplished through Jesus went far beyond the limits of empirical Israel to embrace universal dimensions. Further, it not only related Jesus and his work to humanity beyond Israel but also, by implication, related Israel to the rest of humanity in an out-of-the-ordinary way.

(*d*) *Emphasis on the identity of Jesus.* Luke has already generated considerable momentum concerning the cumulative testimony to the identity of Jesus. These included: 1) the angel's announcement to Mary, 2) Elizabeth's greeting to Mary, 3) the angel's message to the shepherds, 4) the testimony of Simeon (and Anna), 5) Jesus' emerging self-awareness as a youth, 6) the implied referent for John's testimony, 7) the heavenly voice at the anointing, which confirmed all of the above, and 8) the genealogy, which documented Jesus' identity down through the course of human history.

A sermon might explore how our answer to the question, "Who is Jesus?" controls our grasp of who we are before God.

The christological emphasis is so dominant in the passages in this section that it governs the direction of interpretive appropriation. What was definitive for establishing the true identity of Jesus? Ultimately every testimony stemmed from God. The angels were messengers of the divine will and purpose. Elizabeth, Simeon, and John all bore witness informed by a discernment that was possible for them only after they had been filled with the Holy Spirit of God. Even the genealogy which, at first blush, might seem to be an appeal to pride of pedigree, discloses its true import only when it is extended back to encompass the totality of the human story as embraced in the purposes of God at creation.

The question of our own identity may appear to trivialize the majestic testimony of the Lukan presentation until we remember that the question is being raised precisely within the community of faith. What benchmarks decide the issue of identity for us? The ambiguity and lack of clarity evoked by that inquiry disclose the confusing multiplicity of claims to authority for determining who we are. Parentage, schooling, and geographical region; line of work, level of prosperity, and social status; the clubs we belong to, the people we know, and the people who know us; the ideologies, the politics, and the social philosophies to which we give our allegiance; whom we have married, what we have done, what we will do, and what our children do; what we drive, what we wear, what we have read, what we watch on TV; where we have or have not been, where we hope to go; and on and on.

Our culture and our own nurture allow so many voices to compete for our acquiescence in submitting the issue of our identity to their arbitration. And good Christian folks—even preachers—get caught up in the struggle of sorting out which of the competing claims are significant, and which are not. Yet every time we experience that struggle, we may be sure of one thing: We have forgotten our baptism. As the anointing Spirit empowered and consecrated Jesus for his work, the heavenly voice named him for who he was in the light of the saving purposes of God.

At our baptism God names us. We belong to God. We are made new beings in Jesus Christ by divine love. Who are we? All the other above considerations, if entertained as definitive individually or in any combination, bespeak our solidarity with Adam, the disobedient son of God. The call of Jesus is for us to give priority to who we are in the light of his redemptive work and to claim that solidarity which moves beyond Adam to be fused with the new Son of God in whom we are the children of God's new creation.

TEMPTATION OF JESUS (4:1–13)

Luke's story of the temptation of Jesus by the devil in the wilderness is closely connected with Jesus' anointing with the Holy Spirit and his genealogy. It was as the Spirit-empowered Son of God that Jesus was put to the test "in the wilderness," that portion of God's creation most inimical to life and therefore most visibly under the devil's control. Jesus had heard a voice saying, "You are my Son, the Beloved." Now he hears another voice saying, "*If* you are the Son of God . . ." The story relies on three assumptions both Jesus and the devil shared: 1) Jesus was the unique Son of God, 2) scripture disclosed the will of God, and, 3) the devil ruled over the kingdoms of this present age.

(a) *The background to the story in the Jewish scriptures.* Depending on the connection Luke intended between the genealogy and the temptation, he may have been pressing a contrast—between the capitulation of Adam son of God to satanic temptation and the resistance of Jesus Son of God. More obviously in the background is the tradition of Israel's wilderness wanderings after their redemption from slavery in Egypt and before taking possession of the land of promise. The number "forty" occurred frequently in the Jewish scriptures to symbolize an interval of testing and preparation prior to a significant advance to a new stage of salvation-history.

More particularly, Deuteronomy 8:2ff. stands in the background of Luke's version of the temptation. As God was shown there leading Israel in the wilderness forty years, so here the Spirit of God led Jesus for forty days in the wilderness. There God tested Israel to prove its fidelity; here the devil tempted Jesus to pervert fidelity. The three temptations with which the devil confronted Jesus resembled three instances when Israel failed to persevere in single-minded obedience to God during the wilderness wanderings:

1) They rebelled against the monotonous food God provided when they were hungry and murmured against Moses, yearning for the greater dietary variety they had known as slaves in Egypt.
2) They compromised their covenant commitment to God by seeking to serve the foreign gods of Canaan.
3) They put God to the test by demanding that God give them water to drink.

(b) *The temptations exploit Jewish messianic expectations.* The contest revolved around traditional but inadequate and incomplete messianic anticipations of the Jewish people. The devil challenged Jesus to prove his messiahship in conformity with their expectations, and thereby pervert it. Each temptation assaulted Jesus not at a place of weakness and vulnerability, but at the point of his greatest strength—his compassion, his commitment to God, his faith. Nor should we think of them as momentary. They represented the lure of popular but shallow enthusiasm as well as the hostility, isolation, and rejection that would plague him constantly all the way to Calvary.

The diabolic dimensions of the temptations should not be underestimated. What the devil demanded of Jesus was not heinous debauchery, depravity, or outrage. Since proper desires fulfilled in an improper context become just as sinful, he sought to induce Jesus to secure a legitimate end through illegitimate means.

The allure of such a proposal is considerable. If Jesus accepted the devil's lordly authority and subordinated himself to it, his kingly rule over all the peoples of the earth could be gained without conflict with the powers of evil, without rejection and betrayal, without a cross. The potency of a temptation is in proportion to the intensity of the appeal of the goal.

The devil's offers, sometimes couched in biblical language, were countered by Jesus with citations from Deuteronomy, attesting that God's will for God's people and God's intent for the Messiah Son had been sufficiently declared in the scriptural traditions entrusted to Israel. The clarity and discernment with which he appealed to scripture confirmed his effective empowerment by the Holy Spirit.

(*c*) *The testing continues.* Luke concluded the story by asserting that the devil departed "until an opportune time." Undoubtedly he had in mind the period of Jesus' passion when "Satan entered into Judas" (22:3). He did not mean to imply, however, that the devil was absent or inactive until Judas's decision to betray. Luke played upon the gist of the devil's enticements at several points in the further course of his narrative. Galileans lacked bread in the wilderness; Pharisees demanded a sign from heaven. Galileans, Pharisees, and disciples, all three, thought primarily in political, earthly terms of the kingly rule of God that Jesus proclaimed. The devil continued to assault and tempt Jesus also through the distorted demands and the increasingly virulent opposition he encountered.

A sermon could be developed along these lines:

The interpreter may want to invite people to broaden their understanding of the extent, scope, and duration of the temptations of Jesus. The temptations as portrayed in this story really serve as a synopsis of the entire spiritual journey of Jesus as he contended with the allure of popular acclaim and approval wedded to limited and constricting expectations.

Without trivializing the intensity of Jesus' wilderness encounter, it is nonetheless appropriate to point out that all Christians find themselves struggling with similar temptations to dilute the quality and even exchange the object of their commitment during the course of their pilgrimage. There are times when they too, in response to the call of God, are tempted to be satisfied with offering the adequate rather than the best that their disciplined service can offer . . . or, having caught the vision, to succumb to impatience and seek to accomplish God's purposes by means alien to God's character . . . or, to seek to coerce God by taking shortcuts to success.

Ministry in Galilee

Luke adopted Mark's organization of traditional materials around a geographical schema. Most of the events in this section are explicitly described or implicitly assumed to have taken place in and around the region of Galilee. Luke understood that the sending of the gospel to the Gentiles was implemented programmatically only after the Ascension and Pentecost. As he composed this section, he tended to eliminate any references from his source material that suggested otherwise.

PREACHING AND REJECTION
AT NAZARETH (4:14–30)

Luke found a version of this incident in the Gospel of Mark, though Mark placed it later in his narrative, after the public ministry of Jesus had already begun. The reference to works Jesus had done in Capernaum (v. 23) presumes activity that Luke described only later in 4:31ff., and is a dead giveaway that Luke altered the sequence of stories he had found in his written sources. He reordered the sequence of events as he had found them in Mark's Gospel by making this story the initial episode in his account of Jesus' public ministry, and then he expanded Mark's version.

(*a*) *The programmatic function of the story.* In this story Luke highlights some major motifs—several of which he had already introduced—that will be prominent throughout the course of the narrative in both volumes of his work, his Gospel and Acts. These include the preparation for the good news of God's salvation in the Jewish scriptures, the anointing with the Holy Spirit, the gospel proclaimed to the poor, the announcement of the inbreaking of the Messianic Age, the opposition from the Jews, and the mission to the Gentiles.

It would not be too exaggerated to describe this first story as presenting in capsule form the entire course of the ministry of Jesus. It was in the

41

same "power of the Spirit" which had sustained Jesus and enabled him to emerge victorious from his wilderness trials (v. 14) that Jesus preached in the Nazareth synagogue. The Isaiah passage (actually a conflation in which Isa. 61:1–2 was expanded by adding Isa. 58:6) was understood by Luke to voice the emerging self-awareness of Jesus as he began his public ministry. His person and work is in fulfillment of scripture. He will find positive response from some, yet will be received with murderous hostility by others, ones who *should* be the most prepared and therefore the most positive and open to him.

(*b*) *The hostile response of Jesus' neighbors.* The negative reception accorded Jesus by the people of his hometown provided a paradigm for the hostile reception Jesus experienced throughout his ministry from the Jewish people in general and especially the Jewish leaders, with only a few noteworthy exceptions. The same pattern was reflected in Luke's last word, again based on a prophecy of Isaiah and addressed by Paul in Acts to the Jewish leaders in Rome, "this salvation of God has been sent to the Gentiles; they will listen" (Acts 28:28). The episode is a dramatic inaugural tableau depicting how Jesus became the occasion for "the falling and the rising of many in Israel" as Simeon had foretold, "a sign that will be opposed" (2:34).

Preaching possibilities suggested by this passage include:

1. A sermonic comparison with Luke 7:18–23. Jesus will later use the same passage to reply to the inquiries of John the Baptist's messengers (7:18–23). The "poor, captives, blind, oppressed" all represent the righteous remnant in Israel. The people of Nazareth were unprepared to recognize in Jesus the anointed one of God because they myopically did not recognize themselves in any of the Isaian categories.

2. Overfamiliarity can produce dismissive underestimation. "Today," said Jesus, meaning that "even as you heard it this scripture was fulfilled." The word "today," placed by Luke in emphatic position, is the "hour of decision." It is a moment charged with the potential of eternity, but not for them, because they did not "hear" the scripture. They just heard Jesus, Joseph's boy. At least twice more Luke used the word "today" in that very pregnant sense. One is in the story of Zacchaeus (19:1–10) and the other about the thief on the cross (23:39–43). A powerful homiletic appropriation might be accomplished by bringing these stories and the moment of fundamental option each describes into dialogue with one another.

"Today!" Jesus said; "Isn't he something!" they replied. What an extraordinary contrast! Jesus had just told them that right now, even as they were listening, the highest, most precious hopes treasured by their religious tradition down through the years had become reality. And they were saying, "Isn't that nice how well he reads Hebrew. His voice is pleasant and carries well. Such a fine young man, old Joseph's boy. He knows such big words and speaks so well even without notes." Wondering at his gracious words is just not enough. It is insufficient merely to be amazed; wonder by itself misses the point. Their superficial adulation hindered their understanding with discernment.

"Is not this Joseph's son?" is not a put-down. Word of Jesus' extraordinary activity had been spread (vv. 14f.) and had reached Nazareth too. If Jesus had done marvelous things elsewhere, how much more could they expect to enjoy the benefits from their very own hometown boy wonderworker? They were expecting to receive preferential treatment, but were basing their claims on inadequate and inappropriate grounds: personal acquaintance, hometown loyalties, Jesus' assumption of family duties to the community, or common religious affiliation.

3. *Jesus' rejection of attempts to control him result not in repentence but in rage.* Note the significant shift that takes place as the story continues to unfold. Jesus not only rejected their suggestion of special hometown privilege and obligation, he blatantly repudiated any claim for special treatment on national religious grounds. Both the proverbial wisdom and the scripture stories he cited counseled the rejection of their demands.

The prophetic examples of ministry to non-Jews at times when there was great need within Israel made quite clear the universal scope of his work. Jesus' mission extended well beyond the national/tribal limits of traditional Jewish piety. And they *heard that.* He was finally getting through to them, and they did not like it, not even a little bit. His suggestion—that the privileges and benefits they regarded as the exclusive prerogative of Israel were to be usurped by the nondeserving, the noneligible, the non-Jew—drowned out the singularly good news he had just announced on *their* behalf, too.

"All in the synagogue were filled with rage" (v. 4:28) shows that even in a synagogue devoted to the worship and study of the will of God, a synagogue filled with those who knew Jesus better than most, even there the devil's kingly rule and not God's held power. (Luke repeated this observation in the next story of exorcism *in the synagogue,* and, by extension, in the opposition of the religious rulers.)

Luke's description of their driving Jesus out of the city to throw him off a cliff is more than a first-century version of a lynch mob. That was the procedure the law required for the stoning of someone no longer fit to be a member of the community of Israel. They effectively excommunicated Jesus, making him a non-Jew, a Gentile. His miraculous invulnerability demonstrated that human opposition was powerless against Jesus at this point, just as the devil's power had proven ineffective in the story of the

Temptation (4:1–13). So Jesus became the occasion for "the falling and the rising" (2:34) of his own, his hometown folk, a "sign that will be opposed."

Note the change in the reactions of the people who thought of Jesus as belonging to them in a special way. They shifted from rapt attention (v. 20) to unanimous approbation (v. 22a) to great expectation (v. 22b) to angry opposition (v. 28) to diabolically murderous action (v. 29). Such is the peril whenever people claim Jesus for their own yet still reserve the right to dictate what the shape, form, and direction of his rule over them will be. "Today" is as unexpected and startling in our times as theirs—and as little heeded. We are the church, the eschatological community, the people of the end-time. We pray, "Thy kingdom come," we "proclaim the Lord's death until he comes" in the Sacrament, but we are as ill prepared for the authoritative announcement of "today!" as were they.

4. The Isaianic shape of the church's ministry. The passages from Isaiah were not only helpful for articulating the message and mission of Jesus, but are also a convenient summary for the ministry of the church as it seeks to extend the work of Jesus. The church, like Jesus, is the community of the anointed of God. God's Spirit has been poured out upon the church. It, too, has been commissioned to preach "good news to the poor." If Christians are to do that well, they must first know themselves to *be* the poor who have been the recipients of the same good news that has transformed them into God's poor, those whose only locus for trust and reliance is their absolute dependence on God alone.

"Release to the captives" is proclaimed effectively only by those who in the light of the gospel have been led to recognize and claim their own captivation by authorities and powers inimical to God, and who have discovered consequently that the best use of their gospel-effected release has been for them gladly to become captives of God's grace. Only those who remember with terrifying clarity the many times both prior to and since their Christian confession—when they were intentionally blind to the presence of God who willed to renew, to restore, to reassert God's right to rule—are able to announce persuasively how others may become sighted. Those who know themselves to have been liberated from oppression are those best schooled to recognize the diabolical dimensions of all forms of oppression, and are best motivated to commit themselves to the eradication of such oppression no matter what the cost.

Without such a self-awareness, the church's preaching and teaching inevitably become paternalistic, triumphalistic, and ultimately ineffective. The Church preaches such good news well only if, *every time,* it recognizes its solidarity with those who hear the message. The church, still, is poor, captivated, blind, and oppressed. Yet in that very recognition it is released, sighted, set at liberty, and reassured that it is the people of the end-time "acceptable year of the Lord."

THE AUTHORITY OF JESUS (4:31–6:11)

This next cycle of six episodes builds on the multiple traditions used to clarify the identity of Jesus—the focus of Luke up until now. Luke shaped the prior story about Jesus' preaching in Nazareth and the response it evoked to prepare his readers for this shift in emphasis on the authority of Jesus. While continuing to develop the theme of Jesus' identity, that story also suggested the issue of his authority.

The question of authority correlates to the issue of identity. The preaching in Nazareth demonstrated the authority of Jesus in a reverse way. The authority of his preaching ultimately evoked their wrath. His words served to disclose "the inner thoughts of many" and so became for them "a sign that will be opposed" (2:34–35).

Now in these episodes, Luke shifted the emphasis and focused primarily on the nature and extent of Jesus' authority and the varied responses that authority called forth. The assertion with which Luke identified the theme not just for the next story but also for the entire section is found in 4:32: "They were astounded at his teaching, because he spoke with authority."

Miraculous Healings at Capernaum (4:31–44)

The primary reason the synoptic evangelists included stories in their narratives about the miracles Jesus did was because those said something very important about who Jesus was and what God was accomplishing through him. The basic issue to which the miracle stories spoke was not one of pastoral interest in the Christian solution to human calamity. The basic issue was theological: Who controls creation? Who rules in the created order?

Early Christians had learned from late Jewish apocalyptic thought to view their world as caught up in a great struggle for power. Human sin had given to those supernatural powers opposed to God the opportunity to usurp God's right to rule in creation. In the Jewish piety contemporary with Jesus, one of the anticipated works of the Messiah who was to come was the liberating of all humankind—and all of creation—from enslavement to the supernatural powers of evil personified by the devil (Beliar, Satan) and his agents. Through Jesus, the anointed and empowered Son of God-Messiah, God was going on the attack to free creation from satanic enslavement, to reclaim it and restore God's right to rule.

Luke addressed directly the issue of control by focusing on the authority of Jesus. "He spoke with authority" (v. 32) did not mean that people recognized he was an expert about God, the law, and religious matters. Rather, it meant that his word, like God's, accomplished what it said. At Nazareth when he had said, "Today this scripture has been fulfilled in your hearing" (v. 21), *it was so,* and their response determined whether it was for their salvation or their condemnation.

This authority of Jesus, already compellingly encountered in his preaching of the reign of God, was also manifested in mighty miraculous works of power by which he demonstrated the present efficacious reality of the rule of God. For Jesus to establish the kingly rule of God, the kingly rule of Satan had to be destroyed. He had resisted the extension of Satan's rule over his own person during the Temptation. Here he began to push back the devil's hold over other segments of creation.

The section consists of (a) two miracle stories, (1) an exorcism (vv. 31–37) and (2) a healing (vv. 38–39), (b) a general summary of healings and exorcisms (vv. 40–41), and (c) a significant choice Jesus made about the future shape of his ministry (vv. 42–43).

(*a.1*) *A case of demon possession.* This was an excellent occasion to portray the controlling presence of an invading power. It had its counterpart in the anointing of Jesus after baptism, which also depicted the controlling presence of an invading power. So Luke drew the lines sharply. The issue is not "Shall we be free?" Rather, the crux of the matter is, "To whom shall we be enslaved? To whom shall we offer allegiance and give obedience?" Jesus encountered the man possessed with the spirit of an unclean demon (vv. 33–37) in the synagogue on the Sabbath. This made it dramatically clear that no time and place in God's creation was immune to the invasion of demonic rule, not even the time and place especially devoted to the worship of God and the study of God's will.

Note the irony in the question "Have you come to destroy us?" (v. 34). That is exactly why Jesus had come, not just into the synagogue but into the world, to destroy those powers opposed to God and to reassert God's right to rule. The authority of Jesus over demons called forth from them recognition of his messianic identity, "I know who you are!" But getting Jesus' identity right is not enough, unless that recognition results in acquiescence to God's right to rule. *That* the demon resisted, and because of that the demonic control was expelled. "Without having done him any harm" (v. 35) was explicit acknowledgement that the demon, having acknowledged the authority of Jesus, was impotent to do further damage.

(*a.2*) *A healing.* Luke reinforced his point with the abbreviated companion story of the healing of Peter's mother-in-law (vv. 38–39). In the background was the conviction that the presence of disease in the world, which stood for mortality and decay, was additional evidence of Satan's control. The Pharisees taught that tending to human illness on the Sabbath was allowable only if the illness was life-threatening. The crowds conformed their behavior to comply with those restrictions (v. 40); Jesus did not. That both of Jesus' first miracles took place on the Sabbath allowed Luke to voice his conviction that this activity was as appropriate as the teaching and preaching on the Sabbath that had occurred both in Nazareth and Capernaum. Actually from Luke's view, they were all one and the same—effective announcement of God's right to rule.

(*b*) *Summary of additional healings and exorcisms.* This section, verses 40–41, allowed Luke both to broaden and to intensify the impact of the previous stories. With each of his cures Jesus was reclaiming for God additional territory from the realm of Satan's rule. They were dramatic manifestations of the good news that God was reestablishing the realm of the divine. The catchword "rebuke" (vv. 35, 39, 41; cf. also the story of the stilling of the storm, 8:24) tied all three stories together and represented Jesus' authoritative repudiation of any claim of an alien power to have control over God's good creation.

(*c*) *Jesus' decision.* The significance of the final verses of this section (42–44) might easily be overlooked. With them Luke described a major advance in his portrait of Jesus' understanding of his ministry. Jesus rejected the attempts of the people at Capernaum, who had received his ministry so positively, to have him locate permanently in Capernaum. He opted instead for a peripatetic ministry devoted to announcing to people in a much broader region the inbreaking of the end-time rule of God. He chose not to stay and cultivate an acre already restored to God's rule but rather to continue to plow new ground, extending and expanding the rule of God into new areas.

Opportunities for exposition include:

*1. How **not** to preach the miracles.* The "miracle stories" in the synoptic tradition offer the opportunity to clarify and correct potentially confusing assumptions people sometimes hold as to what such stories are all about. Popular piety often finds in the stories about Jesus' miracles the best, most religious answers to specific human problems. When we are ill, we can take medicine or go to the doctor, but the most spiritual thing we can do, they say, is pray to God. If we are good enough or have a strong enough faith, God will heal us just as Jesus healed the leper or the blind man.

This perspective is a type of "Christian scientism" that is not just operative in sect groups but also is visible in some aspects of television ministry and in the emphasis on anointing for healing in some charismatic circles. Jesus' healing of the woman with a flow of blood suggests the real, spiritual solution to hemophilia. The story of the stilling of the storm offers a Christian model for securing protection and deliverance when a hurricane threatens the Gulf Coast. Exorcisms are the best, most Christian answer to psychoses.

Such an understanding of miracle stories can raise some monumental and excruciating pastoral dilemmas. A critical task for us is to avoid exploiting these miracle traditions for misleading and usually disappointing advice on how people are to cope with personal suffering and tragedy. Furthermore, if that is our primary interest in reading the miracle stories, it is likely that we will miss what they were intended to convey in their Gospel context.

2. Conflict at the supernatural level. Interpreting this section will require considerable hermeneutical translation. It presumes a worldview most people would consider primitive and foreign today. Nor are most of us comfortable with "demon" and "Satan" language. Still, films such as "The Exorcist" and "Rosemary's Baby" show us that for many people those images lurk just beneath the surface and readily convey terror. A culture that has in its recent past the experience of the German National Socialist Holocaust, the My Lai massacre, and the Charles Manson cult is more prepared to entertain the possibility of supernatural dimensions of evil and the demonic than were previous "post-Enlightenment" generations.

3. The testimony of the miracles to Jesus. These stories portrayed Jesus reasserting God's right to rule in a creation that had repudiated that rule. If we are to discern the dimension of the miraculous in our spiritual experience, we need to search for every situation that evidenced the subordination of some aspect of God's creation to the demonic and that, in the power and light of the gospel, have been restored to wholeness and health. This includes not only physical infirmities, but also warped self-images; sick relationships; and exploitive, oppressive, and manipulative interactions.

4. Trying to fence in Jesus for our benefit. Another perspective which we might want to invite people to explore together is the way churches tend to try to make Jesus their own exclusive property. How do we seek to constrain Jesus from moving on in the service of God's royal rule? Sometimes overemphasis on ministry to the community of faith eclipses awareness that the community's worship and study are not just to praise God but to equip the community to go forth with Jesus beyond the confines of its own self-identity to engage in service on behalf of God to God's world.

We must be very clear that when we seek to restrict the word of the gospel and the presence of Jesus to our own "in-house" purposes, we have no more success with that restraint than did those folks at Capernaum. Jesus is out announcing the glad word of God's loving rule in all kinds of new and unexpected ways. Our task is not to harness him to our purposes. We just cannot do that. Rather, he calls us to attune ourselves and to give ourselves over to the motivation, guidance, and empowering of the Holy Spirit so that we may discern his work in the world and join him in his efforts.

Call to the First Disciples (5:1–11)

Luke took a tradition that focused on the moment of encounter and the response of faith. He shifted the perspective so that the story not only related the call of the first disciples, but also told of their commissioning for discipleship, with the emphasis on the latter. This story again demonstrated the effective authority of Jesus' word, as did the stories before and the stories that follow. That authority received awed acknowledgement by implication in the beginning of the story and with Jesus' words, "Let down your nets" (v. 4) and "you will be catching people" (v. 10).

(*a*) *Jesus' compelling authority overcomes resistance.* In the introduction Luke prepared his readers for the story's testimony to the authority of Jesus' word. People were flocking around Jesus, eager to hear the word of God from him. He commandeered Simon's boat from which to preach, requiring Simon, who was bone-weary tired and discouraged, to relaunch his craft—*and Simon did it!*

Jesus' next command intensified the impression of the effectiveness of his authoritative word. Jesus directed Simon to move the boat even farther from shore and lower his nets yet once again. Simon's professional experience as well as his human instincts dictated that he ignore that foolishness, cash in for the day, and go home to bed. But Simon found something irresistible about Jesus. With "If you say so" (v. 5), he complied, for the compelling authority of that word superceded the pessimistic expectations of Simon's years of experience as a professional fisherman.

Luke set the ineffective and even reluctant human efforts of Simon and his colleagues in dramatic contrast to the productive word of Jesus. It pointed toward the greater miracle—their decision to respond to his call and follow him.

(*b*) *Simon's obedient response.* Simon recognized Jesus' rightful authority and obeyed his directions. The result was more fish than Simon had seen in his nets at one time in his entire life. The catch was a sign of Jesus' effective authority over God's good creation. Anyone who had such control over creation was lord of creation. Simon knew himself to be in the presence of divine creativity and in need of the salvation Jesus brought.

Simon's experience of Jesus's authority led him to a recognition of Jesus' identity, which then, as always, resulted in a clear grasp of who he, Simon, was before such a presence. "Go away from me, Lord, for I am a sinful man!" (v. 8) was the way Simon articulated his recognition of both identities. It expressed the ingrained apprehension in Jewish piety of a sinner standing in the presence of divinity.

A transgressor was not just unworthy but was in mortal danger of the wrathful retribution of a righteous God. Astonishment led Simon to that recognition (v. 9). But astonishment and amazement are not enough in the presence of such power and authority. Jesus received plenty of that in the reactions from the crowds (for example, 4:32, 36). What was required further was single-minded commitment.

(c) *Call and commissioning.* "Do not be afraid" (v. 10) was the same response to holy awe and fear the angels had given in the nativity stories (1:13, 30; 2:10). They were words of forgiving grace setting aside the legitimate expectations of Jewish piety. And then Jesus told them, "You will be catching people." As central as the task of catching fish had been in their lives up until then, Jesus was able to get through to them that, in the saving purposes of God, people were more important than fish. If Simon and the others were as obedient to that word of authority as Simon had been to Jesus' instructions about going into deep water and letting down the nets, they would experience even more miraculous productivity as they shared in the restoration of God's right to rule in creation (cf. Peter's Pentecost discourse and its results in Acts 2).

Simon encountered and heard the word of God not just in Jesus' words but also in his person. Simon and his colleagues experienced the forgiving grace of God in the person of the Messiah who provided far more than was required, so that when they went to preach the gospel *who they were* confirmed the message they proclaimed.

Options for preaching include:

1. *Jesus' encounter with the fishermen moves them from discouragement through exhilaration to renunciation.* As Luke has related this story, it readily lends itself to application for the community of faith. Considerable care should be taken that Luke's emphasis on commissioning is retained. Jesus came upon the fishermen at a very low moment. They were professionals, and for them a lot was depending on the outcome of their labors. They had done their dead-level best. They had tried every trick of the trade. They had persevered, keeping at it when most others would have given up long ago. Still, they had no fish to show for it.

We know how they felt. We know what it is like to try our very best, do all that we know how to do, and yet still fail. We know what it is like to work hard, to train, to study our field, to get on-the-job experience, then to apply all of the wisdom, knowledge, and skill we have acquired and nothing comes of it. The loneliness of such discouragement and self-doubt is profound.

The alternative, which the story offers, at first seems hardly better. What are we to do when, with God's help, we succeed beyond our wildest imaginings only to discover we simply are not prepared to deal with it? Exhilaration is replaced by consternation when our nets begin to tear and our boat begins to sink and we must finally acknowledge ourselves inadequate to manage the opportunity at hand.

The third, hardest, and most crucial level to the story is the moment when God teaches us, in the midst of abundance, to walk off from it, leave it all, and become a servant of God's royal rule. With the help of his colleagues, Simon finally had managed to get all of those fish to shore. The fishermen were standing in the midst of a record catch of fish. The next task at hand was to get them to market before they spoiled. Only Jesus said to them in effect, "Friends, as good as fish are, ever since the beginning, God has made it crystal clear that people are more important than fish. Come help me net people for God's royal rule." That has to be the most persuasive disclosure of his compelling authority, for "they left everything and followed him" (v. 11). We have not really come to terms with Jesus' call to discipleship and its mandate until we plumb the depths of corresponding renunciation for the sake of service on his behalf.

2. Contrast the situations of the fishermen without Jesus and with Jesus. A meditation might be structured around the outline:

without Jesus:

> night of futile toil
>
> nothing taken
>
> nets empty
>
> discouragement

with Jesus:

> full nets
>
> full boats
>
> full hearts
>
> "Leave it!"

Transgressing Religious Constraints (5:12–6:11)

In this section Luke presented several stories that depicted Jesus as ignoring widely acknowledged religious prohibitions to advance his ministry of restoring God's right to rule in the creation. Although Mosaic law required absolute isolation of lepers from the healthy community, Jesus chose physical contact with a leper. He dared to forgive sins and was rewarded with the charge "Blasphemer!" for presuming to exercise a prerogative religion ascribed solely to God.

Jewish piety regarded tax collectors as being like Gentiles, yet not only did Jesus summon one to be his intimate associate, he also gladly sat down with him and his colleagues in religious table-fellowship. He minimized the highly regarded practice of religious fasting and countenanced the violation of Sabbath restrictions both in defense of his disciples and in order that he might restore a person to wholeness.

By grouping the stories, Luke was able, through the cumulative effect, to sharply intensify our awareness of the emergence and development of hostility from the Jewish religious leaders toward Jesus so that at the conclusion of the section they were "filled with fury" and were beginning to plot against him.

Healing the Leper (5:12–16)

Jesus is accosted by a leper. Neither the leper nor Jesus play the game according to the rules defined by religious regulation.

(*a*) **The leper violated Mosaic law.** "You can make me clean," the leper insisted. According to the law of Moses, a leper was a social and religious outcast, someone to be excluded from participation in the religious community. He should have cowered and withdrawn howling, "Unclean! Unclean!"

It was not that he despised the Mosaic law, but rather that he recognized the authority and power of Jesus to be greater than Moses. It is true that Jesus had become known far and wide as an extraordinarily powerful teacher who was also an effective healer and exorcist. Perhaps that reputation was the genesis of the leper's conviction that Jesus could do something for him. Yet his assertion went beyond appreciation for Jesus' reputation. His perception was something akin to the recognition of the possessing demons (4:34, 41). Frequently Jesus is better known by those clearly under the control of his enemy than by those who acted as though they were his friends.

(*b*) **Despite the Torah prohibition, Jesus touched the leper.** Jesus did not comply with the requirements of Torah either. According to Mosaic law, he should have avoided all contact with the leper lest he become contaminated and religiously unclean, and thereby also excluded from the covenant community.

Moses had the power to exclude, but Jesus has the power to include. That is presented neither as abrogation nor repudiation of Mosaic law. Jesus effected his Spirit-empowered cure in tandem with Mosaic regulations about ritual defilement and purification. The story gave Luke another occasion for underscoring the continuity between the Christian community and its Jewish heritage. Jesus' authority surpassed the authority of the law, yet he adhered to the requirements of the law where it was appropriate to his mission.

Jesus touched the leper. The consequence was not cultic impurity for Jesus but restored wholeness for the leper. Being included within the community of faith was a paradigm for being acceptable to God. If a leper can have access to the healing power of Jesus and be made whole so that he is again eligible to participate fully in the community life of the people of God, *how much more* will other "outcasts"—tax collectors, adulterers, Gentiles, and even Pharisees if only they knew who they were before God—also be included? It is a foreshadowing that Jesus will effect a radical redefinition of the true dimensions and limits of the Israel of God.

Did Luke intend to imply a contrast between the leper who was forced by Mosaic law to hold himself separate from the community of Israel and the Pharisees who chose to separate themselves to avoid cultic defilement and to serve as models of Torah observance? Perhaps. The stories that follow portray Jesus in direct confrontation with the Pharisees. It is striking that the only other story about lepers Luke used (17:11ff.) was also followed by a story about Pharisees. So far, each demonstration of Jesus' power had the result of intensifying people's interest in him (4:14f., 37; 5:1, 15). That sets in sharp contrast the emerging antipathy of the religious leaders.

A possible sermon exposition:

Translate "leprosy" into whatever conveys similar sensations of physical, moral, and aesthetic as well as religious repugnance for today's Christian community. In an area with a prevalence of homophobia, someone with a homosexual orientation might produce a comparable reaction, as will drug addicts in other places. Choose whatever specific prejudice is so menacing to the congregation that it has been bedecked with the garb of religious justification. The story is a terrific wedge to confront people with the recognition that Jesus is not at all impressed, nor is he inclined to be limited, by human criteria for identifying who does or does not have access to the saving and renewing grace of God.

Healing the Paralytic (5:17–26)

This story is the first in a series of conflict stories extending through 6:11 with which Luke presented the emergence and intensification of opposition to Jesus' ministry on the part of the Jewish leaders, especially the "scribes and Pharisees." These stories continue to probe the issue of the identity of Jesus, but from the perspective of the regnant Jewish religious establishment and its suspicious concern about the source of Jesus' ambiguous authority.

Such stories undoubtedly reflect a very real factor of opposition with which Jesus had to contend during the course of his public ministry. In addition, conflict stories about controversies Jesus had with the Pharisees were instructive and encouraging to the early church as it tried to come to terms with its relationship and struggles with the increasingly hostile Jewish congregations in the synagogues dotted throughout the Roman Empire.

Two concerns emerge from the story of the healing of the paralytic. It encourages a proper evaluation of (a) who Jesus was, and (b) what Jesus did.

(a) *The identity of Jesus.* Luke took pains to portray the representative scope of the members of the religious establishment arrayed here against Jesus. These are not just a few maverick malcontents belonging to a radical fringe group out of the Pharisaic party. They are "from *every* village of Galilee and Judea *and from Jerusalem*" (v. 17). In them the total power and perceptiveness of official religious Judaism converges.

These Pharisees and teachers of the law, representatives of the total religious establishment, were there "while (Jesus) was teaching." Yet, they could hear none of that. They embody the ennui, insensitivity, and lack of expectation endemic to those occupying high positions of institutional authority who have become numbed and immune by too frequent and casual contact with holy matters. Of all that Jesus said, they heard only that which promised to justify their opposition toward him.

"Who is this who is speaking blasphemies?" they ask (v. 21). *If* they had heard the teaching, they would not have had to ask, "Who is this?" Still, it was the right question to ask, if only they had not allowed their presuppositions to hobble their perceptiveness and blind them to the obvious answer. The second part of their question, "who is speaking blasphemies?" documents the fact that their presumptions, even before they asked the question, prohibited their raising a neutral inquiry concerning his true identity. They had already arrived at their answer before the question was posed.

Jesus was not fooled for a minute. He knew their game and nailed them in their duplicity. "Why do you raise such questions in your hearts?" he asked (v. 22). The context makes it clear he is referring to the paralysis their presuppositions have inflicted on their ability to be open and responsive to the presence of the power of God effectively at work among them. Luke found in this story another instance in which an encounter with Jesus revealed the thoughts of their hearts (see 2:35).

Luke used the other participants in the story to set the obduracy of the Jewish religious leadership into even sharper contrast. The conviction that led the friends of the paralytic to take unusual measures to present their friend in his need before Jesus contrasted sharply with the critical reserve of the religious leaders. Not only were they persuaded that Jesus could do something to relieve and set right the man's affliction, but, more important, they recognized the *kind* of power at work through Jesus. Jesus knew their conviction clearly and responded to the faith motivating them, as he also knew the duplicity governing the thoughts, attitudes, and actions of the Pharisees and the teachers of the law.

Luke further contrasted the critical stance of the trained theologians, who were more formally informed about the will of God, with the response of the paralytic (and the attendant crowd), who glorified God for the healing and renewing power they had recognized in Jesus. Luke's description of the response of the religious leaders is postponed to the conclusion of the extended section—"They were filled with fury" (6:11).

(b) *The mighty act of Jesus.* According to Luke, the question of what Jesus did revolved around these two pronouncements by Jesus: "Your sins are forgiven you" (v. 20), and "Stand up and take your bed and go to your home" (v. 24). The interrelationship of the two pronouncements depends on an understanding of a correlation between sin and physical sickness or impairment. That correlation is not to be understood in a mechanically causative sense: that is, the man sinned and his paralysis was a sign of his sinfulness, or even was punishment for his sinfulness. Jesus repeatedly went out of his way to discourage people from drawing such a wooden and automatic conclusion.

All physical illness and impairment were understood as symptomatic of human existence in a world subject to the authority of Satan. Sin and sickness both occur in a realm ruled by Satan and subject to the forces of illness and death. When Jesus pronounced the man's sins forgiven, he freed him from enslavement to satanic control so that God might reassert God's right to rule in the man's life. The reign of God is a rule marked not by illness and death but by wholeness and life.

The protest by the Pharisees and teachers of the law so hinged on their judgment that when Jesus said, "Your sins are forgiven you," he was implicitly claiming himself to be equal with God. He was suggesting that he had the power to absolve sin, a prerogative that Jewish tradition taught belonged solely to God. Technically the leaders were wrong, for Luke carefully cast Jesus' pronouncement into the passive, a grammatical circumlocution for referring to an act of God.

Luke portrayed Jesus as making a statement that depended on his unity with God but that the religious leaders mistakenly understood to be autonomous declaration. They heard Jesus presuming to do work that only God can do and therefore claiming for himself an authority superceding all other authority—that of Moses, the law, the Torah, the Temple, and in addition, the authority of the Pharisees and the teachers of the law.

Yet at a deeper level they were exactly right. Jesus *did* share in the authority of God, even though he was making no such overt claim for himself. The irony was that he was employing the same power and authority when he healed the man of his paralysis. His command to the man to "stand up and take your bed and go to your home" (v. 24) was the voice of God asserting God's right to rule in the man's life. It was a clear demonstration and announcement that Jesus *was* who they suspected him of claiming to be. It was a plain affirmation that Jesus in fact *did* exercise the authority which alone could come from God, "the authority on earth to forgive sins" (v. 24). For the man heard and obeyed, and he joined with the crowd to glorify God.

A sermon might take shape from the following:

The paralysis of perception. The danger one must guard against with all such stories like these is a too facile leap from the context of first-century eastern Mediterranean cultures to the contemporary scene. When that translation is done carelessly or inadequately, the result can be the insinuation of a biblically sanctioned anti-Semitism.

The appropriate contrast is not between faithful Christians and a faithless Judaism. The indictment embraces all whose passion for the interests and advancement of the religious institution (church, synagogue, commune, or whatever) obsessively possesses them to the extent that they are blinded to the possibility of recognition and acknowledgement of the presence of God doing healing and restoring work in their midst.

The story invites us to reflect on spiritual perceptiveness during the pilgrimage of faith. The Pharisees saw Jesus primarily as a threat. He claimed an authority that not only eclipsed the authority that they exercised but that went above and beyond the powers of all those religious institutions and establishments from which their warrant was derived. They were not wrong about the identity of Jesus they saw implied in what he did. They *were* wrong to conclude that he should not be acting on such presuppositions. They erroneously saw in him the enemy and usurper of all that they held religiously precious. The story reveals the Pharisees and teachers of the law as being the true paralytics. They were paralyzed by their presuppositions since they had given their loyalty to religion instead of to

God. *All* that seeks to usurp God's authority, to rule in God's stead—even religion—is satanic.

Their imperceptiveness collided with the perceptiveness of Jesus, for he saw their thoughts. He knew not only what they said but what they were thinking. He sought to deal healingly and redemptively with their impairment. Because of *their* sin, they would have none of it. By contrast Jesus saw the faith that moved the paralytic's friends. He saw the man's need and his sinfulness. He intervened redemptively and they heeded his voice of command, recognizing his right to rule in their lives. So they joined company with that expanding company of folk who, like the shepherds, went away "glorifying and praising God."

Call and Controversy (5:27–6:11)

This section, introduced with the brief account of the call of Levi, the tax collector, groups several accounts portraying Jesus in confrontation with the Pharisees and scribes. These religious leaders saw in his behavior a radical critique of those Jewish cultic restrictions and practices they held in such high regard. Both the call narrative and the story relating Jesus at table-fellowship with tax collectors and others described him as defying religiously defined social boundaries. The conflict over fasting and the two stories on Sabbath violation depict the Pharisees as criticizing his behavior for trivializing and even repudiating traditional cultic practice.

In this series of stories, as frequently occurs elsewhere during the course of such hostile encounters, Jesus moved the question beyond the details and limits of the specific incident to a broader and more searching level.

Levi's Call and Banquet (5:27–32)

(a) *Jesus calls Levi to discipleship.* Luke distilled yet further Mark's abbreviated account of the call of Levi. Nothing in the narrative prepares us to expect this incident as there is no indication that Levi had any prior contact with Jesus or his disciples. Nor is there evidence that Levi had a noticeable propensity toward religious precocity.

Levi is not identical with "Matthew" in Luke's Gospel. The Author of the first Gospel is responsible for that identification. Matthew is one of the Twelve—6:15; Levi disappears after chapter 5. The only other occurrences of the name are in Luke's genealogy—3:24, 29.

"He left everything . . . and followed him" is the set phrase for becoming a disciple (v. 28, cf. v. 11). It does not necessarily imply relinquishment of material goods. After all, Levi still had a house and the means to throw a "great banquet" in it. The phrase does indicate renunciation of everything that might impede fundamental spiritual reorientation.

(*b*) *Levi's banquet provokes criticism.* Luke exploited the artful juxtaposition he found in Mark of the call of Levi to the story of the banquet Levi gave for Jesus. Jesus imposed no cultic acts on Levi as mandatory for his becoming a member of the intimate circle of disciples—no requirement for public repentance, no baptismal rite of purification, no sin offering presented in the Temple as prior condition, no restitution of any inflated fees the tax collector might have extorted from other Israelites.

A major dimension to the "scandal" of Jesus' ministry (to the Pharisees especially, but also to John the Baptist and to any really pious Jew) was that neither he nor his disciples made repentance a prerequisite for inclusion in events that expressed religious solidarity, such as table-fellowship. That was the basis for the protest raised on this occasion by the Pharisees and scribes.

(*c*) *The religious dimension to table-fellowship.* By his attending Levi's banquet, Jesus openly displayed himself to be willing, even eager, to enter into significant religious association with those whom Pharisaic teaching and established Jewish religious scruples declared were to be scorned and avoided. Just imagine the motley kind of crowd that would be willing to party with a large group of tax collectors in those days and in that culture!

For the Pharisees, religious piety dictated punctilious separation from such impious rabble lest by association they also become religiously defiled and cultically impure. Table-fellowship with tax collectors involved more than socially associating with undesirable people. According to Jewish piety, with the pronouncing of the prayer over the breaking of bread those assembled around the table were constituted into a religious fellowship. The Pharisees promoted this view, and *that* was their protest. Sharing in such a fellowship with lawbreakers compromised one's religious integrity and involved one in solidarity with transgressors who were displeasing to God.

By his call to Levi, Jesus had already shown himself willing to practice outreach by association, convinced that he was in no danger of religious contamination through contact with sinners. Levi's response to the call demonstrated Jesus to be the one who restores the outcast to community and heals sinners associationally, apart from cultic requirements.

Where there is faith there is already repentance. So faithful response is at least as persuasive evidence of repentance as fulfilling the rubrics of cultic ritual. Repentance accompanies faith because, unless people recognize they are sinners, they will not know they have been called to respond to the present dynamic of God's rule as enfleshed in the Son. That was the religious problem the encounters with the person of Jesus posed for the Pharisees and scribes.

(*d*) *Knowledge about religious matters is not the same as relational knowing and being known by God.* The irony of the situation is underscored by the climactic saying in verses 31f. The "sick" and the "sinners" included tax collectors and transgressors, as well as Pharisees and scribes. The latter did not include themselves in those categories; the former did. The Pharisees' grievance with Jesus and his disciples was that they indiscriminately associated with the wrong kind of people, people who their religion had taught them were unacceptable to God. They thereby displayed that, for all their religious study, discipline, and piety, they did not know who Jesus was or what God was about in and through him. They also did not know that they too belonged to the "wrong kind of people" for whom God had sent Jesus to heal and to save. If they had, they would have been more tolerant of Jesus' association with other sinners and more open to finding ways they could associate with him, too.

The Practice of Religious Fasting (5:33–39)

Fasting, as a commendable act of religious piety, addressed the by-now-familiar issue of conformity to cultic custom from a different perspective. The Pharisees saw in the behavior of Jesus and his disciples an insidious pattern which, under the pretext of reform and correction, threatened to undermine the very core of the religious heritage they were dedicated to purify and uphold.

Their truculent criticisms disclosed their fundamental lack of perception about Jesus. He was not trying to perfect, reform, purify, or advance religion. Through his ministry he was introducing a new order that would not conform to old patterns.

The opportunities offered by this new order superceded the values invested in the practice of religious fasting. Fasting was a prelude to repentance, and faithful association with Jesus already embraced repentance. It was a time for celebrative feasting (as Levi had shown in the preceding story), not penitential abstinence. Fasting would again have its place in the future (the future of Luke's own community, and of ours).

The catena of appended sayings (vv. 36–39) are joined superficially by the catchwords "old," "new," and "wine." Their cumulative effect is to focus on the incompatibility between the expectations of Pharisaic religious reform and the living presence of the saving power of God in Jesus.

The question was not concerning whether Jesus' way or the Pharisees' way was the best. By attempting to impose inappropriate Jewish disciplines of piety on the disciples of Jesus, the Pharisees were in danger of doing ruinous damage to both. The dynamic vitality of kingdom presence did not lend itself to forced conformity to old patterns, values, and customs.

Luke's stress here on the disparity between Pharisaic Judaism and Christianity must be held in tension with his more prominent emphasis on continuity between the two religious perspectives evident frequently elsewhere in his two-volume work.

First Sabbath Controversy (6:1–5)

The next two stories of conflict over Sabbath observance (6:1–5; 6–11) address the confrontation between established religion and kingdom presence from yet a different direction. These incidents should be viewed within the broader context of the other stories in this section on controversies with the sanctioned religious authorities. Jesus was not cavalier about Sabbath observance. He customarily went to the synagogue on the Sabbath (4:16).

(*a*) *The Sabbath and Mosaic law.* The critical challenge by the Pharisees was based on the Torah of Moses, which was recorded in scripture and confirmed by religious custom and rabbinical endorsement. Mosaic law prohibited work being done on the Sabbath, and rabbinical interpretation and expansions of that prohibition specifically included harvesting of crops as one such forbidden Sabbath activity.

(*b*) *The principle of a hierarchy of authorities.* Jesus responded that there is a higher level of authority that supersedes cultic restrictions and allows "doing what is not lawful" with impunity. This issue of an authority that supersedes cultic authority is played out at several different levels: (1) the example of David, (2) the authority of scripture, (3) Jesus' messianic authority, and (4) the sovereign authority of God, the Creator.

(*1*) *The example of David.* The analogy of the David story cited by Jesus (vv. 3f.) illustrates that grave human need takes precedence over cultic regulations, even one springing from the Genesis creation account and grounded in the foundational Mosaic Torah. Who David was, the authority as "God's anointed one" which he bore, and the life and death need of the moment surpassed the normative control of accepted religious regulation.

(*2*) *The higher authority of scripture.* Beyond the precedent of the David incident, the authority of scripture is also involved. The account of David doing "what is not lawful," illustrating that there are considerations that justify the setting aside of cultic prohibitions, is recorded in scripture. The authority of scripture is greater than the authority of the Pharisees, and they simply did not have the power either to change it or to set it aside.

(*3*) *Jesus' messianic authority.* At another level, Sabbath observance was established and maintained:

    1) at the command of Moses,
    2) emulating the model of God's Sabbath rest,
    3) in celebration of God's life-giving and sustaining creativity, and
    4) by extension, in anticipation of the coming of Messiah.

But Jesus *was* the Messiah who was to come. He embodied the authority of God; he incarnated God's sovereign rule; he was the presence and continuation of God's life-giving and sustaining creativity. Jesus was not subject to *any* lesser (not even "religious") authority.

(*4*) *The supreme authority of God.* At yet another level, God is lord over time. God created time, dividing it into night and day, and established the seven-day cycle. God *chose* to rest on the Sabbath; God did not *have* to. Jesus incarnated the presence of God and was reestablishing God's rule over all creation. As God was author of all time, so Jesus was "lord of the sabbath." He, too, can *choose* to rest on the Sabbath although he does not *have* to.

This first controversy story about Sabbath observance reflected an assumption of an implied hierarchy of authority. The Pharisees who presumed authority over Jewish religious practice were, themselves, under the authority of cultic regulations, which were subordinate to the authority of scripture that authorizes them, and whose authority was derived from the God who caused their writing and preservation. Since Jesus' authority was authority that belonged to God alone, his authority was greater than them all.

Second Sabbath Controversy (6:6–11)

The second Sabbath controversy story builds on and intensifies the impact of the first. The setting is even more dramatic, for it was a *healing* done in a *synagogue* on the *Sabbath* (a setting similar to the story of the healing of the man possessed—4:31–37). The story describes the Jewish leaders as seeking a legal basis for instituting official process against Jesus. Jesus discerned their belligerent expectations (as earlier with the healing of the paralytic—5:22, and as Simeon had anticipated—2:35).

(*a*) *The ambiguity of the act of healing on the Sabbath.* The man with a withered hand was another instance of human need, the extremity of which was ambiguous if not obscure. "Saving life" on the Sabbath was permitted by cultic regulations and was recognized as allowable by the Pharisees, but a withered hand did not appear to be a life-threatening condition. If, however, the act of healing the hand was a manifestation of the saving power and presence of God who, in Jesus, is re-instituting divine rule in creation, then it *is* life-giving—in the fullest sense of that term. God, through Jesus, chooses not to rest on the Sabbath God created but rather chooses to work restoringly and redemptively.

Jesus questioned the Pharisees in verse 9: "Is it lawful . . . ?" The question is ambiguous. On the surface it asks about the limits to Sabbath observance as established by Mosaic law, defined by scripture, expanded by rabbinic interpretation, and supported by accepted religious practice. Underneath, the question was the Jewish way of inquiring, "What is the will of God?" Jesus was inviting them to ponder the possibility of conflict and even contradiction between cultic regulation and the will of God. It was a proposition they found hardly conceivable, but it drew the crucial line in the dust: Who best knew the will of God, Jesus or the Pharisees?

(*b*) *Pharisees respond with faithless fury.* The Pharisees did not have enough wit or spiritual perception in the presence of such power and authority to be astonished and filled with amazement (4:32, 36; 5:9, 26). Instead they were filled with fury and plotted against Jesus. It was the beginning of official action to oppose him, which will increase in scope and intensity.

With that response the Pharisees confirmed *themselves* to be breaking the Sabbath, the very transgression they had wrongly attributed to Jesus. By seeking an "accusation against him," they were "doing harm" on the Sabbath; by their furious reflection on "what they might do to Jesus," they were seeking, on the Sabbath, to deny and even "destroy life." And so they betrayed themselves to be not only the Sabbath violators they professed to despise, but even the enemies of the God whom they professed to worship and serve.

Sermon possibilities from this passage include:

1. Religious zeal can hamper spiritual perception. In this section (5:17–6:11) of Luke's Gospel, it is especially important that the congregation or study group experience the cumulative impact of the entire portion. That is always a problem. The section is much too long to be read during worship in its entirety, given the time constraints of the usual liturgical occasion. It is almost mandatory, however, that some provision for that be made—perhaps in the introductory remarks prior to reading the day's lesson, perhaps also by devoting a paragraph to the narrative context early in the lesson or sermon. Some means should be found to call attention to the reiterated emphasis on the established religion standing critically over against Jesus and the dramatic intensification of the hostile relationship that repetition effects.

The section gives forceful expression to the tragedy of the Pharisees in their opposition to Jesus. They took every opportunity to contend with him over who had the more accurate or the more spiritual answer. Their zeal prohibited them from discerning that they were asking a fundamentally different question from what he was interested in addressing in his public ministry. They thought the issue was, "What does it mean to be religious?"

2. *Stringent religious observance is not the same as being faithful.* The program of Pharisaic reform had emerged out of the conviction that prevailing religious instructions and practices were both sloppy and, often, downright wrong. They were persuaded that ordinary Jews were not taking their religion seriously enough. Then along came Jesus, who charismatically caught people's attention in a way the Pharisees envied. However, he seemed to practice and commend a slipshod, indifferent attitude toward accurate, precisely defined, stringent, serious religious observance.

Jesus was interested in evoking faithful, obedient response to the claim of God's right to rule. The question his ministry addressed was, "What does it mean to be faithful?" The Pharisees blundered when they assumed that was just another way of asking the religious question occupying their interest.

We underestimate the competency, intensity, and fervor of the Pharisaic reform movement when we facilely equate it with a preoccupation with externals. The alternatives that the conflict discloses for the life of faith today are not simply the opposition of fastidious observance of religious externals against "heartfelt religion." Both preoccupation with correct religious practice and the pride of personal piety can obscure our awareness of the presence of the claims of the royal rule of God. The gospel mandate challenges us to set all of that aside in the service of being open to discern the claims of God's right to reign in our lives so that the world may be reclaimed for God's sovereign rule.

3. *Punctilious religious scrupulosity impedes ministry initiatives of care and compassion.* God requires the people of the Israel of Christ to join Christ in table-fellowship with those whom God has invited to the life-giving and sustaining feast. That is to occur not as a reluctant acquiescence or an occasional occurrence "by way of exception." God expects from the community of faith not only a willingness "to associate with" the marginalized and despised but also, emulating the model of Jesus' ministry, an aggressive seeking out of them. God expects us to take the initiative to establish meaningful and enduring relationships in the name of the Lord we confess and serve. That is why the church addresses such issues as apartheid,

ministry to AIDS victims and their families, sexual discrimination and disenfranchisement, paternalistic condescension to the elderly and the immature, and so forth.

It is not that the institutional church (the ecclesiastical bureaucracy) has become preoccupied with "social issues" and "political programs" at the expense of attentive fidelity to spiritual concerns. That is once again to assume mistakenly that the question is, "What does it mean to be religious?" As long as *that* remains the primary issue, the claims of correct religious behavior and practice and the claims of the kingly rule of God will be antithetical, for they are fundamentally incompatible and the imposition of one on the other seeking to coerce forced conformity will destroy both new garment and old. Thereby neither God nor the church, neither Christ nor the world, are well served.

CALLING THE TWELVE APOSTLES (6:12–19)

Luke follows his account of Jesus' choosing of an inner group of twelve "apostles" (vv. 12–16) with an abbreviated summary description of healings and exorcisms (vv. 17–19). Together they form a dramatic transition panel that shifts our attention from controversy with hostile Jewish religious leaders to the extended section of Jesus' teaching often called the "sermon on the plain" (see v. 17).

(*a*) *Chronological reference and shift of locale.* The notice "during those days" (v. 12), (a rather general reference, compared to Luke's usually more specific temporal notations), is a Lukan indication that a new phase in the narrative of Jesus' life and ministry is being introduced (cf. 1:5; 2:1; 3:1; etc.). The calling of the Twelve, following immediately on the extended section of controversy stories, suggests an intentional movement toward deepened and broadened positive relationships in the story.

This movement is in counterpoint to the stern motif of the intensified alienation of the official Jewish leadership represented by the Pharisees and scribes. The general description of healings and exorcisms reminds us not only of Jesus' widespread popularity, but also of the power of the Holy Spirit that made him an effective, dependable teacher and healer. It is a grand introduction to the extended speech that follows.

The shift in locale in the two frames of the transition panel reflects typical Lukan symbolism. "The mountain" (v. 12) is a setting appropriate for prayer and revelation—the direction of vertical, divine/human communication. "A level place" (v. 17) indicates horizontal human-to-human communication.

(*b*) *Restoration of Israel.* Luke understood the calling of the Twelve to be a charismatic reconstitution of the Israel of God. It was not so much a supplanting as it was a refocusing of the locus of true Israel. The Twelve become the new patriarchs. To counteract any implication that this was primarily a position of privilege, Luke anachronistically described Jesus as designating them "apostles"—a post-resurrection term reflecting the church's missionary mandate. The Twelve are called not to positions of honor but for mission and witness.

Harmonization of the multiple lists of the Twelve in the several New Testament documents is notoriously impossible. The variety suggests that early on the Twelve held continued importance for the church primarily because of symbolic significance rather than the outstanding, unforgettable accomplishments by individuals within the group (Peter and Judas Iscariot being the most obvious exceptions). It is startling to recall that Jesus, empowered by the Holy Spirit and informed by the counsel of God, selected one to be a member of the inner group of his disciples who would betray him. Surely there must have been more attractive choices in the larger group of disciples.

The following suggests a possible direction for sermon development:

This passage brings us directly before the mystery of the working out of the inscrutable will of God. Jesus was the Son of God and so knew the secret purposes of God. He could discern what was hidden in human hearts. Furthermore, he apparently had been associated for some time with all of those whom he included in the inner group. He had spent the entire night in prayer to know God's guidance and to attune himself to God's will. He then chose the Twelve—and one of those he chose betrayed him! (This aspect of the passage might well be the basis for a meditation at a ministers' or lay officers' retreat.)

Contemporary analogies within the life of the church are legion and are not exhausted by the flagrant scandals frequently making newspaper headlines. We must not be disappointed when persons we have come to regard as specially gifted for leadership or some other responsible function in the life of the church do not measure up. It may be indicative of the extent to which we place our trust in them instead of God.

We would not want to overlook that Peter was also one of the Twelve, and yet he, too, betrayed Jesus through denial at the most crucial hour. Indeed Judas and Peter are representative of *all* of the disciples, and thus are types for the entire church. Yet Peter was forgiven and later became a strong support, even an anchor, for the missionary church. That should counsel us to take seriously the forgiving grace of God. We must not be irremediably dismayed when we, too, betray our calling.

THE SERMON ON THE PLAIN (6:20–49)

Having given advanced notice of the popularity with which Jesus' teaching was received by the people (" . . . a great multitude of people . . . had come to hear him," vv. 17f; see also 4:22, 32; 5:1, etc.), Luke includes at this point in his narrative an accumulation of Jesus' sayings cast in the form of an extended discourse. It has come to be known as the Sermon on the Plain from the reference in verse 17 to his coming down from the hills with the apostles he had just chosen and standing "on a level place."

(*a*) *Not a code for Christian living.* Frequently popular piety has been prone to find in this block of teaching material a dominical description of entrance requirements for inclusion in the realm of God. At its most extreme, this view considers the material to be at the heart of Christian belief and practice. All other theological concerns and issues are considered of peripheral importance when compared to this pattern of behavior. The reasoning goes that, if we can adopt all these attitudes and follow all these instructions, we may be confident that Jesus will claim us before the throne of God as belonging to his circle of disciples. That, however, misconstrues the nature and focus of this material.

(*b*) *Life in harmony with or in rebellion against God.* The first section of four beatitudes and four antithetically corresponding woes (vv. 20–26) warns us away from turning these traditions into a Jesus-defined code for behavior that produces Christians, since both beatitudes and woes are not prescriptive but descriptive. They do not convey blessings or inflict judgment; rather, they describe facets of life lived either in harmony with the restored rule of God, or, conversely, describe dimensions of a style of life deliberately oblivious to that divine rule.

The "blessing/woe" descriptions and the admonitions that follow are not conditions for inclusion in the realm of God. They are representations indicative of what end-time kingdom life is like, even in the present. In the person of Jesus, his mighty deeds, and authoritative teachings, the present time has been infused with the quality of God's eternal future. From now on the potential of the present is measured in terms of God's ultimate purposes.

The calling of the Twelve Apostles sets the stage and identifies the primary listeners of this major address. They are the first level of a multi-tiered audience that also includes the larger group of disciples (vv. 13, 17, 20) and the multitude of people (v. 17; 7:1). That audience extends to include the present generation of believers and inquirers, including Theophilus and Luke's own community (and us!).

(c) *Hearing with discernment.* Especially important is the frequently repeated emphasis on "hearing":

1) "a great multitude . . . had come to hear him," vv. 17f
2) "I say to you that listen," v. 27
3) "not do what I tell you," v. 46
4) "hears my words and acts on them," v. 47
5) "hears and does not act," v. 49
6) "his sayings in the hearing of the people," 7:1

"Hearing" means more, of course, than auditory acuity. It also means something much more fundamental than to "pay attention and obey my directions." "Hearing" is an openness to the presence of the salvation of God that is incarnate in Jesus, and to the reception of the royal rule of God his teaching announced. When the perceptive hearing of Jesus' teachings at this level occurs, only then do his words stimulate and shape the hearer's behavior to conform more to qualities compatible with the presence of the restored rule of God. What one hears from Jesus discloses primarily who one is in the light of God's saving purposes and, only secondarily and by extension, tells how one is to act in harmony with the rule of God.

Ordering one's life in accordance with God's sovereign goodness does not determine how one is regarded by God. Nor is such behavior to be adopted primarily to persuade and convert others to the cause of Christ, or to vanquish evil with good. Any of those latter things may occur as a consequence, but true disciples of Jesus do good to others because God already has done good for them, is even now doing good, and will continue to do good for them in the future.

(d) *Segments of the sermon on the plain.* The "sermon" divides into three subsections of stylistically disparate material: (1) blessings and woes—vv. 20–26, (2) admonitions for kingdom conduct—vv. 27–38, and (3) parabolic warnings—vv. 39–49.

(1) *Blessings and woes.* The first group of sayings conforms in style to similar material found in a broad assortment of Jewish and pagan literature predating Luke. It is reminiscent of the popular "two ways" type of hortatory argument (light and darkness, way of the day and way of the night, flesh and spirit, etc.). The close parallelism between the blessings and the woes is obvious. Although the latter are antithetical to the beatitudes, they are not offered as scare tactics to stimulate a change of behavior in the impious. They describe the opposite of kingdom-quality life. In

addition, the woes, much like the beatitudes, offer assurance and encouragement to the faithful, only now it is by contrast.

Both blessings and woes display the present-future rhythm typical of eschatological (end-of-time, "day of the Lord") material. Future eschatological rewards and punishments are contrasted with present circumstances. Alert commitment to God's future, or the absence of such commitment, controls how one assesses present conditions.

Although some of the conditions listed may have had their origins in the economic, social, or political order, they have been co-opted to express religious content. The present conditions in both blessings and woes have both immediate and extended applications. The poor are materially destitute and, by extension, are those who are totally dependent on God. The rich are self-sufficient and so tend to rely solely on their own resources. (Rev. 3:17 knows the spiritual myopia often attendant to material wealth: "For you say, 'I am rich, I have prospered, and I need nothing.' You do not realize that you are wretched, pitiable, poor, blind, and naked.")

Those who hunger desire food and know by analogy the need for their spiritual nourishment. Those who are full are satiated and insensible to their spiritual starvation. Those who weep do so mourning personal loss but also to mourn their lack of voice under the oppressive structures of a merciless and unjust social order. Those who laugh do so only because, ecstatic over present power, they ignore the crisis of inescapable future accountability.

The blessings and woes section also contributes to Luke's portrait of Jesus and his authority. One who utters such eschatologically informed material implicitly discloses that he has access to the mind of God and is privy to the ultimate shape of human history.

(2) *Admonitions for kingdom conduct.* The second subsection might be characterized as "a profile of kingdom living." It consists of a series of interrelated admonitions and exhortations urging repudiation of acts of retaliation, retribution, and all activity governed by careful calculation of any personal advantages.

Popular wisdom counsels that we should favor those who favor us. The saying goes, "You scratch my back and I'll scratch yours." Give no quarter to adversaries. Take every advantage of their vulnerability; even revenge yourself at every opportunity. "Do unto the other guy before he does it unto you!" Exploit the weaknesses and mistakes of others. "He's just asking to be taken."

In sharp contradiction to such prevailing counsel, this section urges concrete implementation of the love ethic, which is twice articulated in its most extreme form: "Love your enemies" (vv. 27, 35). The segment is artfully constructed by enunciating three general principles (vv. 31, 35, 36), around which specific examples of each principle are clustered (vv. 27–30, 32–34, 37–38).

The entire section requires the presupposition of a faith commitment to the unfolding of God's rule in the world. The summons is neither to prayerful postures or pious activity but to unequivocating love which, of course, must inevitably result in action. The scope and depth of God's goodness and mercy sets the pattern the faithful are to emulate. Because of God's unrestrained abundance and generosity we are to be equally generous, loving and merciful to others. Divine grace helps us to give from gratitude; without that grace, when we give, we give from guilt.

(*3*) *Parabolic warnings.* The third section uses four parabolic analogies to direct exhortations to the community of believing disciples:

1) blind leading blind—vv. 39–40
2) speck and log—vv. 41–42
3) tree and fruit—vv. 43–45
4) houses and foundations—vv. 46–49

The first three address various aspects of the church's responsibility to nurture, train, and exercise pastoral oversight and control. The community needs that, so the task must not be shirked or avoided. Such discipline is effective and upbuilding only when it is exercised in humility by those profoundly in touch with their own shortcomings and lack of perfection. Only then does discipline avoid being destructively judgmental and becomes instead restoringly corrective.

Christian congregations frequently lose that positive view of the role of discipline within the community of faith. Genuine Christian discipline is not an exercise in judging those who are deemed morally defective and inferior by those who paternalistically hold themselves to be superior. The role of discipline is that of mutual admonition, correction, and encouragement in the community. Only then is it an authentic expression of the pastoral care, concern, and love appropriate to the common life of faith shared in the church. Discipline and moral instruction are just as much needed expressions of the love ethic as is the more dramatically radical demand of "Love your enemies!" It is best applied by those firmly in touch with their own need for mercy and forgiveness.

The final parable in the discourse (vv. 46–49) graphically underscores the need for faithful, discerning hearing of dominical teaching and admonitions. True hearing inevitably modifies behavior. Such perceptive hearing will not produce opposition and resistance, as Jesus had already experienced at Nazareth and, repeatedly, from the Jewish religious leaders. Instead, it will move the faithful disciple/community to actions shaped by Jesus' authoritative instruction.

JESUS EMBODIES DIVINE PRESENCE (7:1–50)

Sophisticated and accomplished author that he is, Luke advances his portrait of Jesus on several levels simultaneously with the stories he included in this section.

By placing this sequence of stories immediately after the extended discourse of the sermon on the plain (6:20ff.), Luke used the context to compel recognition that Jesus himself, in his person and in his ministry, incarnated and disclosed authentic divine presence. He taught authoritatively and accurately about the nature of life in harmony with the presence of the end-time reign of God.

These narrative illustrations of sermon on the plain themes show that he also embodied that harmony. Verses 7:1–10 and 36–50 show him loving his enemy. In 11–17, because of an encounter with him, someone who weeps now laughs. From verse 24 to the end of the chapter, he is seen loving those who "hate and revile" and regard him as evil. The story of the sinful woman at the Pharisee's banquet (vv. 36–50) movingly illustrates the admonitions "Do not judge!" "Forgive!" and "Be merciful!"

Also related to the sermon on the plain material is the artful interplay of the John the Baptist traditions (vv. 18–35) with the story of the Pharisee's banquet (vv. 36–50). John is harbinger of the rule of God and subordinate to divine presence, so he is included as one of the "blessed . . . who takes no offense at (Jesus)" (v. 23). By contrast, the critical and judgmental Pharisee, Simon, is an example of one who will not hear Jesus' words and act on them (6:47) and so shows himself to be one of those who "rejected God's purpose" (7:30).

At another level, the stories in this section enhance Luke's portrayal of Jesus as one who is liberated from constricting ritual prohibitions. They provide further evidence that Jesus will not be boxed in by the artificial restrictions of cultic taboos. As an embodiment of the presence of God's royal rule, he is willing to enter into a gentile's house (v. 6), touch the bier bearing the defiling corpse of a dead man (v. 14), and appreciatively receive, in public, the intimate, loving gestures of a sinner (v. 47).

At a third level, Luke used the stories in chapter 7 to engage another facet of the critical question concerning Jesus' identity. The acclamations in verse 16 ("A great prophet has risen among us!" "God has looked favorably on his people!") give this concern sharp focus. Do the two mean the same thing? Is Jesus a prophet? What kind of prophet is he? Who says so, and why? What is his relationship to the prophets of old, or to John the Baptist? What kind of person does it take to perceive that he truly is a prophet, an Elijah-like prophet, even the End-Time Prophet—and more?

Healing the Centurion's Slave (7:1–10)

"I've been a Christian all my life. I was born into a Christian home and raised by Christian parents. I was baptized into the church and nurtured in Sunday school and youth group meetings. I was confirmed when I reached the usual age and made my public profession of faith in Jesus as my Lord and Savior. I went to youth camps and conferences. During college and for several years afterward I drifted away, partly through indifference, partly because I was distracted by other things. But then I married a Christian and have returned to a close walk with Jesus. Each day I try to let him come into my heart."

So what? All those things have significance, of course, but not ultimately. The story of the healing of the centurion's slave orchestrates a head-on collision with such popular profiles of personal piety. It tells us that proximity to Jesus does not enhance one's chances for inclusion in the royal realm of God. Who one perceives him to be—and what one does about it—makes the difference.

(a) *The idea of "distance."* Think for a moment of how distant the centurion was from Jesus. He was physically distant since he had never seen Jesus face to face before, nor did he see him in the story. Actually Jesus never came into the physical presence of the slave who was ill, either. Nor, as far as we know, did he even speak the word of healing the centurion was persuaded would be sufficient. Although a great multitude of people had just heard Jesus give an extended discourse on the quality of kingdom life, the centurion was not among them. He had never heard Jesus; he had just heard about him. He was culturally and religiously distant from Jesus by not being a Jew. He had bound himself to service under an authority other than that Jesus embodied.

The story is structured to underscore that distance. The first delegation (Jews), while ostensibly seeking to reduce the distance ("He may not be one of us, you see, but he is in a strategic position and is friendly toward religious Judaism, don't you know"), emphasizes that very distance by speaking commendingly (and condescendingly) of him. The second delegation (friends), as well as the message he sent through them to Jesus, serves to maintain the distance. In spite of all that, the Gentile centurion and Jesus were nearer to each other than most of Jesus' own ethnic people.

Many Jews had heard Jesus and seen him do mighty deeds of miraculous healing, and some had even touched him—but did not know him.

(b) *Jesus' response to opinions about the centurion.* The story contains a fascinating interplay of contradictory opinions about the centurion. The Jewish delegation extols those virtues they found particularly commendable. Were those qualities therefore equally pleasing to God? A strand of Jewish piety held that God's favor could be earned through extraordinary generosity, but the more informed levels of Jewish theology never bought into it. The centurion's self-effacing evaluation of himself, taking into account who Jesus actually was, was as accurate as it was irrelevant.

Jesus was impressed neither by the centurion's reputation nor by his self-assessment. What caught Jesus' attention was what the centurion's message, sent by way of his friends, revealed about the strength of his faith, and what it disclosed about his perceptive valuation of Jesus and the power present in his person.

The centurion, no stranger to authority, had much regard for the authority he discerned in Jesus. In fact, he was certain that Jesus' utterance of the powerful word was sufficient to cure his terminally ill slave. He recognized in Jesus a quality and scope of authority that does not require his physical presence to be efficacious. That strong conviction caught Jesus by surprise and he "was amazed." That is what he had been looking for all along but found so seldom—and had hardly expected to find here.

A sermon might be developed from what follows:

Several commentators point out that this story anticipates and prepares for the Peter and Cornelius episode in Acts 10 (e.g., C. H. Talbert, *Reading Luke*, [New York: Crossroads, 1982], pp. 79ff.). The account follows the "salvation by way of the Jews to the Gentiles" sequence, which Luke will develop intensively in the Acts narrative. " . . . God shows no partiality, but in every nation anyone who fears him and does what is right is acceptable to him" (Acts 10:34f.). Bring these two stories into conversation (the contrasting responses of Peter and Jesus are also instructive). Doing so could provide an opportune occasion to invite the community to consider subordinating what it hopes God sees in it in favor of placing primary emphasis on what it sees in Jesus. Who knows, we may catch him by surprise again! We may be certain he is just as eager to be amazed over our faith, too.

Healing the Widow of Nain's Son (7:11–17)

(a) *Luke's narrative line is advanced.* It was strategically advantageous for the development of Luke's story line for him to include this story next in the sequence. The story vividly illustrates a major theme in Jesus' sermon on the plain, as was indicated in the introductory paragraphs to the discussion of this chapter. It reminds listeners of the Elijah associations (cf. 1 Kings 17:17–24; 2 Kings 4:18–37), which marbled Jewish messianic expectations. It also gave a specific instance of Jesus restoring someone from the dead. Both aspects are central to the material that follows immediately concerning John the Baptist and Jesus.

Luke takes pains to ensure that his hearers know that plenty of witnesses are present. A large crowd plus all the disciples are with Jesus, and another large crowd is with the funeral procession. When the two columns meet, Luke expects us to visualize a considerable throng.

(b) *Jesus, like Elijah, restores life.* Jesus, the empowered agent of God, brings the creative and restorative power of God, the life-giver, to bear on this pitiful scene of death. Both powerful word and potent touch are efficacious; the man is restored to the life that had been interrupted. The mighty act evokes the considerable affirmation from the crowd that he is more than a prophet—he is a *great* prophet with access to life-giving power.

Jesus had referred to the resuscitation miracle of Elijah in his inaugural sermon at Nazareth (4:26–27). The dependency of this story on that same tradition enables it to serve as confirming evidence of one aspect of his messianic identity. Jesus fulfills and completes the prophetic role of Elijah. In addition, he personifies divine salvation.

Preaching on this passage might explore the following:

"A great prophet has risen among us!" What would it take these days to get a congregation to say that about someone? (What would it take to get *you* to say that?) Would a charismatic healing during Sunday morning worship do it? Would it take a resuscitation at the funeral home? How are you going to pull that off? And how are you going to get the lid back on in the unlikely event that you do pull it off?

What would it take to evoke acknowledgement of Jesus as a great Elijah-like prophet with power over life and death, the incarnate visitation of divine salvation? If a group in your congregation insisted "A great prophet has risen among us!" would you be glad? Luke would have—as long as they were referring it to Jesus, and as long as they went beyond just that in their faith acclamation—maybe to include "God has looked favorably on his people." Those two statements could mean the same thing but, for Luke, the second says more than the first. He has already introduced the idea of God "looking favorably on his people" at the beginning of the nativity hymn Benedictus, attributed to Zechariah (1:67ff.), where it stands in synonymous parallelism to God's raising up a Davidic "horn of salvation" (literal translation of v. 69a; cf. also 1:78b).

Invite the congregation to rethink and redefine its understanding of authentic experiences of the miraculous in the life of believers and in the contemporary community of faith. Where do we witness life being brought forth out of death? Perhaps it is with a person who had been stunted by guilt and self-hate, but who found in the Christian faith a renewing perspective of self-affirmation emerging from the startling conviction that God loved her/him. Perhaps it is in a dry-rotted marriage relationship that discovers a new lease on life because of a Christ-stimulated recovery of the importance of living for the nurture and well-being of each other.

What would it take? News of a congregation once on the brink of self-destruction from prolonged conflict and polarization that has a renewed commitment to the common life in the body of Christ? An implemented Palestinian-Israeli accord incarnating mutual respect emerging on the affirmation that a common love for God surpassed all differences? When concrete walls and iron curtains suddenly come down, we *have* to give Christ the glory because, despite our forty-year struggle, none of us has ever been able to make it happen ourselves.

Why are we so limited and so narrow in our definitions and perceptions of what is authentically miraculous in the faith life of a person or congregation? To open that up, and then to exercise such newly activated skills for discernment, may well lead us to confess Jesus as the "great prophet" — or even more. It will also protect people from gullible exploitation by religious hucksters in public life and in the media.

John the Baptist and Jesus (7:18–35)

Who was this Jesus, anyway? Was he or was he not a prophet? Was he or was he not *the* prophet of the end-time? Was he or was he not Elijah, returned to usher in the end of history, to herald the day of the Lord, to make final preparations for the establishment of God's royal rule on Mount Zion?

(a) *John the Baptist's uncertainty.* John the Baptist, presumably still in prison (cf. 3:20), really wanted to know. He had been patient for a considerable period of time, giving Jesus every chance, granting him every latitude. But it still was not clear if Jesus really was the "One" whom John hoped he was, and John did not know if it was because Jesus *would* not act like the Expected One, or because he *could* not.

In any event, John's time was running out. Even after all the hoopla attending his birth (cf. 1:5ff, 57ff,), the notoriety of his public ministry (3:1ff.), the scandal in court circles (3:19), and religious enclaves (vv. 30, 33), John still struggled with the specter of the possibility that somehow he had gotten his signals mixed and had not done what God had called him to do—or, at least, not with the right person.

Was Jesus the prophet, Elijah redivivus, or not? "Well," Luke hemmed and hawed, "yes and no." Or, perhaps better, "Yes, and more!"

(b) *John's disciples to find out.* John sent his disciples to ask Jesus, "Are you *the one who is to come,* or are we to wait for another?" (vv. 19f.), which expressed more than a little uncertainty. (Of course, if he had been convinced beyond doubt, why did he still have disciples who were following him instead of Jesus? Why had not he himself become Jesus' disciple? Luke and his community as well as other contemporary Christian groups—for example, the community of the Gospel of John—were still puzzling over that one.) "The one who is to come" was language molded by Malachi 3:1, and popular Jewish piety had long since referred those expectations of end-time agent to the person of Elijah, who was to return as harbinger of the Day of the Lord.

It was clear how John the Baptist envisioned the returned Elijah was to act. In his preaching (3:16f.), he had stimulated the expectation that, as radical a call to repentance and renewal as his own ministry was, *the one who was to come* would escalate the stridency with which he announced divine wrath and the intensity with which he inflicted divine judgment. That is what Elijah was supposed to do. But Jesus had not baptized anyone with the Holy Spirit and with fire. (There was no way John could know that he just had not waited long enough.) Jesus had not inflicted winnowing judgment on anybody yet. Or had he?

At a more subtle level, Jesus and John together had accomplished judgmental discrimination (v. 30). Some who had rejected John's summons to repentance also rejected Jesus' proclamation of the presence of God's regal rule and took offense at him (v. 23). They thereby showed they did not belong to the "people prepared" John was to "make ready . . . for the Lord" (1:17). If they did not listen either to John or to Jesus, then they *had* to oppose them both and ultimately the God whom they served, which *was* divine wrath and judgment.

(c) *Similarities between Jesus and Elijah were ambiguous.* Was or was not Jesus the Elijah figure? On the one hand, yes. Luke had just told the story of the raising of the widow of Nain's son (vv. 11–17) to make that clear, but Jesus' reply to the question John sent through his disciples incorporated that event into a much broader context. That restoration was just one of a whole list of mighty deeds and occasions of salvation proclamation corresponding to what the Isaiah literature had described as the anticipated activity of the end-time suffering and saving servant of the Lord. Jesus had been trying to get that across to people ever since the beginning of his public activity (4:18–21).

Furthermore, if anyone deserves to be thought of as the Elijah figure who is precursor of the end-time coming of the salvation of God from on high, it is John himself. Talk about announcing divine wrath and pronouncing judgment! That fits him to a T, as Jesus insisted in the next section of comments about John (vv. 24ff.).

Does Luke hint here that one reason John was uncertain about Jesus was that John underestimated the scope and misconstrued the function of his own ministry? He saw himself as the master of ceremonies, announcing the impending appearance on the stage of Elijah Redivivus, who would serve as precursor of God's end-time agent of salvation. But *he,* in fact, was Elijah, and the one he thought to be Elijah was, in fact, the Christ. If you do not understand this about John, you will not have a clue about who Jesus really is and so will miss what God is bringing to fulfillment through him (vv. 29f).

(*d*) *The "lesser to the greater" argument.* Jesus had just been acclaimed a great prophet—and more (v. 16). He acknowledges here (v. 26) that John is a prophet, yet more than a prophet. John himself testified that Jesus was more powerful than he (3:16). Had he meant only that Jesus was a greater prophet than he? The hierarchy of evaluation informing this tradition seems to be, in ascending order: (1) human beings (all those born of a woman), (2) prophets of old, (3) John, the prophetic forerunner of Malachi 3:1, (4) believers in the realm of God, and, (5) greater than them all, Jesus. The critical transition in the hierarchy is marked by those who by faith recognize and acknowledge in Jesus' person and in his ministry the presence of kingdom power.

Jesus' words about John in verse 28 are not a put-down. The comparison is between one's status in the human community and one's status as citizen of the realm of God. The greatest one of those in the human community anticipating the coming of God's salvation is surpassed by the least member under his established royal rule.

A sermon on this text might explore the following:

Jesus disconcerts us, too. He just will not do the things we want him to do, or act the way we think he ought to act. We have loved him since we were tots, but life is still tough—and he should do better by us. We have confessed him as Lord and Savior and praised God's name, but still we get sick, our kids still do drugs, neighbors and colleagues are condescendingly arrogant, and we still get audited by the Internal Revenue Service!

The tyranny of irrectifiable presuppositions prevents perceptive insight. Set categories used to define a person, and preconceived ideas of how that person must act and function, pose the danger of blinding us to recognizing the rich majesty of who that person really is. So we may miss what we yearn to see the very most.

John the Baptist was flirting with myopia such as that. The Pharisees also had that problem, carried to the extreme. Like John and the Pharisees, we, too, sometimes cannot understood who Jesus really is because we miscalculate who we are.

If John could just have looked beyond his disappointment that Jesus was not doing what John expected (and had publicly advertised), he might have been able to see more accurately who Jesus really was and what God was doing in and through him. That would surely have led John to recognize his own accomplishment of those Elijah-like things he missed in Jesus' ministry.

We may find it helpful to divest ourselves of preconceptions as well. Perhaps we could suspend our prior expectations and come to know Jesus as he chooses to disclose himself to us. Certainly we are then in a better position to know who we are in comparison with his perfect humanity, and more accurately perceive what he is doing among us as Savior and Lord. Or, better, perhaps we can finally give up feeling it necessary to make such projections as those at all, so we, too, might know ourselves as being embraced by his beatitude on those "who take no offense" at him, a beatitude within which he surely also intended to include John.

A Penitent Woman Attends Jesus (7:36–50)

The story of the sinful woman lavishing affection on Jesus while he was at table in a Pharisee's house dramatically illustrates the mercy, forgiveness, and absence of judging emblematic of life lived under the royal rule of God (cf. 6:36–38). The parable encased in the story exemplifies the admonitions about lending as seen from the kingdom perspective of the sermon on the plain (6:34f.). Finally, the story describes a striking case in point concerning the type of Pharisee who, for all of his good intentions, took offense at Jesus (v. 23) and "rejected God's purpose for (himself)" (v. 30).

(a) *A Pharisee's invitation.* Unlike the more consistently negative Gospel of Mark he used as a source, Luke included several traditions that portrayed officials from various levels of the Jewish leadership in neutral to positive postures toward Jesus. They were more curiously interested than hostile. Simon the Pharisee had apparently heard the popular opinion that Jesus was a prophet. (Luke had just considered—and considerably nuanced—this opinion.) Simon was understandably curious, if a bit skeptical about that. After all, prophecy had supposedly ceased in Israel many years back, and it was not expected to be revived until the end of days.

Simon invited Jesus to his house, to include him in a somewhat formal and festive occasion for table-fellowship. This meant that he was willing to enter into an intimate religious association with Jesus (and expected his other guests to do so, too). He did this at considerable risk, hosting Jesus even though Jesus regularly breached accepted religious custom, taunted Simon's colleagues, and had the reputation for being a glutton who sought out occasions to eat with (in other words, engage in intimate religious fellowship with) tax collectors and sinners (7:34). Jesus consistently showed himself prepared to enter into religious community with sinners (even when they happened to be Pharisees). So hosting this dinner was an extraordinary and precarious initiative for Simon to take. He was so close and yet so far.

(*b*) *A woman's intrusion.* We are not to think of the woman as barging into the house in a disruptive, obtrusive manner. It was the custom for the host of a formal meal to leave the house open so that the uninvited also might come in, sit along the wall surrounding the invited guests, observe the festivities, and perhaps enjoy a choice leftover or two from the table. She became obtrusive (in Simon's view) only by the extravagant expressions of affection she lavished on Jesus, burlesqued by the tawdry reputation that accompanied her person.

"Well, that settles it," Simon thought to himself. "If Jesus were a prophet, he would know all about her and he would not put up with any of that hanky-panky for a minute. If he only knew who she is!"

"Simon," Luke wants his hearers to think, "if you only knew who Jesus was, you would have known long before now that he was more than just a prophet. And you would be right down there next to her, wailing and washing his feet with your tears, too."

(*c*) *Before Jesus, the "customary" is suspended.* Commentators puzzle over the sequence of the woman's experience. Did her great love cause her to be forgiven great sins? Or did her great love result from her having been forgiven great sins? That is a critical problem only for those still engrossed in the possibility of coercing God. Luke was not interested in that. "Blessed are you who weep now for you will laugh" (6:21). In the saving economy of God, the sequence is incidental. The future tense is eschatological, and the eschaton has invaded the present in the person of Jesus. It is a parable told in the future present tense. This woman was weeping and laughing at the same time. Her weeping was her laughing; her laughter was her tears.

Clearly the woman's priorities were revised. Notorious sinner that she was, she would not have dared previously to intrude upon the circle around the table, for the Pharisaic presence awoke guilt, shame, and a fear of their searing, indignant, righteous scorn. Now she hardly knew they were there thanks to the "presence of the kingdom" whose mercy transfixed her, whose grace held her captive. "Amazing grace—how sweet the sound!" And so she greeted Jesus—celebrated religious fellowship with him—with actions so extravagant, so far beyond normal social protocol, that Simon would have had to discern who Jesus really was to appreciate and match them.

(*d*) *Simon's imperceptiveness.* What never even occurred to Simon was that Jesus knew more about the woman than Simon could even begin to imagine. Furthermore, Jesus knew just as much about Simon, although Simon did not have a clue about that, either. So Jesus told the parable. Still Simon did not "hear" what Jesus was saying. He felt himself to be catechized and, petulantly, he resented the impudence.

Simon made several critical mistakes in identification that day. 1) He did not know who Jesus was. 2) He correctly identified the woman as a sinner (both Jesus—vv. 47f.—and Luke—v. 37—agreed), but he failed to recognize her as a forgiven sinner and member of the royal realm of God. And, even worse, 3) he failed to identify himself (and everyone else sitting around the table and along the wall that day) as equally reprehensible sinners who were just as much in need of God's mercy as the woman. The reason Jesus accepted the invitation and came to dinner that day was to offer to Simon, and to anyone else, the same kind of opportunity for admission to the realm of God as the woman received.

More tellingly, for Simon to enter into religious table-fellowship with Jesus without discerning who Jesus was made his very invitation to that fellowship a lie before God and showed that Simon, too, was a sinner. Theoretically Simon, the Pharisee, still could have found himself in the parable Jesus told as the one forgiven little (if nowhere else). What a blessing it would have been for Simon to love Jesus even a little! But, sadly, he did not know himself to have been forgiven, or that he even needed to be forgiven. Neither he nor his crowd knew who Jesus was (v. 49).

Some sermonic suggestions:

The story fairly preaches itself. First, invite the congregation to "put on" the story, to enter into it and to participate by feeling what happens when one is the woman, when one is Simon, and when one is a guest. Second, invite them into the parable told within the story. Explore what it is like to be the one forgiven much, the one forgiven little, and the creditor who forgives. Finally, retell the story at next Sunday's Eucharist, or even at next Wednesday's family night supper, but develop it so that Jesus, the sinful woman, and Simon the Pharisee gather around a new table as co-hosts and summon the others as invited guests—those sitting around the walls and those out in the streets who could not find a place, as well as those who did not dare (or care) to come and sit at the table in the royal realm of God.

HEARING AND DOING THE GOSPEL (8:1–56)

Have you ever noticed that sometimes you will hear someone say something you know you should find important but the whole thing is so vague and remote that you can hardly force yourself to listen? Then, at other times, all it takes is a carefully crafted phrase, a startling juxtaposition of ordinarily unrelated words or images, an unusual and unexpected simile or metaphor—sometimes less than any of that—and suddenly an unanticipated world of meaning and insight rushes in on you and your mind reels with the marvel of it while your breath comes in ragged gasps.

According to Luke's Jesus, that is not accidental when it occurs in response to gospel proclamation and kingdom presence—neither the enlightened "Aha!" of perception nor the bored disengagement.

Hearing (auditory reception) but not hearing (perceptive appropriation) and, therefore, not doing (the integrated acting out of the perception) is a general human experience. We wish we could control our hearing better. We yearn for the "turned-on-light bulb" experiences even when we cannot orchestrate them with regularity. When they come, they stimulate and challenge for the moment, but are they real or illusory? Will they endure?

The experience provides a common point of departure for the leader and congregation in exploring the material of chapter 8. Only faithful, attentive, and perceptive hearing of the good news of the reign of God produces those acts by the disciple that reflect kingdom presence and power. Precisely that is what sets the reliable disciple distinct from all others.

The chapter portrays Jesus as the model to emulate. He has integrated in his person the message of the royal rule of God with the accomplishment of mighty deeds through divine power and presence. Here he teaches the kingdom (vv. 4–21) and does kingdom deeds (vv. 22–56). Disciples are to hear discerningly and to see perceptively, and then they are to go and do likewise (9:1ff.).

Jesus' Itinerant Ministry (8:1–3)

This brief paragraph of narrative connector provides transition in the story for the material to follow. Luke describes women that share prominently with men both in the benefits and in the responsibilities of belonging to the realm of God.

The section anticipates the tradition of Jesus' true family (vv. 19–21). These women and the Twelve, at least, already belong to Jesus' true family. The Twelve hear and see Jesus preaching and doing kingdom business, and as they *really* hear, they also will be expected to do. So the section looks forward to the commissioning of the Twelve (9:1ff.), and of the Seventy (10:1ff.), and of Luke's own community (Acts 1:8), and of everyone who really hears the good news of the sovereignty of God.

This brief section could well serve as the theme passage for a series of studies/sermons (or a retreat weekend) that would explore each of those other passages listed in the previous paragraph, for recovery of vivid engagement with the missionary/evangelistic/service mandate.

The Parable of the Soils and "Hearing" (8:4–21)

Luke adapted Mark's version of the parable of the soils considerably. He liked what he found in Mark but had substantial reservations. Evidently he considered Mark's version to be too negative and critical of the disciples. So Luke reworked the story as well as the interpretive material attached to it, which he had also found in Mark. C. E. Carlston (*The Parables of the Triple Tradition,* [Philadelphia: Fortress, 1975]) provides a very thorough comparison and analysis of the details of the two versions.

(*a*) *The message of the parable.* The parable speaks analogically of the uninhibited and uncalculatingly faithful announcement of the message of the restored rule of God. How that declaration is received has eternal implications. The announcement has been authorized by God, and, given the eschatological nature of the time, there is an intense urgency for the proclamation to be made without delay in as many places and to as many people as possible.

It is not for the proclaimer to decide whether the hearers are ready or not, alert or inattentive, worthy or undeserving. Let the message be broadcast and trust the outcome to God, for God will bring results with an astonishing yield from what may appear to be unimpressive and unlikely beginnings. The story can thus serve both as an exhortation for responsive reception to those hearing the announcement of the reestablishment of God's sovereign rule, and as a word of support and encouragement to the "disciples" of the church (including Luke's own community), who are charged with making that regal presence known.

(*b*) *Allegorical explanation of the parable.* The story appears to distinguish between different classes of seed, but the intent is to refer to the differing fates of the same seed in various soil conditions. The allegorical interpretation (vv. 9–15) heightens the tone of encouragement by offering consolation to the Christian community that has experienced inexplicably mixed results from its gospel proclamation. Some who heard responded and endured, some responded and then fell away, renouncing their commitment under risk of trial or persecution, while some never responded. No one could tell for sure which direction they would take ahead of time, or why they chose that way after the fact.

An exegetical clue from Jewish scriptural traditions (v. 10b) suggesting a solution to the theological problem of why some people believe and some do not was found in a major prophetic motif especially prominent in Isaiah. This "see\not see; hear\not understand" perspective grew out of the "hardening" theory frequently encountered as a solution to human obduracy in the Old Testament narratives. People do not believe and disobey, because their hearts are hardened. Unresponsive disbelief and unstable belief in response to the preaching of the gospel are embraced in the divine command to preach the good news of the reign of God. The *result* of the act of gospel proclamation is theologically recast as the *purpose,* in order that God's will is not portrayed as frustrated by human disbelief.

God is not to blame; the devil made them do it (v. 12). The explanation suggests that parables are enlightening to believers but judgmentally obscure to unbelievers. Consequently, members of the Christian community must not become discouraged if their labors in preaching the good news are not uniformly effective. They must persevere with even greater zeal, fidelity, and urgency, and be content to let God order the results.

The text suggests a couple of ways a sermon might take shape:

1. Announce God's royal rule whether or not people respond in faith. The first application was a collection of independent Jesus sayings Luke found in Mark and edited. The collection has a double thrust: 1) Do not worry about how others respond—just be sure that you hear the message of the good news of God's rule with perceptive acceptance; and 2) God causes the gospel word to bear fruit in you not for your private benefit or personal enlightenment alone. Your "hearing" is so that you may participate in the further proclamation and get on with it. That is the whole purpose of your belief in the first place.

2. Fidelity to the Word of God controls inclusion in Jesus' family. Luke's second application is through his repositioning and reworking of the "family of Jesus" tradition (vv. 19–21) he had found in Mark. Commentators concur that Luke did not understand Jesus to be rejecting further association or connection with his biological family. Jesus did agree with John the Baptist (3:7–9) that one's response to the presence of God's kingly power took precedence over relationships defined by physical, blood descent. Luke shows what is determinative for him as he changes Mark's version of Jesus' words from *do* the will of God (Mark 3:35) to "*hear the word of God and do it*" (v. 21). Perceptive hearing and faithful doing are mutually confirmatory.

Stilling the Storm (8:22–25)

The stories Luke placed together from here until the end of the chapter all have a similar theme. Jesus, by his word, his presence, and his physical contact, imposes the order of God's rule on the demonic chaos pervasive in the world and especially in human lives. He restores order and harmony in nature (vv. 22–25), in a person's mental health (vv. 26–33), and in a person's physical and family life (vv. 40–56).

Do the disciples belong, without qualification, to Jesus' family (cf. v. 21)? Have they fully integrated the "secrets of the kingdom" (cf. v. 10)? Do they hear with enough clarity and discernment, and see perceptively enough, that they are prepared in any circumstances to go and do the work of kingdom proclamation with fidelity and integrity? Although Luke is more subtle and subdued about that issue than is his source document, the Gospel of Mark, still he will not allow it to be decided prematurely in his narrative. (In Luke's next chapter, Jesus indicates that responding to the call to discipleship *never* is decided once and for all times but is a daily challenge, the outcome of which is taken for granted only at great spiritual peril—9:23f.)

(*a*) *The disciples' terror contrasts with the tranquility of Jesus.* Hardly had they pulled away from the shore in their small boat when Jesus—whom they were to emulate—modeled for them the tranquility that comes from perfect trust. He went to sleep in the shalom of God. It was not that he had overlooked the gale warnings in the weather reports, nor that he was such a landlubber that he did not grasp the perilous vulnerability of being out on the sea in an open boat. It was, rather, that he knew God was in control, and he was willing to rely on that knowledge absolutely. He expected the disciples to exercise such trust also.

When the storm hit, they were not phlegmatic about its potential. It is hard to be calm in the midst of a threat like that. They had seen too many sudden, severe squalls on that lake before. Besides, the waves rapidly became so turbulent that the boat, filling with water, was perilously near swamping. They were in imminent danger. The point of the story, however, is that they were in *worse danger* before the first cloud ever appeared in the sky or the first gust of wind came, heralding the approaching storm.

"Jesus! We're going under!" The disciples do not even take the time to criticize Jesus for his indifference toward their peril (as Luke had read of them doing in Mark). They are flat-out scared and in a desperate panic.

Their hysterical cry betrays that they have not heard or seen with the clarity Jesus covets for them. They do not really know who he is. If they did, they would not be anxious. God was reasserting royal control over the creation through Jesus who had the power to establish that rule. God was in control—even when it did not appear to be so (as when Jesus was asleep!).

(*b*) *Order out of chaos.* For the story to have full effect, we need to recover an appreciation of the scriptural themes at play. God's control over chaotic waters is a frequently encountered motif in Jewish scriptures that has its biblical origins in the creation account of Genesis 1. When Jesus "rebuked the wind and the raging waves; they ceased, and there was a calm" (v. 24b), he was restoring order to primordial chaos (represented by the stormy waters). This chaos had been reintroduced into a world that had chosen to renounce God's right to rule. So the story makes a considerable statement about Jesus' identity. It discloses that this agent of God, who previously had shown that he possessed the supernatural power to restore life and to forgive sins, also has the power to reimpose God's natural order on chaos, as occurred in the first creation.

(*c*) *The chaotic waters mirrored the disciples' inner chaos.* Of more critical concern in the story than the storm on the waters was the chaos within the disciples. This is where Jesus yearned to reestablish the orderly rule of God. They resisted where deluge and demons and disease and death itself could not resist his authority.

Even though they talked like disciples and sporadically tried to act like disciples, they had not yet seen and heard with the clarity, consistency, and discernment required for true comprehension. "Where is your faith?" he asked (v. 25). He was saying, "Do you not see that you still are in danger of perishing?" That continued to be so even though the wind and the waves were now calmed.

The disciples did not "do" what they had heard (cf. 6:46ff.). They divulged that his word had not taken deep enough root for them to know calmness, trust, and peace in a time of severe crisis (cf. v. 13).

To continue to hold back, and not offer absolute trust and reliance, discloses that the question of Jesus' true identity still is unresolved. "Who then is this?" (v. 25) the disciples asked. If *anybody* knew, *they* should have known. That question of identity has been raised frequently before in Luke's narrative (4:22, 36; 5:21; 7:19, 49). It will be raised again (9:9), and even again pointedly to the disciples by Jesus himself (9:20).

Sermon possibilities on this story include:

1. Chaos within betrays a vulnerability that resists the order of God's shalom. From this marvelously dramatic story, a pastoral lesson could be developed that speaks to the turmoil caused by crises in human hearts and in human faith. However, care and sensitivity must be used to guard against trivializing the intense pain and agony such crises cause.

As panicked as the disciples were, they seriously underestimated the danger they were in. They did not realize that without faith and trust in Jesus and in God they were not only at the mercy of a violent meteorological phenomenon, but were in grave danger of being overwhelmed by those malevolent forces opposing God and the good order of original creation responsible for the chaos, pain, and death in the world.

2. *The disciples' panic compared with Jesus' later agony.* An intriguing and instructive contrast may be discovered between this story and Luke's later depiction of Jesus' agony on the Mount of Olives.

In the present story, Jesus tranquilly sleeps embraced in the shalom of God. The disciples' terror reveals their propensity to cultivate solidarity with chaos.

On the Mount of Olives (22:39–46), the grief sleep of the disciples betrays continued solidarity with chaos marked by their refusal to respond to Jesus' bidding them to be at one with him in the fellowship of prayer. His own anguish over the looming threat of chaos, attested to both physically (v. 44) and verbally (v. 42a), is resolved by his surrender to the shalom of God (v. 42b), confirmed by the angelic ministration (v. 43).

The Gerasene Demoniac (8:26–39)

This story of the healing of the man possessed with multiple demons movingly complements the previous account. In that story, the disciples had panicked at the dangers of the storm out on the lake. Jesus had been more disturbed by the storm in their hearts, turmoil that testified to reservations in their commitment to him as disciples and in their allegiance to the reign of God which he, through his own person and ministry, was reasserting in the world.

(a) *The demons' response to the presence of Jesus.* The demons have the question of Jesus' identity solved better than do the disciples. They know who Jesus is: "Son of the Most High God" (v. 28). That is the same phrase the angel used in the annunciation to Mary (1:32), so they have to be right. (Previously, a demon had accurately recognized him as "the Holy One of God" [4:34].) Not only do they know who Jesus is, they know what he can do (vv. 31f.), and they know who is in control. God yearns for the rest of creation to acquire that knowledge and to take it at least as seriously as do the demons.

As well informed of Jesus' identity as the demons were, that did not contribute to their well-being. It is not enough to know who Jesus is—you have to be transformed by that recognition. Although they were subject to Jesus' authority, they chose not to surrender themselves to it. They sought, instead, to evade such divine presence through escape.

Early Jewish Christians undoubtedly told the bit about the pigs (vv. 32f.) with a great deal of relish for the joke that it was. To the Jew who observed cultic dietary restrictions, pigs were where demons belonged. When the pigs rushed down the slope into the water, (a fit place for pigs), where the demons could expect to encounter and be rejoined with the forces of chaos, they encountered instead the order Jesus had just imposed and so remained, albeit unwillingly, under the control of God's royal authority.

(*b*) *Economic anxiety distracted from spiritual perception.* The Gerasenes from the region, alerted by the herdsmen, did not know who Jesus was, either, but they did know his power. They knew what he had done to them, and they did not like it one bit. Economic considerations were partly to blame, since they were more agitated over the loss of their swine than they were excited over the recovery of their countryman.

It is demonically easy to be more concerned with pigs and profit than about people. Control over their own economic well-being concerned them and can concern us more than the clear disclosure of the reassertion of God's royal rule, which the restoration of the possessed man's well-being heralded. It is not too flip to observe that it can be costly to encounter Jesus, depending on where one's values are vested. Preoccupation with "treasure" tends to dim one's detection of the divine and to blunt one's enthusiasm.

Since they did not know who Jesus was, it is no wonder they were "seized with great fear" (v. 37, see v. 35). The reason he was able to do what he did was ambiguous. Maybe the reason he could drive pigs berserk by ordering around a whole host of demons was because he was a demon of higher rank. Given what those demons had done to one man, just think what he might do to them all! When you are not clear about who Jesus is and have not surrendered yourself, you are vulnerable to the counterfeit credibility claims of all kinds of fantastic conclusions.

(*c*) *A new witness to the order of God's shalom.* The man possessed of the demon legion was as good as dead, not just physically and socially but also spiritually, when he found Jesus. He lived an "un-life," ostracized and in isolation among the tombs under the control of death-givers, when he "saw" Jesus, the life-giver. He knew Jesus' power, he knew Jesus' authority, and he also knew Jesus' goodness. He assumed the posture of disciple (v. 35), the only one in that crowd of Gerasenes to become a disciple that day. Understandably he longed to be with Jesus, for that is where a committed disciple belonged.

Jesus proposed a different role for his discipleship. As little as he knew about Jesus, and as new as his knowledge was, he knew what counted. Jesus commissioned him to testify to God's deeds, and he did it gladly because he *knew who Jesus was* and had surrendered to him.

"Declare how much *God* has done for you," Jesus instructed him, and, restored, he went back to his home in the city, telling all who would listen about "how much *Jesus* had done for him" (v. 39). To him, God and Jesus were one and the same, and Luke does not disagree. The healed man heard Jesus' words, abbreviated as they were, and did them. That is what a faithful disciple does.

A sermon suggestion follows:

Moving from this story about the demoniac in its first-century setting to the faith concerns of a contemporary faith community can be accomplished easily. The story vividly illustrates the radical transformation that occurs in a person's life when Jesus is allowed to impose God's order on the chaos within.

That transforming order is what Jesus' disciples needed fully to experience. Until they did, they were in as much danger of running amuck—of being "out of sync" with God, the world, and their own society—as was the man who was possessed.

Jesus' authority and power are superior to the chaos of a fallen natural order and greater than a crowd of demons. There are, however, the limits of divine condescension. When fear intrudes and counsels caution and reserve, even rejection, there is just not much Jesus can do except to grieve and wonder what has happened to trusting faith. The disciples were learning about that (vv. 22–25) and would learn even more. We are learning all about that, too.

Pervasive feelings of double-mindedness, lack of integration, a loss of control over the events and relationships of one's life, coupled with a sense of tepid, shallow, qualified commitment to faith in God, encourage people to open themselves for convergence with this story. The pastoral trick is to help them claim that for themselves without dunking them in forcibly.

The issue of Jesus' identity again plays a part. Until you understand who Jesus is, once and for all, without reserve, and surrender yourself to that recognition, you simply are not in a position to allow the peace, harmony, and order of God that Jesus incarnates and brokers flood into your life.

Power over Sickness and Death (8:40–56)

What an accomplished narrator Luke is! He introduces this section by describing the glad reception with which the crowd welcomed Jesus back into Galilee, a reception standing in sharp contrast to the way he had been received by people in the land of the Gerasenes. They may not have been precisely clear in Galilee about who Jesus was (see 9:19), but they certainly were not afraid of him. Now Luke artfully intertwines two miracle stories in such a way that the impact of both is enhanced.

(*a*) *The mortally ill daughter.* Jairus, a local religious leader, has an only daughter who is dying. (Luke likes "only child" language. It heightens the pathos of the incident and emphasizes the compassion of Jesus [7:12, and see 9:38]). So here is Jairus, a respected community leader, who is desperate and absolutely convinced that Jesus can make all the difference.

Jairus abandons his posture of haughty aloofness and prostrates himself before Jesus, imploring him to go to his house. (He is not content to ask, as was the centurion [7:1ff.], for a powerful word spoken from afar.) What will Jesus do? Leaving the critical question unanswered, Luke fades the camcorder over to the crowd scene with the invalid woman. It effectively increases the narrative tension, thereby elevating audience interest.

(*b*) *Jesus is diverted by the ill woman.* In vv. 42b-48, an invalid confronts Jesus, and during the incident the element of religious defilement is very pronounced. The invalid is a woman and a hyper-orthodox Jewish male would avoid touching any of them "just in case." Furthermore, she had been bleeding over an extended interval—way beyond the normal menstrual occurrence which, in and of itself, profanes. According to Leviticus 15:19–30, she cultically defiled everything and everyone she touched. She touches Jesus—but he is not defiled, and she is healed! Luke was drawing here on the view that the possessions of a person who was empowered to accomplish miraculous deeds could impart something of that power (see Acts 5:15 and 19:12, which reflect a similar view).

The woman's act, far from being reprehensibly irreligious and intrusive, is the most personal and profound testimony she could offer about her perception of who Jesus is. Her conviction that he had the power to heal her was so great, and her need to be healed so desperate, that the situation transcended whatever scruples the cultic restrictions and prohibitions evoked within her. She saw who Jesus was, she recognized what he could do for her, she forced access to his presence, and she claimed the restoring rule of God, which he incarnated, in her life.

Jesus' query caused such turmoil in the crowd and among the disciples that the woman confessed what she had done and why. Her agitation reflected residual recognition that at any other time such a confession would have earned her indignant chastisement for breaking the law and causing defilement. However, in that case she could not have testified, as she does here, that she has been healed.

Instead of sharp rebuke, what she hears are words of confirmatory blessing. "Daughter," Jesus calls her (v. 48), indicating that she belongs to Jesus' family (see 8:19–21). That was a more profound affirmation of her restoration to health than any declaration uttered by the priest, accompanied by sacrificial offerings as required by the law to confirm her cure.

(c) *Jesus' attention tardily returns to Jairus's daughter.* An impressive and moving encounter—but it took time. In the interval, Jairus's daughter died. The opportunity for a timely miracle to guard her from death, which had seemed to be her father's last hope, was now patently lost. "Not so," corrected Jesus "Your final hope, your only hope, for you as well as for her, is your trust in God who has empowered me to make right what has gone wrong in creation."

In verse 52, Jesus said the child was "sleeping," and they laughed at his ingenuous imperception. Again defying cultic prohibitions, Jesus reached out, touched the corpse, and spoke. Weeping Jairus did not have much time to ponder. He chose, he believed, he laughed. "Blessed are you who weep now, for you will laugh" (6:21b)—not the laugh of arrogant incredulity at the absurd, but the laugh of exhilarated abandon at the recognition of God-originated life where before they had been able to see only death. "Her parents were astounded," Luke observed (v. 56). What did Peter, John, and James make of it? What did they think? Were they able to share in Jairus's laugh?

A stunning nature miracle and a singularly spectacular exorcism, a healing and a resuscitation—one following on the other. Do the disciples get it? Can they see who Jesus is? Can they discern what God is doing through him? Do they see what God longs to do for them through him? Can they commit themselves unequivocally to what they see and hear? Can they do what Jesus says? With the Jesus stories in the next section (chapter 9), Luke will test that out. His findings are not univocal.

COMMISSIONING THE TWELVE (9:1–6)

(a) *Jesus empowers the Twelve.* Jesus gave "power and authority" to the Twelve. He equipped them with the same spiritual resources of kingdom presence with which he himself was empowered. He charged them to be agents through whose healing and preaching activity the rule of God was to expand. He entrusted to them ministry functions similar to his own, sending the Twelve out as extensions of his ministry. They had witnessed his work, heard his preaching, and been schooled in his teaching. Now they, too, were to preach (a crucial emphasis Luke apparently added here, since it was not in his Markan source) and do mighty works of healing.

This assignment was no trial period, no supervised ministry internship, no field education project, no tentative period of candidacy, or interval of limited licensure. God spurns such caution, even when the church dares not. Give God the least chance and God will go for broke all the way every time.

Since Jesus is willing to take such a gamble, he requires them to lay something on the line as well. Jesus always expects that. They are to demonstrate their complete trust in God down to the minutest detail of their behavior. Such reliance on God is compromised when they have travelers' checks squirreled away in the secret compartment of their wallets "just in case."

(b) *Prohibition to provide in advance for needs.* Jesus prohibited the disciples from making those prudent advance preparations any experienced traveler would take in anticipation of unexpected needs that might conceivably arise on a trip. Concern over maintenance and support can be distracting, but beyond that they must completely trust God, even to the extent that they rely absolutely on God to use others to provide whatever they require (as Jesus, himself, was doing—8:1ff.). Such visible vulnerability displayed an unqualified reliance on what God provides that is necessary to the posture of faithful discipleship in every circumstance.

This voluntary dependency was to be Exhibit A in support of their preaching about the claim of God's royal rule to which others must respond in faith and trust. As Eduard Schweizer (*The Good News According to Luke,* [Atlanta: John Knox Press, 1984], p. 152) observes, "only disciples who concretely live their trust in God by renouncing all forms of security are credible."

Not only are the disciples to depend totally on what God provides through the generosity of others for their sustenance, they also are not to be offensively particular about their accommodations. They should accept whatever hospitality is offered and not try to upgrade that which God has provided through their hosts to meet their needs.

(c) *Prophetically withdraw from hostile reception.* The disciples also must expect an occasional hostile reception. When that occurs, given the urgency of their assignment, they are not to take time to be peacemakers nor enter into an extended exercise in conflict management. That is not their mandate. Instead, they are to break all semblance of contact with those who reject the presence of God's sovereign claim in their preaching and healing. They must leave, taking absolutely nothing away from there. Even the dust of the place should not be carried off. That is not an act of indignant disdain. It is a prophetic action warning of divine judgment— "a testimony against them" (v. 5).

The disciples' preaching and teaching, their powerful, miraculous acts, their demeanor and response to the way they are received, all are integral to their ministry. In every way possible, they are to reflect God's royal rule already effectively established in their lives. Who they are and what they represent as empowered agents extending the ministry of Jesus makes a claim for God's right to rule and imparts either blessing or judgment depending on the reception they are accorded.

(*d*) *Outcome of Jesus' initiative.* What was the result of this gamble which Jesus took with his followers who, prior to this, have not proven to be as single-mindedly perceptive, discerning, or committed as he might have wished? How did his hazard turn out? The Twelve did what they were told to do. They heard his words and did them—with alacrity and thoroughness (v. 6). The story gives Luke opportunity to balance his portrayal of the disciples, which was beginning to look negatively lopsided.

We do not know how long they were at their mission work, or how successful they were (v. 10 is disappointingly vague). Luke wants us to think of them as causing a noticeable enough stir which, added to the impact of Jesus' own personal ministry, caught Herod's attention (v. 7).

Sermon suggestions for this story include:

1. *The hazard of discipleship.* Given the portrait of the disciples' ambivalence and vacillation in their faith relationship to Jesus Luke has sketched thus far, we could label this incident "Jesus Takes a Gamble." The presentation might then remind the faithful that this is precisely what God through Jesus does with every one of us. Furthermore, the history of the church (and of our own personal pilgrimage) documents that Jesus loses more often than he wins.

The good news is that he comes to terms with that risk. Even though the gamble may not always pay off, he does not lose hope that we will finally trust him. Considering what is at stake, he is willing to take the gamble again and again. It is the Second (New) Testament appreciation of divine forbearance and grace.

2. *The cost of being called.* A terrific stewardship sermon may be developed from this passage around the perspective of complete reliance on God for what one needs, but we should also be aware that it may wreak havoc with "increase in salary for the preacher" negotiations. That is why authentic, sincere lay testimony is so effective. No one is paying them to testify. Historically, the same perspective supported the emergence and cultivation of the religious vow of poverty. People who have learned to depend on supernatural resources rise above their visible potential to meet exceptional expectations. God counts on that and exploits that gladly, even if it is risky.

JESUS' IDENTITY FURTHER DISCLOSED (9:7-50)

This concluding section to the first major division in Luke's narration, that of Jesus' public ministry in Galilee, makes explicit some additional aspects of the identity of Jesus. Luke's auditors have been exposed to most of them in the Infancy and Preparation for Ministry sections (1:26–4:13). Now Jesus is made known to his disciples as the Messiah of God, and the suffering Son of Man, the chosen Son of God, and the servant greater than Moses, who is about to embark with the new Israel on the new exodus.

Herod's Perplexity (9:7-9)

It is a hard thing to detect when anyone, but especially a leader with political power and authority, is asking the right questions for the wrong reasons. Motives are notoriously elusive for others to discover, and chancy to inquire after or to call into question, since one can so easily misunderstand or be misunderstood. Still, it is only prudent to recognize that properly articulated formulae do not always tell the entire tale.

(*a*) *Herod's perplexity over Jesus.* This story again raises the question of Jesus' identity, a question Luke teaches us must be continually rethought and answered anew. It cannot be dismissed as having been already resolved. It is not so much an informational question as it is a confessional issue requiring regularly reiterated confirmation.

Herod was alerted to the ferment in the region. The reports he had been receiving corresponded to those popular opinions about Jesus that the disciples shortly were to report directly to Jesus (v. 19). The activities causing unrest provoked Herod to ask the right question: "Who is this about whom I hear such things?" (v. 9b). That is the question everyone should ask who hears about Jesus and what Jesus and his disciples are doing in the neighborhood. They should really hear and recognize that activity as evidence for what God is doing in the world.

Herod's bewilderment about the identity of Jesus leads to what, at first blush, appears to be the proper and pious response: "he tried to see him" (v. 9c). That is the proper reflex. If you are uncertain, or unconvinced, about the truth claims of the gospel, or when you do not know what to make of Jesus, do not let it pass. Go and find out by putting yourself in his presence.

(*b*) *Herod's hidden interests.* Nevertheless, Herod's question emerged not simply from positive perception nor from neutral curiosity. Subsequent references in Luke's account make clear that Herod was not even remotely open to hearing an accurate answer to his question. Luke understands an underlying malevolent current to his curiosity (13:31). The Evangelist will allude to this present story in the trial scenes prior to Jesus' execution (23:8).

The reaction of Herod later during the trial of Jesus (23:8ff) makes very clear that Herod's desire to see Jesus was not so innocently inquisitive. He was not really in the least inclined or prepared to see Jesus. He just wanted a show—some spectacular entertainment. "Jesus, show me you're no fool/walk across my swimming pool!" (Andrew Lloyd Webber, *Jesus Christ Superstar,* The Really Useful Group, plc., 1971). Instead of seeing Jesus for who he was, Herod saw only a powerless agitator with political pretensions who did not deserve serious consideration.

Possible ways for sermon construction include:

1. To rightly know ourselves, we must first know who Jesus is. This passage directs our attention to the fundamental option with which God through the gospel confronts us. It is not enough to ask "the right question" about the identity of Jesus. We must realize how the asking of that question impinges on our self-understanding. The question having been asked, it should be clear that the one coming into question is the questioner.

When we understand who Jesus is, information is disclosed to us about ourselves which, often, we do not care to acknowledge. Furthermore, when we find the right answer to "the Jesus question" and learn who Jesus is, we find ourselves exposed to mandates and missions, to ministry and ministrations we used to avoid as irrelevant, boring, or repulsive.

2. The two *Herods and Jesus.* We could take a real flyer by violating that canon of Synoptic interpretation that counsels us to avoid the urge to merge material from the three Synoptic Gospel accounts. It might be fun to compare the earlier Herod in the Gospel of Matthew with this Herod in Luke. The prior Herod said the right things for all the reprehensibly wrong reasons, too (Matt. 2:8, 13), with deadly consequences (Matt. 2:16ff.). So this Herod asked the right question (Luke 9:7ff.) for the wrong reasons with deplorable results (13:31; 23:8ff.). That may commend careful pondering of what our reasons and motives are, before we pose the question of Jesus' identity—for when we learn the answer to that question, we too can either mock and destroy, or submit.

Feeding the Five Thousand (9:10–17)

Immediately after Herod asked about the identity of Jesus (v.9), Luke told the story of the miraculous feeding. He found details in Mark's version that fascinated him—details reminiscent of Moses and the "wilderness wanderings" traditions in the First (Old) Testament. He will use each of the stories in this concluding section to the Galilean ministry to emphasize and exploit that. It is the key to understanding what he portrays theologically in the next "Journey to Jerusalem" portion of his narrative.

(*a*) *Luke's narrative sequence and the problem of place.* Luke reduced Mark's extended account of the execution of John the Baptist by Herod (Mark 6:16–29) to three terse words (v. 9). This let him put the story of the miraculous feeding immediately after Herod's question. So he signals to his hearers that a significant new insight into the issue of Jesus' identity was about to be provided.

Commentators have made all kinds of attempts—some terrifically tortured, others terribly tentative—to account for why Luke, who can be so subtle and precise in his literary style, pictured Jesus going with the apostles into a city [v. 10], then calling it a "deserted place" [v. 12] more bereft of available provisions than small villages and country crossroads.

I think he was working too hastily through Mark and at first intended to skip this story, too—maybe to include it later in his narrative. So he jumped from Mark 6:16 to Mark 6:45. *Then,* noticing that he was missing a really good bet for advancing his solution to the question of Jesus' identity, he included the miraculous feeding account, but he neglected to delete the reference to Bethsaida from his computer's hard disk.

It is certainly a dramatic story. The Twelve apostles reported the positive results of their mission (v. 10). Jesus showed his solidarity with them by continuing his ministry with the crowd that was identical to the ministry he had entrusted to them (v. 11, see v. 2). Things were on a roll!

Success, however, has its own problems. Double the membership of your congregation and see what adjustments have to be made, and how many extra meetings you have to attend!

(*b*) *The disciples refuse to follow Jesus' directions.* While the logistical need of the moment was gustatorial, it gave rise to a singular opportunity for Jesus to deepen their perception of kingdom presence and, thereby, to advance God's rule. Why would the Twelve not do what Jesus told them to do and "give them something to eat" (v. 13a)? They had Jesus' authority and power, they could preach the good news, they could cure diseases and even cast out demons. Why not be instruments for God's miraculous, nourishing, physical sustenance?

The Twelve could not meet the need because they thought their resources were limited to what they could see, count, and weigh. And what they counted in their hands was pitiful compared with all of those whom they counted into groups of fifty. It was more than they could handle, they thought. Their cardinal, faithless blunder was that they thought they had to handle it on their own.

A possible sermon venture on this aspect of the story:

You might recall with the congregation the crisis meetings of the budget committee of the official board when needs surpassed visible resources by far. Or they may remember together those times when enticing opportunities had frustrated rather than challenged them, because it just was not at all clear that the community of faith was up to pulling it off. Recall times when the harvest was great, the laborers were few—and the denomination hardly had enough wherewithal even to keep the scythes sharpened and the training classes for novice mowers supplied with curricula, much less support the actual work.

(c) The twelve baskets of leftovers show that the miracle is not over. Jesus organized the event. He gave the disciples ushers' and waiters' work to do. (Nothing wrong with that—it is *diakonia,* ministry.) Grace having been said, the bread was broken, the fish was fragmented, the pittance passed, *and all ate their fill!* When the Twelve picked up after the meal was finished, they had more than enough leftovers to do it again. Their problem was that they did not realize their baskets had been just as full when Jesus told them, "You give them something to eat" (v. 13). The church frequently has similar difficulty discovering that today.

Were any of those five thousand hungry men (plus their women and children) grateful? Did anyone leave a tip? How many wished that there was a McDonald's around the corner, instead? Nevermind! The critical issue now becomes: What are you going to do with that twelve-basket surplus? And what does the whole event tell us about Jesus, and about ourselves?

It is such a profound story, drawing as it does on numerous First Testament passages and traditions that describe God as promising to feed the people of Israel (e.g., Ps. 78:19f.). These traditions depended on the Genesis creation accounts, but were particularly focused and shaped by the many miraculous provisions of sustenance during the wilderness wanderings of the exodus. At least some of the hungry horde on that high hill had been nourished better than they could remember ever having been before—not since they were with Moses in the wilderness.

Another sermon might be developed along the following lines:

This passage suggests a very obvious liturgical context for preaching. Early on, the community of the Easter faith invested this story with eucharistic meanings. It is most obvious in the description of Jesus' words and actions (v. 16). It is also frequently evident in early Christian art. That interpretation was an obvious connection for the early church to make. They saw in the story of the miraculous feeding more than echoes of First Testament traditions describing how God miraculously provided food in the wilderness. They found similar marvelous nourishment every time they gathered to celebrate the Lord's Supper. People still do.

The experience of spiritual satiety does not occur for the afterglow of contentment alone. Being so richly nourished requires us to look again at Jesus, see him for who he truly is, and reaffirm our vows of allegiance to him. *That* movement triggers self-reflection. It is partly self-examination, partly genuine remorse, but, above all, it produces resolve to change. It requires reflective refitting of the dimension, direction and depth of our discipleship. The pastoral role is clear: Do not let them leave the Table without their making some concrete commitments about what they are going to do with those twelve baskets of nourishing fragments in excess.

Peter's Confession (9:18–27)

(*a*) *Various popular opinions about Jesus' identity.* There is no question about it. Jesus certainly had made an impression with his peripatetic ministry in the region, his authoritative preaching, his marvelous healings and exorcisms, his astounding provisions for that huge, hungry crowd—not to mention all those extraordinary things he had his disciples doing in his name on behalf of the sovereignty of God. It is no wonder that people were talking.

The differing identities assigned to Jesus by popular opinion (v. 19) all had one thing in common: They unanimously acknowledged that, whoever he precisely was, he was clearly an agent empowered by God to proclaim God's word and disclose the divine will. They suspected he had something to do with end-of-days events and the reestablishment of God's realm in Zion. It was quite a reputation for a small-town boy to have acquired.

(*b*) *Jesus requires his disciples to identify him.* As intrigued as Jesus may have been by those multiple prevalent speculations, he had the disciples rehearse them as a foil for what came next. That is what they say, but are they right? That is what other folks are thinking; what do you think? "Who do you say that I am?" (v. 20).

There it was, laid right out on the table, and the disciples had to deal with it—otherwise, what did they think they were doing in following Jesus? It was a question the disciples had asked themselves time and again (e.g., 7:25), from the beginning on. They had pondered it, worried about it, changed their minds about it, evaded it, postponed it, discussed it. They did not always like or understand the answers they found. It was the question Herod the Tetrarch had asked before (v. 9), but the way Jesus put it now, it was time for the disciples either to "fish or cut bait."

They looked at one another, then took deep breaths as Peter fronted for them: "The Messiah of God!" There, can you believe it? They had said it.

Of course, Luke's audience knew that answer already. They had heard that this was the one whom Simeon was waiting to see when Mary and

Joseph brought the infant Jesus to him at the Temple (2:26). It exaggerates the irony of the later account at the crucifixion when the scoffing rulers use the exact same phrase in what they thought was a "contrary to fact" condition (23:35). Besides, Luke's listeners had heard the story in its entirety again and again. Still, you could not help but hold your breath to see what the disciples were going to say.

(*c*) *In identifying Jesus, the disciples identify themselves in relation to him.* When he used the phrase, "the Messiah of God," Peter (and the other disciples through him) acknowledged Jesus to be the anointed and empowered end-time agent of God. He was the one who had come to usher in the restoration of God's regal rule over Israel and the whole of creation. That confession was a considerable statement for them to make—not just about Jesus, but also about their relationship to Jesus.

With that acclamation they certified that they really were his disciples and they were committed to following him. Only those who truly belonged to the royal realm of God (or the demons whom that realm opposed) could know him to be the Christ of God. It is going to take much more, including their experiencing his humiliation and their witnessing his suffering, death, and resurrection, for them to begin to fathom what their confession really meant. Still, they had finally said it, and that was enough for the moment. Actually, in God's eyes, it is quite a lot.

(*d*) *The necessity of Jesus' suffering as the Messiah.* Jesus knows full well that they still have a lot to learn and experience. His command to silence (v. 21) provides for an extended interval in the narrative for this learning to take place. You might say that Peter's confession was somewhat precocious (or "inspired"). After all, the returns are not all in yet. If Herod had asked the right question for all the wrong reasons, Peter gave the right answer for incomplete reasons.

The suffering Son of man passion prediction (v. 22—the first of several such predictions Luke included in his Gospel) interprets a crucial additional dimension to the content of Peter's confession. What it means for Jesus to be the Christ of God will be evident only after he has undergone humiliating trial, execution, resurrection, and ascension into glory. (Actually, it is going to take living through all of that for them to begin to grasp fully what it means for them to be Jesus' disciples.) That dire forecast is so sharply at odds with any of the multiple popular expectations of what the Messiah "who was to come" would be like that it is only after the resurrection that the risen Christ can help his followers to sort it out and meld the two traditions (24:26f.).

The confession of Peter (and of the other disciples) concerning Jesus, and the startling interpretive amplification Jesus appended to it, are accurate, necessary, and complementary responses to the question Herod had asked (v. 9). With this account, Luke begins to negotiate a shift in emphasis of the christological focus of his narrative so that the question of the identity of Jesus includes the question of the necessity of his passion: Why must the Christ of God suffer and die? As pious Jewish traditions remembered Moses' suffering and death as pivotal to his role as the divinely empowered agent of God, so Jesus' suffering was an even more critical component of his ministry and mission. Thus the pericope also prepares for the next major division of Luke's narrative: the journey to Jerusalem, which begins with 9:51.

(e) *The necessity of the disciples' suffering as Jesus' faithful followers.* Luke left out Mark's story about when Jesus had to rebuke Peter, perhaps partly because he thought Mark was too harsh on the disciples. But Luke also wanted to connect intimately the disciples' extraordinary confession with the Jesus sayings about the nature of true discipleship (vv. 23–27). Inextricably related to the issue of correctly identifying Jesus is the issue of the correct identity of the true disciple, a theme to which Luke's narrative will return in the healing of the epileptic boy (vv. 37ff.) and the stranger who exorcises (vv. 49f.).

If "the Christ of God" confession, nuanced by "suffering Son of Man" content, is shockingly unexpected, also unnerving is the corresponding assertion of the necessity of suffering self-renunciation for the true disciple. True disciples do share the power and authority of Jesus and, therefore, something of his popular acclaim. They share in his suffering fate, too. Following Jesus means more than learning from him or emulating his acts of ministry. It also includes a passion that shares in his passion.

(f) *The nature of discipleship.* Each of the five Jesus sayings about the nature of true discipleship lend themselves to contemporary reflection and application:

> verse 23: To be a true disciple is to school oneself to stand consistently for God's rule and purpose no matter what the cost. When that posture of discipleship is properly assumed, the risk is not occasional or extraordinary but omnipresent.
>
> verse 24: This verse is a compellingly catchy expression of the paradox that preoccupation with self-survival is fatal while surrender to Jesus, and to the redemptive program God prosecutes through him, is to live life at its fullest and richest potential.
>
> verse 25: This verse recalls the second temptation (4:5ff.) and is a pithy exhortation for the true disciple to reorder priorities to conform to convictions.

verse 26: The true disciple cannot be selective either about the timing or about the scope of the content of his\her confession. Only the disciple who consistently claims Jesus in every circumstance will be claimed and vindicated by Jesus in his end-time role as judge.

verse 27: Rather than refer this saying to any event or series of events observed by some of the disciples that Luke will relate further on in his narrative, this verse is best understood as referring to true spiritual "seeing," which reflects in perceptive recognition of the presence of God's kingly rule.

The cumulative effect of all of the sayings is more important for Luke at this stage in his narrative. As the "suffering Son of Man" exegetes the disciples' confession of Jesus as the Christ of God, so the issue of discipleship shifts from the question of whether finally to respond to Jesus in faith, to the question of grasping what that response means for one's life and witness. The loyalty of the disciple to such a "suffering Son of Man" Messiah demands daily renunciation of all that detracts from single-minded obedient devotion to the Christ and to the redemptive program of God he implements.

The Transfiguration (9:28–36)

Luke has built considerable momentum into his narrative leading up to this moment. Who is Jesus? The Pharisees argued, the disciples wondered, John the Baptist puzzled over it, and the hometown folks had worried about that, too. Both Herod and Jesus asked it point blank. Peter, responding for all the disciples, could hardly believe what he heard himself say, especially so after Jesus interpreted Peter's testimony by imposing the meaning of necessary suffering and execution, an interpretation foreign to the wildest imaginings of the disciples. Now in this episode the best and highest, most authoritative personages of the entire holy history of Israel wondrously appear as a prelude to the climactic moment confirming Jesus' interpretative instruction, the testimony of the very voice of almighty God.

(a) *Inauguration of a new Exodus.* Many commentators on Luke's Gospel have been timorously tentative about drawing too close a parallel between Jesus and Moses, between the Sinai/Mount Horeb traditions and the events at the mountain of divine revelation. The cumulative effect of the imagery compels such a comparison. It is more than just the mountain parallel. Jesus' altered appearance and "dazzling" (v. 29) garments are, like Moses on Sinai (Ex. 34:29–35), reflected manifestations of the presence of God. The cloud of divine presence (v. 34), the revelatory heavenly voice (v. 35), the "exodus" about which Moses and Elijah spoke to Jesus (v. 31) all were exodus motifs. Even the booths which Peter proposed constructing were to commemorate the wilderness wanderings of the exodus. All were symbolic of a "new exodus" tradition.

David Moessner, (*Lord of the Banquet,* [Philadelphia: Fortress Press, 1989]), has demonstrated persuasively that this recognition is absolutely fundamental for an understanding of the ten-chapter travel narrative, which begins at the close of chapter 9. Moessner views it not simply as a didactic prelude to the passion but as a "new exodus" culminating in Jesus' suffering, death, and resurrection through which God delivers a "new Israel" to a new promised land of salvation. Even Jesus' prediction of his vicarious suffering (v. 22) and his cry of frustration (v. 41) bracketing the transfiguration account reflect Moses traditions (Deut. 4:21f. and Deut. 32:5, 20 respectively). The view that Jesus was a prophet like Moses, only greater (cf. Deut. 18:15–19), was of central importance to Luke and to his community, as is amply evidenced in Acts 3:22–26.

The "glory" of Moses and Elijah (v. 31) and of Jesus (v. 32b) is the glory of God's royal rule restored in the creation. It corresponds to the glory God invested in creation prior to the Fall. The privileged disciples see in Moses and Elijah and, above all, in the transformed Jesus the manifestation of the glory of creation restored. But they see it only hazily, as in a dream, (being half-asleep [v. 32]), which corresponds precisely to Luke's carefully crafted portrait of disciples who see but only occasionally, and then perceive only vaguely. Accordingly, Peter's suggestion for the construction of booths (the Jewish Feast of Booths commemorated the Exodus and the giving of Torah at Sinai) was far more profound than even he realized.

(*b*) *Jesus supplants both Moses and Elijah.* It should not be overlooked that, according to Luke's version of the story, the Moses and Elijah figures separate from Jesus before the theophany. In Luke's Christology, Jesus supplants them both. Moses and Elijah represented the past heritage and religious tradition of empirical Israel. Through Jesus, God is reconstituting Israel. He is more than Elijah, as Luke had already argued in 7:11ff. Now he is shown as more than a prophet like Moses.

(*c*) *Divine ratification of Jesus' true identity.* The cloud reproduces a frequent First Testament symbol for the presence of God. Consequently the disciples' fear as they entered into the cloud was what any pious Jew would expect to experience when coming into the presence of God. Evidence elsewhere of the disciples' imperceptiveness was the infrequency with which they responded in the same way to the presence of God in the person of Jesus (7:16, 8:25 are examples).

The voice from the cloud gave the ultimate answer to Herod's (and the disciples'—and *our*) question, "Who is this?" "Listen to him!" (v. 35) is God's ratification of the emphasis Jesus had frequently put on hearing his words and doing them (v. 26, cf. 6:46ff.; 8:4ff., 21, etc.), especially the connection made to his teaching about his passion (v. 22). Jesus is the Chosen One of God (cf. Isa. 42:1) who speaks with an authority greater than that of either Elijah or Moses. From now on, people—especially the disciples (and the church that hears the words of Jesus in the disciples' testimony)—are to listen to him.

That the disciples "kept silent and *in those days* told no one" (v. 36b) ambiguously expressed several dimensions of Luke's presentation. They kept silent because 1) they perceived the true significance of this dramatic event and its crowning divine disclosure only dimly, 2) Jesus had told them not to tell (v. 21), and so they were being obedient, 3) the drama was still in the process of unfolding and so the message was still incomplete, but that would soon change (see 24:48–49; Acts 1:8).

A sermon on this story might take shape from what follows:

Luke's skillful presentation serves as a warning that no one can afford to be content with initial perceptions of Jesus no matter how pious or innocent or sincere, no matter how powerful and persuasive those first perceptions might appear. Who Jesus is and what it means to be his disciple are connected concerns whose content is so vast and so complex as to elude being exhausted by a lifetime of devoted inquiry.

Clearly, as it was with the disciples (vv. 1-6), so we, too, cannot wait to be sure we have understood the truth entirely before getting on with Jesus' mandate to extend his ministry. But neither may we set the Jesus question aside as already having been fully, or even adequately, explored. The most telling sign of ossified discipleship is pervasive ennui at the prospect of pursuing any further the scope, depth, and quality of one's perceptive engagement with the Jesus question: "Who do you say that I am?" As long as that question is passé among the adult membership of a congregation, that membership will desiccate and, eroding, be dispersed.

A Healing Exorcism (9:37–45)

They were disappointed in the disciples all around—everyone involved in the story.

(*a*) ***The disciples disappointed everybody.*** The father whose little boy was possessed was, of course, terribly disappointed. He had been led to believe that, finally, there was hope his most fervent wish would be realized.

It was reported that extraordinary things had been occurring in the area for some time, mighty deeds of healing and exorcism done not just by Jesus but by his disciples, too. At long last the father hoped that his family shame and public humiliation, as well as his deepest personal agony, might be set right. However, when he asked them for help, the disciples could not do it.

The crowd was disappointed. Rumors of the wondrous activity done at first by Jesus and then by his disciples had fired people's imaginations. The word spread swiftly, and everyone was telling stories. If they had not seen it personally, they knew someone who had, or knew someone who knew of someone who had been there. Now some of this charismatic leader's disciples were in the area, and the people flocked to them in hordes. "Come on," they encouraged the man whose boy was afflicted, "after what they have already done, they can surely handle your situation. It will be a snap for them." However, the disciples could not do it.

The disciples, too, were disappointed—and embarrassed. They had thought that they were finally beginning to get it right, as an inkling of understanding about Jesus had begun to emerge. Of course, there were still contradictions and confusions, but they felt they were finally beginning to get the hang of it. Some of them had just recently preached and healed and cast out demons with astonishing effectiveness. Now was no different—or should not have been. But, when asked, they could not do it.

Jesus was disappointed—and more than a little exasperated. He should have expected it, of course. Again and again in the long history of God's efforts to accomplish God's purposes through human instruments, those who were chosen agents had proven themselves inconsistent. They were not always up to it. How abysmally frustrating for Jesus! He must have known just how Moses had felt (cf. Deut. 32:5, 20).

Jesus had taught the disciples, trained them, carefully brought them along, and finally taken the risk and equipped them, thereby empowering them to extend what he was doing. At first it looked as if they had caught on, as if they had bought into his mission and were making it their own. They did what he said, how he said to do it, and when he told them to. But now, confronted by comparable need and similar opportunity, they had somehow disengaged. They could not do it.

Perhaps even God was disappointed. The time was ripe to reverse the trend toward rebellion and revolt that had pervaded the creation almost since the beginning. The time was ripe to reassert God's right to rule, to inaugurate the restoration of God's reign over all. To accomplish that purpose, God had "gone for broke," sending the best most precious resource, the unique Son, to broker the transfer of authority. The disciples were about the best that this Son had been able to find and recruit, so far. He had commissioned them to aid him in extending God's royal rule. Now God wanted to rule in this boy's life, but there was a usurping, competitive power present there that had to be expelled. And the disciples could not do it.

(*b*) *The disciples' failure did not defeat God.* Luke's version of this story significantly qualified his portrait of the disciples. Even though they had acknowledged Jesus to be "the Messiah of God" (v. 20), even though some of them had been successful as empowered agents of Jesus, extending his healing and preaching ministry (vv. 1-6, 10), that did not mean they had "arrived" as instruments of God's regal rule.

Luke sketched the situation to evoke maximum sympathy for both father and child. He portrayed the child, the only son of the father, as a helpless victim invaded by those powers in the world inimical to God who usurp God's right to rule and cause pain, suffering, havoc, and chaos. If anyone deserved the healing power of the restored rule of God with which Jesus had empowered the disciples (vv.lf), *he* did.

The disciples cannot cast the spirit out, but all is not lost. Although God through Jesus invites the disciples to share in the reestablishment of the sovereignty of God, still God is not dependent on them. The healing of creation and the restoration of the rule of God are going to happen, and it is up to the disciples to decide whether they can give themselves completely enough to faith in God and to trust in Jesus' words so that they really are fully involved in the work of restoration.

Disappointed, perhaps, still God was not surprised. God knew what to expect. Even if God counted on those whom Jesus had recruited as the ones most likely to serve his purposes, God knew they were not ready yet to invest themselves with consistency and fidelity in the enterprise of restoration. Before they reached that point, they had a whole lot more to learn, a whole lot more to experience, a whole lot more personal transformation to undergo.

Disappointed, perhaps, still God was not defeated. Even though the disciples could not do it, there was still Jesus. And there was the father's hopeful trust, born and sustained by desperation, still intact in spite of disappointment. So Jesus, casting out, did heal and restore, and that saving activity extended beyond the troubled boy. All who were there—the father, the crowd, the disciples—experienced the healing presence of God's royal rule. So, in the final analysis, none—not the father, the crowd, the disciples, Jesus, or even God—was disappointed.

(*c*) *The disciples still could not fathom the necessity of Jesus' passion.* Luke closely tied another prediction by Jesus of his impending betrayal to the crowd's (including the disciples') awe-filled response to the wondrous exorcism-healing. Kingdom presence was compellingly evident at such moments. Since the majesty of God was clearly discernible in deeds of miraculous healing, how much more was that majesty to be displayed plainly in Jesus' approaching passion? If the disciples could see kingdom presence in the healing event, why could they not sustain the perception with consistency?

Jesus' words to them, "Let these words sink into your ears" (v. 44a) was solemn prophetic admonition recalling the urgent command of the divine voice on the mountain: "Listen to him!" (v. 35b). With this passage Luke indicated why the disciples could not cast out the tormenting spirit from the troubled boy. As far as they had come in following Jesus, still there were crucial moments when, hearing, they did not (even would not, and could not) understand (cf. 8:10). Not yet do they know all the secrets of the rule of God, for at times their hearts, too, are hardened. The culminating sign of their wavering fidelity was that, not wanting Jesus to know of their lack of comprehension, they thought that they could conceal it from him.

The disciples' inability to understand the passion prediction, their being hindered (by God!) from understanding it, underscored their need for yet stronger faith. So the passage set the stage for the considerable amount of teaching Jesus will give them during the impending extended journey to Jerusalem. Such an interval of intense private instruction putatively promises to place them in a much better position to grasp the meaning of the events they are to witness in Jerusalem.

Discipleship Misunderstood (9:46–50)

This material must be heard in the broader context of the Gospel story to appreciate its full impact. It would be easy to overlook how seriously Luke has qualified his otherwise positive portrayal of the disciples in their relationship to Jesus and to the rule of God that he proclaimed. The cumulative effect of the entire section brings that negative evaluation home. The disciples do not hear, see, or obediently do what they have been told to do. They do not understand, and they do not know their lack of understanding. They are not humble, they seek to deceive, and they are not open to the presence of saving power. Why does Jesus even bother with them?

In these two brief incidents, Luke shows us disciples with tarnished credentials who neglect concentrating on deepening their perception of Jesus and amending their sense of their own discipleship accordingly. They instead dispute over the pecking order in their fellowship and seek to guard the guild from outside competition.

(a) *"Who is the greatest?"* In the first incident (vv. 46–48), the disciples bicker about their relative rank in the realm of God Jesus is establishing. In spite of their clearly disclosed inability to hear with comprehension and, consequently, their impotence to do the work of the new order, they are preoccupied with prestige. The squabble effectively diverts them from their primary business, which is to devote themselves with single-minded concentration to being formed for a discipleship marked by consistency and integrity.

Jesus had just recently outlined for them what that discipleship necessarily must be like (vv. 23–27), but they had not accepted it. So he tried again, using a little child for a "show-and-tell" object lesson. True discipleship devoted to the service of God's royal rule renounces competitive rivalry for rank and prestige in favor of self-effacing humility, the most consistent expression of which is other-directed service. Instead of seeking esteem, the more acceptable goal is to esteem the least impressive person by recognizing that that person's sponsor and advocate is God. The true disciple must be willing to hold in high honor the weakest, most impotent member of the human community, and, especially, the community of faith.

(b) **Who guards the gate to discipleship?** The second incident (vv. 49–50) displays the disciples preoccupied with protection of traditions and preservation of prerogatives. The language used ("we tried to stop him" [v. 49b] and "do not stop him" [v. 50]) was technical language the early church used in the rite of initiation into the Easter community, baptism. Luke's community knows that language well. (Luke used the same technical language at other points in his narrative where the issue of allowing entry and access was critical, cf. 18:15; Acts 8:36, 10:47.) So the audience hears Luke raising the issue of who it is that controls entry into the realm of God.

The glaring irony in the incident is that the stranger whom the disciples were excluding was more effective as an extension of Jesus' ministry than they were at the moment. He could successfully exorcise while they could not (see v. 40). Instead of the disciples being able to affirm that and celebrate it by including him into their fellowship, they resented it. Infidelity impedes openness to the inclusion of "others" into the disciples' fellowship. But that does not govern access to the fellowship of God's royal realm.

A sermon might probe the following:

It is always perilous to presume that only those confirmed and in good standing in the church know where God's reign is actively being restored in creation—and through whom. The Holy Spirit is not restricted by charters for church order or printed, amended, and revised "standards for procedure." Nor is the Spirit limited to accomplishing God's work through the jealously guarded channels of established ecclesiastical bureaucracy. God *may* choose to work through those institutions on occasion, but when God does, it is, as always, startling evidence of God's unpredictable and unharnessed grace.

Journey to Jerusalem

Luke 9:51–19:27

$\mathbf{L}$uke's perceptive literary eye knew a good thing when he saw it. He found the description of Jesus' journey from Galilee to Jerusalem in his Markan source (Mark 10:1–52), recognized its potential for helping him to realize some of his literary and theological goals, and, in adapting it, expanded the travel account into a more prominent and significant feature of the Gospel narrative than had Mark.

What took Mark one chapter to relate occupies almost ten chapters in Luke's version, extending from 9:51 through 19:27. The journey narrative provided Luke with a literary vehicle for incorporating into his story sequence a considerable collection of additional Jesus stories he apparently knew as self-contained, independent traditions, both oral and written, with little or no narrative setting. Of the total journey section, all but the last bit (19:1–27) comprises what has become known as Luke's "special section," a narrative segment unique to his version of Jesus' public ministry.

Theologically, this juncture in the narrative provided Luke with what for him was *the indispensable perspective* for a right and complete understanding of the full significance of the stories he included. Prior to the beginning of the journey, Jesus told his disciples twice of his impending passion (9:22, 44), emphasizing its inescapable necessity. At the conclusion of the journey Jesus will approach and enter Jerusalem where, shortly thereafter, that passion will be accomplished. Throughout the journey, all of the events and instructions take place under the sign of the cross and require belief in the cross event (crucifixion and resurrection) as the prerequisite for full comprehension of the stories.

The journey is an "exodus" trip moving unavoidably toward the exodus event to be accomplished in Jerusalem (v. 31) at Calvary. His deeds and sayings during the journey are instruction and training for his disciples in the way of the Lord, and, therefore also, the way of discipleship (vv. 23ff.). The journey provides both "a revelation of God's dominion

107

and a catechesis in discipleship" (David Tiede, *Luke*, [Minneapolis: Augsburg Publishing House, 1988] p. 196).

Jesus, traveling toward Jerusalem to his crucifixion, instructs his followers, the disciples, and confounds his adversaries, the religious leaders, all under the shadow of the cross. The disciples must process all of this as well as the events that are pending in Jerusalem in their understanding of Jesus as the Christ of God (v. 20) if they are ever to begin to grasp the awesome dimensions of obedient discipleship. For the religious leaders, and anyone else still holding back, the interval offers one last chance yet to repent and believe.

It is important to notice that, as we will see below, the journey account begins with additional misunderstandings about the nature of discipleship (9:51–62). This suggests that although Jesus, anticipating his death and resurrection as conforming to the will of God, was determined to go to Jerusalem, his accompanying disciples are far from comprehending that significance (v. 45). It discloses where they are now and how far they have yet to go.

Journeying is a motif we readily recognize in our times. Given the multiple modes of mobility that are taken for granted as available in our culture—trains, ships, buses, automobiles, excellent roads, and above all, airplanes—travel is part of most people's activities these days. People may easily travel to the mountains or the seashore for a change of scenery. Often we go on a journey to another region or country for a limited, temporary exposure to another culture. A trip may be undertaken because something significant is going to take place at the destination, such as a business meeting, a class reunion, a major sports event, or a new job. Frequently, we travel to be with family, colleague, mentor, lover—people who are important to us.

A trip can be utilitarian, a means to an end. A journey can be its own end, a formative, nurturing interval. Journeying can be an apt metaphor for significant dimensions of the human experience.

A young Swiss girl I know who traveled to the United States with an American family had never, prior to that trip, been more than forty miles from her mountain village home. The journey to America, the goal of which was to help her learn the English language (and, for the American family, to acquire inexpensive baby-sitting), was formative for her. She was liberated from what she considered stern family restraint, learned to be self-reliant, experienced unanticipated socially and culturally enriching occasions, and came to view her own life from a significantly different perspective. The journey seemed to make the entire world accessible to her. It changed her life.

Jesus' journey to Jerusalem was utilitarian, a means to an end. It was necessary for him to get to Jerusalem where his passion was, of God's necessity, to occur. Luke portrayed the trip as a formative journey for the disciples as well. While they traveled together to Jerusalem, Jesus instructed his followers, shaped their faith, prepared them for the nightmare of the cross (his and theirs), disclosed dimensions of discipleship to them, and motivated them for mission. It changed their lives. So too can it change ours, *if* we have ears to hear and eyes to see.

REJECTION AND REPROACH IN SAMARIA (9:51–56)

As the first major segment of Jesus' public ministry began with rejection (by the hometown folks at Nazareth, 4:16–30), so Luke depicted the second major stage as inaugurated with rejection also. Of course, the third major portion, the public ministry in Jerusalem (19:28–21:38), has the rejection motif running throughout as an intensified undercurrent in anticipation of Jesus' arrest, trial, and execution.

The story of Jesus in Samaria and the section that follows (vv. 57–62) both have as their primary focus the consideration of how *not* to be disciples:

1) 51–56 — by inflicting retributive destruction

2) 57–62 — with qualified, conditional following

Luke's vocabulary compels recognition of the single-minded intentionality with which Jesus "set his face to go to Jerusalem" (see Ezekiel 21:1–2 for a typical First Testament passage that shaped the "Bible language" Luke used so well). In the Greek text *face* is used three times; various forms of the verb *to go* appear four times; *Jerusalem*, as the destination, is given twice. "To be taken up" (v. 51) is a phrase that includes the geographical and the theological significance of 1) the journey, and 2) the events to occur in Jerusalem culminating in 3) Jesus' assumption into heaven. The tone of firm, unshakable resolve on Jesus' part is inescapable.

(*a*) *Samaritans diverted by Jesus' destination.* The Samaritans' reaction to the prospect of the coming of Jesus among them illustrates how "religion" can retard religious perception. They could not see who Jesus was for pique over where he was going. Fiercely competitive with the Jews over the issue of the proper place to worship God, all the Samaritans knew was that Jesus was coming to them on his way to *Jerusalem.* They would have nothing to do with that. Misconstruing the significance of his destination, they overlooked the meaning of his advent and his presence. In rejecting him, they rejected the saving power of the kingly presence that the God whom they claimed to serve more perfectly at Gerizim willed for them and was sending to them.

The divine response to the Samaritans' negative reception was far less severe than the disciples (who had, after all, been schooled from childhood to despise Samaritans) would have it. Samaria was later given a prominent place when the risen Christ commissioned his disciples (Acts 1:8), and it proved to be fertile territory for the message of the missionary church (Acts 8:5f., 14ff.). Both the procedure for approach described in the incident and Jesus' response to the Samaritan rejection anticipate the procedure and the response to rejection he would recommend in his instructions to the Seventy (10:1ff.). This may reflect a missionary methodology familiar to and even used by Luke's community.

(b) *The disciples' desire for retribution was demonic.* The primary emphasis in Luke's version of the incident falls on the disciples. Jesus had sent them ahead, Elijah-like, to prepare the way of his coming. Consequent to the Samaritan rejection, they offered, again in an Elijah-like manner, to call down consuming fiery judgment (see 2 Kings 1:9–16). Luke may have wanted us to see in their assumption that such a thing was appropriate (Jesus had already instructed James and John otherwise in verse 9:5) and that they had the power to do it, evidence of an arrogant and distorted misunderstanding of what Jesus intended when he spoke of the least one in God's realm being greater than the Elijah-like John the Baptist (7:28).

Jesus not only prohibited the vindictively retaliatory response proposed by James and John, he *rebuked* them. That is more than a disciplinary "slap on the wrist." "Rebuke" is the word Luke often used to describe what Jesus did to overcome all who opposed the power of the rule of God (4:35, 41; 8:24; 9:42, etc.).

Such a potent response was called for because the disciples had not "heard" (and, therefore, "done") Jesus' teachings about the posture of non-retaliation in the realm of God (6:27–29, 32–38). It was additional evidence of the disciples' imperception and, therefore, their lack of empathy with Jesus and his mission. Hearing the word means doing it; *not* hearing and doing constitutes a rejection at least as flagrant as the Samaritans' rejection.

The Samaritans rejected Jesus by not receiving him. The disciples ostensibly "received" him but betrayed their rejection by not believing and obeying his teaching. That rejection indicated their solidarity with all those people and powers who were actively opposing Jesus and the saving purposes God was accomplishing through him.

A preaching suggestion follows:

Elijah-like power is seductive. How we yearn to control such clout and to use it in the name of God! Now as then, most "hell-fire and damnation" pronouncements say more about the impaired spiritual health, sensitivity, and security of the pronouncer than about the divinely decreed deserts of the target audience. Ranks of righteous "Rambos" slaying demonic dragons right and left to vindicate and defend the honor of God is a grotesque posture for anyone to assume who claims to have no help in heaven and on earth, save the Lord.

The same posture can be much more subtle. Blatant excommunication is so crude and unsophisticated, yet there still are pressures one can apply. Paternalistic judgments, whispered criticisms and condemnations, avoidances, exclusions, the withholding of affirmation or compassion, meager encouragement, grudging praise, superior aloofness from all attitudes, behavior and procedures that differ from "the way *we* do things"—all are ways we have of indicating how we would change things around if God would only let us.

Discipline is an indispensable expression of mutual responsibility and reciprocal pastoral concern being made concrete for specific situations and particular people. Discipline is the community of faith ordering its common life in a way that is responsive to the lordship of Jesus Christ. We suppress or ignore it at our peril.

The purpose of the exercise of discipline in the Christian fellowship, however, is not to provide us with a religiously sanctioned way to punish those we judge to have behaved badly. Nor is its purpose to destroy others who think differently than we do, or to ostracize or quarantine them until they conform. How much less is its intended purpose to advance, promote, and serve our prejudices.

Although cross-bearing servanthood may have little surface appeal, still, Christ-centered other-directedness, according to Luke, is what authentic discipleship is all about (6:23ff.).

RADICAL DEMANDS OF DISCIPLESHIP (9:57–62)

Jesus has begun his "exodus." He has single-mindedly "set his face to go to Jerusalem" (v. 51). He will not turn aside, and he requires similar categorical commitment from the disciples—and from any who would follow him. His way becomes their way now—no exceptions, no postponements, no tentativeness.

The three sayings in verses 57–62 sound as if they may well have circulated as self-contained, independent units in the oral tradition (even, possibly, in prior written form). Grouped together and placed at the outset of the journey to Jerusalem, they provide powerful commentary on the need for unqualified discipleship. To assume the posture and role of disciple requires unequivocal dedication, whether that role was sought by the prospect or whether the initiative came through an invitational call by Jesus. *Nothing* must be allowed intervening, diverting precedence.

(a) *The meager material rewards of discipleship.* Saying number one (vv. 57–58) highlights the likely lack of creature comforts and security for those devoted to the service of God. Jesus offers little of that and is even the cause of increased deprivation and discomfort to his followers. The way of discipleship appears as rootless insecurity. Absolute dependence on God, even for lodging and for daily sustenance ("give us each day our daily bread"—11:3) is a chancy thing when one's faith is tenuous. As always, of course, it all depends on where you locate your security. That is the whole point for announcing the reassertion of God's rule over creation.

(b) *The urgency of instantly responding to Jesus.* Saying number 2 (vv. 59–60) probably does not imply that the potential disciple's father had just then unexpectedly died and that leave was being sought to attend to pressing and unavoidable family responsibilities. Rather, the person agrees to join with Jesus and his enterprise sometime in the indefinite future whenever his father will have died and he has fulfilled his familial obligations and received his inheritance. Jesus' reply to his request for delay underscored the element of present and immediate urgency to embrace the claim of God's rule. "The dead" are those so preoccupied with satisfying the expectations of the world (culture, family, job, religion) that they are unresponsive or only marginally touched by the compelling presence of the reign of God in the person of Jesus.

(c) *Acceptance of the call to follow Christ supercedes all other obligations.* Saying number three (vv. 61–62) not only reinforced the theme of a call to radical, single-minded obedience but also served Luke's interest in depicting Jesus as both distinct from and greater than Elijah. Elisha was plowing when Elijah "mantled" him, but Elijah permitted him to say goodbye to his family before he apprenticed himself to Elijah (1 Kings 19:19ff.). The call to kingdom service incarnate in the person of Jesus is an opportune moment that displaces all other interests. Equivocate, and the opportunity may well be lost.

Suggestions for application of these sayings follow:

The attitudes toward the present claims of the gospel and the rule of God that these sayings express are always germane. They are particularly appropriate as meditative foci in classes for: 1) officer or teacher training, 2) new members, and 3) youth confirmation.

Discipleship in the service of Jesus and the royal rule of God which he, in announcing, inaugurates is permeated with the end-of-the-old-world urgency to preach the claim of God's rule without delay to as many people as possible in as many places as possible. Would-be disciples must count the cost and be prepared well in advance for resolving the claims of competitive, conflicting loyalties. When such conflicts arise, the true disciple knows how priorities are to be ordered.

Pastoral sensitivity must control the stress on urgency. The radically absolute nature of discipleship dare not be diluted. The dimension of urgency must not be used to cut short considered consent, much less to manipulate premature decisions, for people may not be ready. Freedom to demur, acknowledged in a timely and kindly manner, may well encourage confident commitment later. When that occurs, the sovereignty of God is well served even if current statistics are not quite so impressive.

SENDING THE SEVENTY (10:1–24)

Again Jesus sends out a group of disciples, equipped with similar power and authority to that which he exercised. They go as extensions of his own, restoring and proclaiming ministry. It had worked so well before (chap. 9); why not repeat and even expand the enterprise?

(a) *The worldwide aspect of Luke's numerical symbolism.* Of course, from "twelve" to "seventy" was more than simply numerical expansion of the force functioning in the field. For Luke and his hearers, those numbers were ciphers with deeper meaning. The "Twelve" stood for the mission to empirical Israel; the "Seventy" symbolized the proclamation of the gospel to the rest of the inhabited world.

The second stage—the mission to the entire world—was the effort to which Luke's community was committed and in which they were involved. That second sending out held intense interest for them. We are very interested in that phase, too, and for similar reasons. The mission of the Seventy represents a missionary mandate we share with Luke and his church.

(b) *This story depends on the sending of the Twelve.* Luke is the only Evangelist of the four to tell of a mission of the Seventy. Comparison of the details of this account with his description of the commissioning of the Twelve in chapter 9 (see the earlier discussion of that passage) has led many Lukan scholars to surmise that Luke depended on the previous pattern to construct this second "sending out" narrative. That conjecture is strengthened as we identify details of Luke's story of the Seventy that are not in his story of the Twelve but were applied to the

Twelve in the written sources he was using, or appeared elsewhere in those source documents.

The only details unique to Luke's story of the sending of the Seventy are the number "seventy" (v. 1a), the reference to the role the Seventy serve as forerunners preparing the way for Jesus (v. 1c), the repeated admonition to eat whatever is offered (vv. 7b, 8), the saying on hearing and rejection (v. 16, but comp. Mark 9:37), the spectacle of the fall of Satan (v. 18), and Jesus' interpretive exhortations (vv. 19–20).

The choice of the number "seventy" may well have been related to the story of the choosing of the seventy elders who were empowered by God to assist Moses (Num. 11:16ff.). Surely Luke's primary understanding was the connotation of completeness and universality the number conveyed in scriptural tradition and to Luke's community.

(c) *Disciples went in pairs in advance of Jesus.* It is likely that going out in pairs was a widely followed procedure for itinerant preachers in the spread of early Christianity. Jewish missionaries traveling in the Diaspora had developed a similar practice, no doubt reflecting the requirement in Jewish law for two witnesses to establish the veracity of testimony, but also having its practical dimensions of mutual protection, support, confirmation, and care. In the book of Acts, Luke will repeatedly describe Christian missionaries as going out two by two.

Preparing ahead for Jesus to come into a town (v. 1c) was a practice Luke had described as being already in place at the beginning of the journey narrative (9:51–52). The Seventy assumed Elijah-like functions that Luke had previously portrayed as focused in the work of John the Baptist. So the disciples now are to become forerunners who prepare the way of the Lord.

Luke's Bible (the Greek version of the Jewish scriptures) frequently used harvest imagery to direct attention to the end-of-the-ages ingathering and judging of the nations of the world. Jesus had begun that process and was now expanding the work force to seize the opportune moment. As pressing as the season for proclamation was, Jesus did not relax the stringent job qualifications required of a messenger of the good news of the royal rule of God.

(d) *The urgency of the disciples' assignment.* As were the Twelve previously (9:1ff.), so now also the Seventy are totally dependent on God for protection and sustenance. Disciples in the process of carrying out their mission are in a precarious, vulnerable position in a world still committed to allegiances opposing God's purposes for creation. The time (anticipated in Isaiah 11:6) has not yet come when lambs may lie down with wolves in tranquillity.

Jesus' instructions to the Seventy were just as uncompromising as those he had given before to the Twelve. Provisionless, honoring their absolute trust that God would supply all that they needed, they were to be consumed by the urgency of their assigned task. As it had been with Elisha's servant, Gehazi (2 Kings 4:29), so it is to be with them. Their mandate is so momentous they dare not tarry, even for civility's sake. Social dallying will not do. Passing the time of day, exchanging gossip, swapping opinions on the weather are friendly things to do, but time-consuming. Anyone commissioned with such an urgent message has neither time nor words to waste on small talk.

Jesus sent the Seventy out not to cultivate cordiality but to pronounce peace. If those listening are put off by the abruptness, or are not open to the announcement of God's act to restore to wholeness, they expose themselves to God's regal judgment, for their unreceptiveness leads them to be excluded from the benefit of God's saving blessing.

The Seventy must avoid going from one house to another, for that, too, could compromise the reception of their message. People might suspect that they were trying to exploit their situation as empowered messengers for personal comfort or gain. (Verse 8 may even reflect and commend the laid-back attitudes of early Jewish Christian missionaries toward the observance of Jewish food regulations with varying degrees of rigor by their hosts.)

The main point of the instructions Jesus gave to the Seventy (vv. 2–12) was that simply the appearance in a community of messengers bearing the good news of God's rule was an event of eschatological urgency. How the community responded announces its spiritual fate—the blessings or the judgment of the sovereignty of God. The way in which the community receives the messengers anticipates the reception which Jesus will be accorded when he comes among them on his way to Jerusalem and the cross. Their reception of him governs the way they will be received by King Jesus at the end-of-time judgment. (The contrasting fates of the sheep and the goats in Matthew 25 has the same point.)

Should any of the Seventy experience rejection, it was no more than what the Twelve had been cautioned to expect (9:5), indeed no more than Jesus himself had repeatedly experienced, the latest instance occurring just prior to this pericope (9:53). In every case, those judging wrongly about the presence of God's claim to rule are themselves judged by that presence.

The unambiguously compelling clarity of kingdom presence is so vivid that only the worst kind of willful imperceptiveness could misconstrue it (vv. 13–16). To get the full force of the "woe" pronouncements, we need to substitute for Chorazin, Bethsaida, and Capernaum the name of the town where we live: Pittsburgh and Peoria, Tulsa and Tucson. Just as the missioners must hear and comprehend Jesus' words of kingdom command, so those missionized must hear with perception the preaching of the rule of God. In rejecting the claim of the message, they reject not only the authorized bearers of the gospel but also the One who is the content of the gospel and, finally, the divine ruler who sent Jesus, God (v. 16).

(*e*) *Jesus' response to the report of the disciples.* So off the Seventy go, and upon returning they report back. What they have to relate is so extraordinary they can hardly restrain themselves. They are ecstatic at the control they exercised, in Jesus' name, over the fearsome and vicious agents of those supernatural powers that had usurped God's right to rule.

Jesus looked beyond the details of their reports and celebrated the cosmic accomplishment their activities heralded, namely, the end-of-time event when all of creation will have been liberated from Satanic enslavement and restored to the beneficent reign of God. (The authority of the Seventy over serpents and scorpions intensified a wilderness wanderings motif [Deut. 8:15; cf. Ps. 91:13; Acts 28:3–5] that illustrates the protective presence of God that now accompanies Christian missionaries into even the most hazardous places and among the most hostile people.)

Do not let your success go to your head and skew your perspective, Jesus warned (v. 20). It is not simply what you can do in Jesus' name by faith, empowered by the Spirit, however astounding to you and to others that may seem. After all, *you* do *not* do it—God is doing it through you. Even more astonishing than the use God makes *of* you when you let him (what God through Jesus does through you) is what God through Jesus does *to* you. God "naturalizes" you into citizenship in his royal realm. The end-of-ages restoration is reality for you right now. So rejoice!

With the *makarism* (the beatitude) of verses 23–24, Jesus affirms that the disciples are not only living in the time of fulfillment of the promises of God but are participating in its actualization—indeed, are serving as instruments for its accomplishment. It illustrates concretely what Jesus had said earlier when he favorably compared the disciples to John the Baptist (7:28).

Preaching possibilities include:

1. Announcing the good news is every Christian's task. There is hard work for the interpreter with this passage. Somehow people in the community of faith must be disabused of the notion that the "Twelve" and the "Seventy" are select groups within the larger group of disciples who follow Jesus and who say, "Some people have a gift for evangelism but it is not everybody's cup of tea." For Luke, the "Twelve" is the entire church directing its efforts to alerting empirical Israel that its heritage anchored in God's promises to Abraham is being fulfilled. The "Seventy" is the church in its entirety, including Luke's own community, announcing the inbreaking of God's royal rule throughout the length and breadth of God's creation.

What inclusive symbol can we use to confront Christians with the claim that proclamation of the gospel has on the energy, interest, and ownership of *everyone* in the believing fellowship? Jesus frees us all to do that. The task of making that announcement with clarity and winsome urgency is not restricted to just those "Seventy" over there. It belongs to all of us.

2. The qualitative character of gospel urgency. The issue of urgency raises another tough task for the exposition of the account. How might we reclaim that first-century sense of urgency so that it compels us aggressively, even impatiently, to announce good news and pronounce peace? Earliest Christians were captivated by the conviction that the interval of time left before the end of the world was exceedingly short. Eventually congregants wearied of hearing about the end of the world coming soon, when nothing apocalyptic seemed to be happening. Calendar-controlled urgency carries that peril. It was a major problem with which the Second (New) Testament church had to deal. Although sects still try from time to time to resurrect that sense of "short interval" urgency, most of us are not caught up easily by that. The need for urgency is there, only now there is a qualitative rather than a durational dimension to it.

Who knows when Jesus will come again? Still, *he will come!* God has raised Jesus from the dead. He is exalted to the place of highest authority next to God. He will come again to judge the living and the dead. These convictions control the quality of kingdom life we are called to live. These convictions compel a sense of missionary urgency to announce to others the opportunity that they too may live lives permeated with the quality of God's royal rule.

What would happen if, on a Sunday morning, at the 11:00 A.M. "holy hour," this passage was read, a brief prayer said, then *everybody,* from organist to usher, from little Sue to old Uncle Ben, was sent out two by two with a name and an address on a 3×5 card, and instructions for one of them to say in fifteen minutes or less how and when their faith in Jesus as their Lord and Savior became vital and immediate for them?

Some of the flock would perhaps deposit the 3×5 card in the litter bag in the car and head for home, muttering all the way about the crazy preacher who seemed to insist on upsetting people. Even they would be learning something very important about themselves which, if graced with sustained reflection, might precipitate some change for the better later on.

As the people gathered again, bringing who knows whom with them, there could be soup and sandwiches, glad singing of some old favorites, a brief explanation of the beatitude in verses 23–24, a short litany expanding on the prayer in verses 21–22, and a benediction. Brochures about the church's program and invitations to visit could be placed on the sandwich trays.

While the people were out visiting, the minister(s) could assemble any visitors and adamant nonparticipants in the church parlor and meet with them there while everybody else went out. That way, folks would not think that they were only "helping the preacher out with *her* job."

What would happen? Who knows what might happen? The event certainly would not exhaust the multifaceted potential for evangelistic outreach. But at the very least, people would not continue to think that evangelism was the business of only those seventy over there.

THE LOVE COMMANDMENTS
AFFIRMED AND ILLUSTRATED (10:25–42)

Luke has structured this section in a subtle, sophisticated way. In the exchange with the lawyer (vv. 25–28), the two love commandments—love of God and love of neighbor—are described as complementary to each other and comprehensive to the godly life. The parable of the Good Samaritan (vv. 29–37) illustrates the second: to love one's neighbor as oneself; the story of Mary and Martha (vv. 38–42) illustrates the first: to love God with one's entire self. Charles Talbert describes the two illustrations as "an exposition in haggadic [illustrative story] form, and in reverse order, of the two great love commandments of 10:27." (See Charles H. Talbert, *Reading Luke: A Literary and Theological Commentary on the Third Gospel*, New York: Crossroad, 1982, p. 120).

The Two Love Commandments (10:25–28)

(a) *The lawyer's contentious inquiry.* The atmosphere for the encounter between the "lawyer" (one trained in the technical interpretation and application of Mosaic law, or a scribe) and Jesus is hostile. The lawyer asked Jesus, "What must I do to inherit eternal life?" to "test Jesus" (v. 25). Still, Luke was intrigued by his question. He will describe the ruler as putting the same question to Jesus later (see 18:18).

The motive aside, the scope of the lawyer's question was too limited. He wanted a definitive description of how the present practice of piety controlled a future reward. Jesus challenged him to recall that it was present obedience and allegiance to the rule of God, by which one's life is permeated already with the quality of the eternal, that had always been the essential option in Jewish spirituality at its best.

(*b*) ***The charismatic catechizes the professional.*** The tables are neatly turned. The lawyer, the professionally trained expert in Torah who is accustomed to being accorded attentive and reverential acquiescence, finds himself catechized by the charismatic "amateur" whom he had arrogantly confronted to interrogate, expose, and discredit. Jesus' response sharply raises the question about who is in the best position to "know" the law: the one schooled in interpretive technique or the one who has unrestricted access to the will of God. Here is a dramatic illustration of how God hides "things from the wise and the intelligent" (cf. v. 21).

Jesus: "How does your Bible speak to your question?"
          "How does "Moses" respond to your query?"
          "What does God make known to you through Torah?"
Lawyer: God says to love God with everything you are and have."
          "God says to love your neighbor as yourself."

He knows his Bible!

If the combining of those two love commands out of the Jewish traditions in the Pentateuch was not original with Jesus, it was nonetheless profound. (Mark and Matthew ascribe the merging of the two to Jesus himself, but that combination was already current in popular Jewish piety.) Juxtaposition of the two requires recognition that how one regards and relates to one's neighbor reflects one's attitude toward God.

Unperceived by the elaborately trained lawyer is the more fundamental perception that both affirmations have credence, separately and together, only for the one who knows himself/herself to be a member of the covenant people of God. That covenant relationship is what makes possible a life that partakes of the quality of the eternal.

Jesus: "Do this and you will live."

The lawyer is a child of Abraham, a member of the covenant people of God. All he has to "do" is order his life and his actions consistent with who he knows himself to be by the covenant mercies of God, and with what he knows himself to believe. "Truth is in order to goodness." Right theology issues in right action. Righteous answers require righteous living. All that is necessary is integrity, harmony, and consistency between creed and deed.

Sermon options on this passage include:

1. *The love commandments commend covenant love.* "Do this, and you will live" (v. 28) ought not to be read as even theoretical acquiescence on Jesus'

part to a belief in a righteousness that is contingent on Torah observance. Loving both God and neighbor is celebrative confirmation of one's participation in the saving covenant initiated by God. Coming to terms with what God is accomplishing through Jesus—independent of our appreciative awareness, our activity, or our desire—liberates us from being exercised by the question, "What must I do?"

2. *What the lawyer should have asked.* The learned lawyer phrased his question badly. If his purpose had been other than solely trying to make points on behalf of "the guild," if he had really known who Jesus was, if he had discerned the presence of the royal rule of God in him, his question might have been, "Lord, having been granted eternal life through God, what may I do now to serve and to promote God's reign?" It is a question we almost always have the most difficult time posing accurately when we are talking to Jesus and to God, but also when we talk to one another about Jesus and about God.

It is easy for us to disparage the lawyer's preoccupation with issues of formal theology in order to evade the exercise of the clear implications of the faith he claimed to serve. Those who have paid their dues can grasp what is at stake in this exchange with all its complexity and risk. By "paid their dues," I mean those who have discipled their minds to Christ and the service of the gospel, disciplining themselves to think logically and speak coherently about their faith and its implications for service—a service they themselves practice.

Unlimited Love of Neighbor:
The Good Samaritan (10:29–37)
(Year C—Fifteenth Sunday in Ordinary Time)

An injunction imposing upon the lawyer the requirement to "do" something (v. 28) was not really what he was looking for, even though that was the structure of his original question. He wanted a rigidly reasoned and stringently argued formal debate about "issues in religion." He wanted to have Jesus vulnerable and exposed on *his* turf. He needed to recover the theoretical tone to the conversation.

(*a*) *The problem of precisely defining "neighbor."* "Who is my neighbor?" was the question the lawyer next posed (v. 29) to divert attention away from the demand for radical obedience and redirect it toward religious discourse. Neither a humanitarian question nor a question of identified and defined ethical responsibility, it was a religious question that had proven a popular focus for scribal debate, a question asking after proper limits for cultically acceptable association. What are the discernible and defendable boundaries of the people of God? Who shares with me common membership in the community of faith? Who is included, and who is excluded? By extension it posed the problem of what were the definable limits of God's mercy and grace.

The usually accepted delineation was ethnic—"my neighbor" includes all of those who share the same racial, cultural, and religious heritage as me. However, not everyone accepted that definition. There were Pharisees who wanted to restrict the boundaries to include only those who were religiously observant according to the practices and rubrics the Pharisees themselves defined. The Qumran covenanters limited the term to include only those who belonged to their religious sect. *Everyone* would have included Moses and the prophets, and, of course, the Messiah. The lawyer's professional training and energy were primarily devoted to debating such legal definitions.

(*b*) *Love for neighbor knows no limits.* It was not an idle or an abstract query, this question the lawyer asked Jesus. A lot more was at stake than he realized. If "neighbor" is defined inclusively, in terms of need, instead of exclusively in terms of blood lineage or religious party affiliation, what will scribes and lawyers and the entire lot of religious legalists do for a living? Furthermore, the lawyer was at a terrific disadvantage in trying to snare Jesus through the intricacies of debate about precise limits for categorizing those who are acceptable to God—for Jesus' disciples knew (and so did Luke's community—and so do we) that "Who is my neighbor?" ("Whom am I required by my love for God to love?") was being asked of the One who had already unambiguously required his followers to "love your enemies" (6:27–35).

If love of neighbor is correlative to love for God, then it, like love for God, can know no limits, for God's love for us knows no limits. One must know the limitlessness to God's love experientially, as the *only* explanation for one's *own* inclusion, if one is ever to love God without reserve. That experience, which absolutely prohibits us from arrogantly assuming that divine election is the result of preferential selection according to our inherent worth, controls our openness to the inclusive extent of the term "neighbor" as an appropriate description of the scope of those eligible for our love. Conversely, it is only in our uncalculating service to those in need that we begin to explore experientially the breadth, depth, and scope of God's love and thereby are moved to remove all vestiges of inhibition to true worship, making unreserved love of God possible.

(*c*) *What limits may legitimately restrict one's duty as neighbor?* At first blush, the story Jesus told in response to the lawyer's question about the identity of "neighbor" does not seem to be quite on target. The lawyer asked, "Who is the religiously acceptable object of love?" Through the story Jesus redefined "neighbor" as the subject, the doer rather than the object, the recipient of compassionate, loving ministry. For the lawyer to hear the parable as an answer to his question, it was necessary for him to see himself in the person of the Samaritan.

Clarifications of the details of the parable of the Good Samaritan are available in any good commentary: 1) the dangerous road; 2) the Jewish cultic restrictions on contact with a corpse, lest ritual defilement result; 3) the healing properties popularly ascribed to wine and oil; and 4) the startling suggestion that a (presumably Jewish) innkeeper would take orders from a Samaritan.

The beginning of the story implies a narrow definition of the scope of "neighbor." A (presumably Jewish) man was savaged by (presumably Jewish) thieves. All were children of Abraham and were taught to honor Moses. Along came a priest followed by a Levite. Both were children of the covenant, both were schooled in Torah, both had devoted their lives to the cultic service of the worship of God, both were so committed to the laws of purity that they felt compelled to risk neglecting love for neighbor and thereby violating love for God lest they become ritually unclean and unfit for cultic service. Who among them all, out of love for God, was loving toward their neighbor?

Up to this point it sounds for all the world like a typical anti-clerical story. Those hearing it for the first time, other than the lawyer, would now expect the one who does give assistance to be a Jewish peasant, uninstructed in the finer points of the law, unintimidated by threat of defilement. He would be one of God's "poor ones," untutored and unlettered, yet one who knows in his heart of hearts that he is loved by God and loves God. That knowledge compels him to be lovingly compassionate toward the injured, "half-dead" neighbor. What a caustic critique on the "professionals," who out of overexaggerated devotion to the letter of the law violate the spirit of the law and thereby betray themselves into transgressing the revealed will of the God whom they have dedicated their lives to serve!

(*d*) *"Neighbor" is anyone who out of love for God meets need with love.*
Instead, along comes a Samaritan. What a jolt! How revolting!

We do not hear the shock factor because we are too far removed culturally. "She is such a good Samaritan" extols exemplary compassion. A home for the homeless is named "Samaritan House." The "Good Samaritan Program" provides regular free meals and clothing for street people. The term, solely shaped by this story, is synonymous with empathetic charity.

"Samaritan" to those who heard the story first meant detested half-breed, despised defiler of true religion, abhorrent distorter of the precious heritage of the faith, loathsome perverter of covenant community. *Nobody* would have dreamed of defining "neighbor" to include Samaritans. It would have been scandalous enough for Jesus to have made the Samaritan the recipient of compassion from a pious Jew. For him to reverse those roles and portray the Samaritan as the model of one who integrates love of God and love of neighbor, as the model whom true believers are to emulate, was outrageously shocking at the first telling of the story.

The Samaritan, of all people, in contrast to the Jewish *personae* in the story, "hears the word of God and does it." When Jesus asked the lawyer, "Which . . . was a neighbor?" (v. 36), the lawyer has to resort lamely to circumlocution to avoid associating the term "Samaritan" with any expression of approbation. Among those listening, the ones who could hear beyond the shock were forced to conceive of the unlimited scope of God's love evoking a reciprocal love from them which *would not tolerate boundaries that exclude* others.

It is particularly striking and significant that Luke portrays Jesus as using a Samaritan as a model for commendable kingdom behavior so soon after Jesus himself had suffered a concrete experience of Jewish/Samaritan antipathy when a Samaritan village rejected him (9:51ff.). Here we see that the religious question was already receding into the background for Luke and his community, and the role of "Good Samaritan" as exemplary moral model was moving to center stage.

"What behavior produces eternal results?" "Whom must I include, and whom may I exclude?" Both of the lawyer's questions betray how distant he was from recognizing the presence of God's royal rule even when he was standing before its personification, the One who alone defines both inheritor and neighbor. Even though the lawyer had access to all of the right theological information and could almost automatically answer profound religious inquiry, he did not "know" theology in the sense of embracing and integrating that data as the ground for defining essential relationships.

The parable illustrates that "doing in order to inherit eternal life" is misdirected religious energy. The Samaritan's behavior (which the lawyer acknowledges) is that of one who knows himself to have been already named an inheritor of eternal life and, as such, loves God and neighbor not to "get" it but to celebrate it.

Sermonic exploration of the parable might be shaped as follows:

An illuminating imaginative exercise can be orchestrated by inviting people to enter into the parable in the role of various of the *dramatis personae,* other than the Samaritan.

Think of the injured man in the ditch, knowing himself to have been assaulted by "his own," absolutely dependent on the compassion of one of those whom he had been indoctrinated all of his life to loathe. When have we been surprised by the presence of uncalculating compassion from unexpected directions, an experience that has forced us to redefine and maybe even renounce our penchant to define and maintain rigid boundaries?

Think of the thieves who saw the traveler not as "neighbor" but as easy victim to their violence and greed (and, perhaps, desperation?). Remember those occasions when we have met and dealt with others not for who they are in the light of the gracious goodness of God, but for what we can gain by abusing and exploiting their vulnerability.

Think of the priest and the Levite. Recall those moments when we have allowed the constraints of religious performance or church requirements to divert us away from giving practical expression to the faith we acknowledge through compassionate service.

Think of the innkeeper—perhaps the first to have been transformed by the Samaritan's example. When have distorting stereotypes been disclosed to us for the sham they are, and in the disclosure have dissolved, opening for us fresh ways of thinking and appreciating? On what occasions have we been schooled by the gospel to fill a supporting role that undergirds and extends the sensitive, compassionate, innovative ministry of another?

Unlimited Love of God:
Mary, Martha, and Jesus (10:38–42)

How would *you* have felt, if something like this had happened to you? What would *you* have done? The two sisters were already behind in the housework chores as it was. Along came this crowd—unannounced and unanticipated. (Even if Jesus had sent messengers on ahead to let them know [cf. 9:51f.], that still was not much of a warning.) And what a gang! The context of Luke's narrative implies that there were close to a hundred (cf. 10:1, 17, add the Twelve and Jesus plus a few more, probably—Luke is the only one to tell this story, so we cannot really check to see if that is what he had in mind). No wonder Martha was nervous, harried, and distracted—and even a greater wonder that Mary was not.

(*a*) *Two different responses to Jesus' presence.* It happened, after all, in a culture that highly prized the exercise of hospitality as a God-pleasing duty—even toward complete strangers. But these were not complete strangers. Jesus was leading the crowd. Martha knew Jesus, she loved Jesus, she wanted to honor Jesus by doing the very best she could for him and those with him on such short notice. She needed all the help she could get.

Where was Mary? There she was—at Jesus' feet, assuming a posture of discipleship (see 8:35 and Acts 22:3), which for her, in those days and in that culture, was absurd, even scandalous. Rabbis generally avoided contact with women whenever possible and would have disdained accepting such a one as a disciple. Only someone like Jesus, radically inclusive as he was, would have welcomed and encouraged something like that.

All things being equal, Martha would have liked to have taken the time to edge nearer to Jesus (only to the fringe of the throng, though, *not* at his feet) to hear his teaching, too. But something had to be done about the meal! Martha's perception of Jesus and of her relationship to him was still at the level of the women who had been content to attend to his needs (cf. 8:2f.). All things were not equal, of course. Martha's need for Jesus' presence and his words were greater than his and his companions' need for her fancy food.

(*b*) *Two perceptions of what the occasion required.* The story played Mary and Martha against each other by way of contrast, an artful accompaniment to the previous Good Samaritan parable. In that story the priest and the Levite had gone to inhumane (even irreligious) lengths to conform to the formal requirements of the law, while the Samaritan, ignoring entrenched antipathies, acted in harmony with the essence of the will of God, which the law had been given to reveal. Here in this narrative Martha is distracted with meeting the requirements of the canons of hospitality while Mary subordinates all other considerations and duties to her appreciatively absorbed recognition of who Jesus really is.

Mary is single-mindedly devoted to Jesus and the presence of God's claim to rule, which he both announces and mediates. Martha allows the dictates of hospitality and the making of elaborate provision for physical human needs to deflect her concentration from the uniqueness of who Jesus was and what he really required from her as he did from everyone: attentive obedience. Preoccupation with assembling what she thought he needed from her obscured her awareness of what she needed from him.

It was not only imperceptive distraction; there was perhaps something insidious to it. There usually is when we miss the moment of encounter with Jesus and that claim of God on the total devotion of our lives that he brings. Martha's distraction was caused not just by the demands of hospitality, not just by what was needed for physical sustenance. She was intent on laying out an *elaborate* meal—a *real spread.* She wanted to make an impression, put on something that folks would talk about for a long time to come. She was so concerned about what Jesus would think about her that she neglected to attend to what *she* needed to recognize, know, and think about him—and about God who was being made known in and through him.

Jesus is *there—at Martha's house*! What does she want from him, of all that he has to offer? Well, all she can think of is she wants him to send Mary over to lend her a hand so that Mary would be reprimanded and Martha vindicated. Martha's protest is really a ploy for self-justification at Mary's expense. Martha tried to impose her priorities onto Mary by demanding that Mary be required to acquiesce to the service obligations of the hospitality customs, too. It is yet another way of giving expression to the "*What must I do* to inherit eternal life?" (v. 25) perspective.

(c) *Jesus commends Mary and reproaches Martha.* Jesus' reprimand (vv. 41f.), however, vindicated Mary and reproached Martha instead, primarily for her myopia toward his presence and what that offered, but also for her obsession with ostentatious display. Jesus' disdain for elaborate provisions reflects in his own behavior the instruction he had given to his disciples for undemanding acceptance of simple fare (10:8).

The reproach also has a second dimension. "Need of only one thing" is ambiguous, with a deeper meaning. Mary has unhesitatingly chosen the posture of single-minded, unreserved, attentive discipleship. That is "the better part" of which Jesus will not allow Martha's distracted demand deprive her. Mary receives Jesus rather than trying to provide for Jesus.

(d) *Jesus, not Martha, is in charge, even in her house.* The story *does* illustrate the first of the two love commands with which the lawyer had responded to Jesus' query (v. 27). It sets in sharp relief the radical demand for total, unequivocal, indivertible devotion as the only constructive response to the presence of the reign of God.

When Jesus comes, the primary concern is not ostentatiously displayed hospitality and politeness. When Jesus comes, Martha is displaced as host even in her own house—just as, later, "both Zacchaeus (19:1–10) and the two men from Emmaus (24:13–32) will find their role as hosts preempted" [Frederick W. Danker, *Jesus and the New Age*, p. 225]. Jesus rules—he is in charge.

Martha wanted to honor Jesus. The only way to honor him is Mary's way: to hear and to obey, attending to what he offers. We would like to think that Jesus got through to Martha, that inspiration happened, that Martha let the Seventy cut their own cukes and the Twelve form their own falafel while she came and sat with Mary at Jesus' feet. Perhaps she did. Perhaps we will, too.

PRAYING TO GOD (11:1–13)

"Lord, teach us to pray," one of the disciples of Jesus asked, ostensibly because they had enviously observed the strength and vigor of the spiritual discipline in which John the Baptist had schooled his adherents. Maybe some of Jesus' disciples had been privileged to have experienced that tutelage themselves earlier. But surely they would not have addressed the request to Jesus if they had not also seen something compellingly desirable in the vitality of his practice of prayer.

(a) *Jesus responds to the disciples' request.* So Jesus replied, "When you pray, say, 'Father . . . ' " Luke's version of the material we have come to know as the Lord's Prayer tradition is less elaborate than the more familiar version we have learned from the Gospel of Matthew (cf. Matt. 6:9–13) and which we frequently include in corporate worship. Matthew's version of the prayer is permeated with end-of-time overtones, as is his entire Sermon on the Mount. Luke commends the prayer to his community as a paradigm for doxological and petitionary prayer that embraces crucial concerns of the ongoing day-to-day quest for a faithful walk in harmony with the will and purpose of God.

We should note, first, the communal nature both of the request and of the dominical response. It was not inaugurated as a practice toward the perfecting of private piety. The first person plural is prominent throughout the pericope. "Lord, teach *us* . . ." "When you pray, say: 'give *us* . . . , forgive *us* . . . , for *we ourselves* forgive . . . , do not bring *us* . . .' " Even private prayer requires that corporate consciousness and self-identity.

The form of address, "Father," is remarkable in its simplicity, especially when we compare it to the elaborate and flowery forms evident in both Jewish and Roman prayer styles contemporary to the first century, C.E. The Aramaic expression that stands behind the form was boldly innovative, even startling to Jewish piety. It is the familiar term of affection small children would use in referring to their paternal parent, instantly recognizable to Aramaic-speaking Jews and Jewish Christians. It would never have occurred to them in the wildest stretches of their imagination to use such a term to address the majesty, holiness, and power of the righteous almighty God. Yet, following Jesus' example, it served so well to express reverence and obedience in a context of informal intimacy. God was not distant and unapproachable; God was close and attentive and lovingly concerned.

(b) *The first three petitions.* Eduard Schweizer alerts us (*The Good News According to Luke,* [Atlanta: John Knox Press, 1984], p. 191) that the first three petitions in the prayer correspond, in reverse order, to the three temptations Jesus himself had struggled with in Luke's narrative at 4:1–12, and that the fourth petition reflects the conclusion (4:13) to the temptation scene. That observation suggests that the content of our prayer, as well as any instruction in the practice of prayer we would offer to others, ought not to be abstract and theoretical but rather solidly anchored in and shaped by the most pivotal experiences of our own spiritual life.

The first two petitions are equivalent. When we reverence the name of God with integrity and consistency, our lives are thereby so ordered that the rule of God is acknowledged, established, and made evident to others by the quality of the life we live. Together those petitions entreat God for empowerment that the faithful might know continuity in their daily walk with the faith they profess in God. Such charismatic empowerment is solely a gift from God (see v. 13).

The entreaty for daily sustenance (v. 3) is not so much a request as it is a confession of absolute reliance on the dependable provisions of a faithful God. As such, the prayer petition reflects the attitude of complete trust that Jesus had commended to his disciples when he, earlier, had sent them out (cf. 9:3; 10:4). In the background of this appeal echo reminiscences of the Exodus tradition and of God's life-sustaining daily supply of manna. Willingness to depend each day on that sustenance was a test of one's confidence in the trustworthiness of God.

(*c*) *The two concluding petitions.* Absolute reliance on the God who reigns in our lives necessarily shapes our dealings with others (v. 4a). We do not coerce God to forgive our sins by being magnanimously merciful toward others. Our acts of forgiving mercy are expressive of that reciprocal relationship in which our trust in God is met by God's faithful mercy toward us. Our forgiveness of what others owe us is both a celebration of God's pardon which we have already received and an anticipatory extension of the mercy with which, we are confident, God will continue to meet us.

"Do not bring us to the time of trial" (or, "Lead us not into temptation")—verse 4b—is hardly a plea for God to desist from deceiving and misleading us. It recalls that Luke had pictured the Holy Spirit leading Jesus into the wilderness where he was tempted by Satan (4:1–2). God's fidelity then and now is no guarantee that we will not be tempted even on God's initiative. But it does assure us that neither Jesus nor we are deprived of God's sustaining presence as we struggle daily not to violate but rather to conform to the just requirements of the revealed will of God. It is so fundamental a prayer that Jesus will urge it upon his disciples again later (cf. 22:40, 46).

(*d*) *Aphoristic analogies commending the practice of prayer.* Verses 5–8 present a metaphorical caricature which, with good humor and according to the logic of the "from the lesser to the greater" argument, attests to the importance of prayer as a spiritual exercise. Shameless refusal to take "no" for an answer is justified when the need is so severe that ordinary social convention is inappropriate. If such perseverance is effective in producing the necessary result in human affairs, how much more is God eager to welcome and respond to faithful petitions?

Pursuit of the posture of prayer as a habitual discipline cultivates our confidence that God responds beneficently to faithful prayer, as verses 9–13 urge with another "lesser to the greater" analogy. Not even *evil* parents will deceive their hungry children with destructive gifts in place of those that nourish life. How much less will God respond with condemnation when we ask for life-giving mercy! How much more will God give life-sustaining gifts, daily bread, merciful forgiveness—above all, the Holy Spirit!

Sermon possibilities on Luke's Lord's Prayer tradition include:

1. Our double-mindedness about prayer. "Teach me to pray!" People do not seem very much inclined to make that request these days. Practicing the posture of prayer is not popular. Oh, you can stir up a good row over prayer in public schools, all right. It is fitting for the football team, the number of unsportsmanlike conduct calls against them notwithstanding, to kneel in prayer after the game, particularly if they have won. In our culture, prayer tends to be a social formality, though not without its uses. It is a good way to get folks quieted down so the meeting can begin, and it does bring effective closure to the adjournment process. Beyond that, passionate prayer is for fanatics, the feeble, and the fey.

Or is it? Witness the plethora of how-to books for deepening the devotional life, some in the fourth or fifth printing, in the Christian bookstores peppering our community shopping areas. Publishers would not be producing them if someone was not buying them. "Teach me to pray!"

Or, again, witness the persistently pervasive popularity of "quick fix" media religion, which shows amazing resiliency and elasticity in its recovery from repeated disclosures of flagrant monetary and moral mendacity. There is little human community involved in such phenomena and little common engagement in costly self-spending in service to others out of love for God. Still, the prayer requests flood in, usually accompanied by not-really-affordable donations because, since we do not know how to do it ourselves, we are eager to enlist the services of anyone who claims she or he does. "Teach me to pray!"

Pastoral counselors hear the same story again and again, bedecked in so many guises: intense isolation, deep depression, an unrevisable sense of personal unworthiness and unlovableness, fearful frustration with an acknowledged inability to communicate and to be receptive to the communications of others, an unexorcisable mood of melancholy meaninglessness to one's life, a haunting conviction that no one cares. Prayer has been tried—haltingly, stutteringly—but it felt so futile. Someone has said it is like a stage technician speaking into the microphone: "Testing, testing, one . . . two . . . three . . . Can anyone out there hear me?" Nobody really believes in stuff like that these days. Still, if we only knew how, just maybe . . . ! "Teach me to pray!"

It is difficult even to know how to ask about that. We recognize something authentic in the intellectual renunciation and psychic liberation from our own earlier immature, simplistic religious perceptions, persuasions, and dependencies. Yet our confidence in the legitimacy of that authenticity is diluted by nostalgic yearning for similar certainty right now, this moment, in these particularly trying circumstances, and produces rage or morbid resignation at how regularly that earlier certainty eludes us.

2. *The request and parish ministers.* "Teach us to pray!" It is a tough task—particularly when pastoral professionals prefer to devote time and energy to more visibly productive and institutionally rewarded activities. Cultivating contemplative composure and practicing prayer are elusive disciplines. The presupposition for their pursuit is renunciation.

"Teach us to pray!"

It is a difficult request because prayer is either so public and formal, or it is so personal, so subjective, so private. In those rare moments when the request is proffered, one reason that preachers find it to be a tough task to respond helpfully may be because the request strikes through a chink of vulnerability in their own authenticity. They pray a lot, formally and in public, and often, they do not know how to pray.

One of the most popular continuing education course offered for ordained ministers and other professional church leaders is on spirituality, spiritual direction, spiritual formation, and development of the devotional life. The guild, too, asks, "Teach us to pray!"

The disciples asked Jesus to school them spiritually because they had seen how John the Baptist's followers were fortified by their practice of prayer. Surely another reason why they asked Jesus was because they had observed his prayer discipline and they knew how it sustained him. They yearned for him to share access to that prayer dimension of his trusting relationship with God as a renewing resource for their own spiritual growth. Maybe the reason that few people make a similar request of their preachers these days is not that they do not yearn for it, but that they have no clue that such praying to God is a meaningful and helpful component in the pilgrim walk of pastoral professionals.

Prayer is not the perfection of a religious technique. Prayer is attitude molded by conviction. It presupposes a reliance on God's interest in and concern for us and for our well-being, even when that presupposition defies demonstration either to others or, even, to ourselves.

Prayer begins with but is not constricted nor exhausted by a pervasive, humbling sense of personal and communal inadequacy and willful transgression. What that sense produces is not paralyzing guilt but profound gratitude. In spite of who we truly are and know ourselves to be—and know that God knows, too—in spite of all of that, we are sure God yearns for and delights in our address. So God encourages us to form the totality of our life and being according to the trust and reliance in God that Christ commends to us. And God gifts us, too, with the presence of the Holy Spirit who makes that transformation possible.

3. *Reconnecting with the Lord's Prayer.* The Lord's Prayer tradition is so familiar as to be almost automatic and, paradoxically, at the same time so remote. An enriching exercise for a prayer group whose members have learned to trust one another would be to read together this less well-known form of that tradition as it appears in Luke's Gospel and to listen to the content with openness of heart as well as head. Then, have the group recast the petitions in contemporary terms reflecting its intent in categories that would compute without clarification in the pew and in the discount store aisle, to one's children, and to one's spouse.

HEALING THE EVIL WITHIN (11:14–36)

"What is going on here?" Is that an expression of idle curiosity? Or is it a question born of more than simple inquisitiveness? It can be a query after the fundamental nature of things. It can be a way of asking, "Who is really in charge?" It can be the lens through which enlightened recognition of reality is focused, if one is open to such insight.

(a) *An ambiguous act elicits confusion.* Confusion was inevitable, I suppose. The affliction of muteness was ambiguous. Although demon possession was more readily conceivable to them than it is to us today, still, muteness *could* have been the result of an act of God (cf. 1:20–22). (It could also be simply a natural disorder—cf. Mark 7:32–37.) However, that was not the issue.

It was the ambiguity to the act of restoration that caused the uproar. A "mighty work" accomplished in a culture where spiritualism prominently shaped the operative primitive scientism by which experiential phenomena were understood is vulnerable to conflicting interpretations. A successful exorcism—while often regarded as an extraordinary, commendatory accomplishment—could be seen as evidence of the exercise of a superior demonic authority to which lesser demons were subject.

(*b*) *How one decides shows who one is.* Once the accusation of demonism was raised (v. 15), sorting out the ambiguity became a litmus test, Luke proposes, for the acuity of one's spiritual discernment. Accurate resolution hinged on an openness to inspired insight that leads observers to perceive the presence of the power of God's majestic rule in the mighty acts of Jesus.

The remainder of the material Luke included in this section explores the explanatory alternatives the event evoked in those observing the occasion and the implications of those alternatives.

Both those who misinterpreted (it was all done "by Beelzebul"—v. 15) and those who were uncertain what to think (so they demanded "a sign from heaven"—v. 16) betrayed by their very lack of discernment that they were as enslaved to the power of Satan as was the man possessed. The sign of the restoring power of God at work in and through Jesus becomes for them the "sign that will be opposed" as Simeon had warned in the Nunc Dimittis (2:34). It would have been better had they, too, been mute.

(*c*) *Jesus exposes the demonic dimension of wrong conclusions.* For the ones seeing a demonic dynamism at work in Jesus, his response was scathing. In the first place, it does not make sense to surmise that Jesus was serving as an agent of Satan when he cast out the demon because then Satan would be working against Satan's own purposes. Secondly, they habitually tolerated, perhaps even on occasion patronized, popular Jewish exorcists who presumably claimed harmony with the will of God in their work. If they saw no evil force in them, they should have seen with clarity the power of God operative in Jesus. Such confusion betrayed their antipathy to the presence and claim of God's royal rule (v. 19).

The inbreaking of the reign of God is both for restoration/salvation and for judgment. How one responds to the presence of that claim for allegiance and obedience discloses the individual consequences of encounter with the divine right to rule (vv. 20–23).

Myopia to the true spiritual dimensions of such an event leaves one exposed and vulnerable (vv. 24–26). Renunciation of allegiance to Satan is not enough. One must go beyond that; one must choose for God. Even if they had recognized the power of God working through Jesus, that was not enough. They had to affirm God's right to rule in them, too. Otherwise, one is susceptible to even more severe satanic enslavement ("seven" signifies "complete, total"). The need is not simply to expel but to supplant. God must be allowed to rule actively where Satan once held sway.

(*d*) *Jesus castigates the demand for more evidence.* To those others who sought to resolve the apparent ambiguity by demanding a corroborating display (v. 16), Jesus' response was equally unequivocal (vv. 29–32). They wanted to see something more authenticating than a mere exorcism miracle (which, for anyone who can see, clearly discloses kingdom presence and power). They wanted something stupendously spectacular! Luke's audience could hardly miss hearing the same satanic challenge being posed again here that Jesus already had forthrightly resisted (4:9–12).

Jesus recalled before them the "sign of Jonah," and the corroborating incident concerning the Solomonic visit by "the queen of the South." Both of these were incidents treasured in the religious memory of Israel which described non-Jews who showed remarkable spiritual perception, far greater than did these Jewish contemporaries who were observing Jesus and his work.

The Queen of Sheba recognized the divine wisdom in Solomon and went to considerable trouble and expense to put herself in the presence of that wisdom. By contrast, in Jesus, a more transparent personification of divine wisdom has come to the present generation of people, and they are for the most part oblivious to or confused about that presence.

The "sign of Jonah" in Luke's view was displayed in the person of Jonah as the empowered agent of God, and in Jonah's authoritative preaching which promoted a conversion, prompting repentance from the Ninevites. The critical note lies in the realization that the "Son of man," as sign, stands before these Jews and, unlike the pagan Ninevites with Jonah, they do not have a clue as to who Jesus is or what he signifies.

(e) *Further of "Jesus' true family" tradition.* Luke bound together the two sharp critiques against those who mistook the implications of the exorcism with a brief story (vv. 27–28—similar to the story in 8:19–21) that underscored the necessity for attentive, obedient hearing of God's word. The section concludes (vv. 33–36) with a collection of Jesus' "wisdom logia" that illumine the person and preaching of Jesus as the "something greater than Solomon/Jonah," even as the "word of God" which is to be heard and kept. These interpretive passages focus attention on the supreme importance of response to the word of God with a perceptive, receptive, obedient spirit.

The development of a sermon from this text might consider:

The section offers the opportunity to caution people pastorally against longing after personal revelations and yearning for private mystical visions of Jesus that give self-credence to publicly professed piety. In Jesus, God has accomplished a self-disclosure with all of the clarity and completeness we require. Our task is to study him and his teaching.

The fundamental question for us, too, is not a superficial "What is going on here?" but a reverent perusal of what this passage discloses to us about who, really, is in charge—in our lives, our relationships, our churches, our society, our world. We are to bring an openness to that task that derives its confidence from our conviction that God is faithful and trustworthy, and will not mislead us. God longs for us to find in the person and message of Jesus a clear disclosure of who God is, and of who we are and what we are to be about in the purposes of God.

JESUS REBUKES SOME
RELIGIOUS LEADERS (11:37–54)

In this final section of chapter eleven, Luke redirected the critical gaze of Jesus from the imperceptive segments of people in the crowds and focused it on some Pharisees and on the lawyers within their religious "party." The function of these lawyers was to provide technical legal counsel concerning appropriate contemporary applications of Torah.

Coming under sharp scrutiny is the tendency of those in this "party" to allow themselves to become religiously distracted from service to God by their zeal for consistent, unqualified obedience to the demands of the Mosaic law. When that zeal led them to be themselves diverted—and to use their authority to divert others from the proper offering of worship and glory to God—their very love of the law became demonic, deserving divine judgment.

(*a*) *Invitation and conflict.* The narrative setting for this protracted rebuke is a meal at the home of a Pharisee (v. 37). Table-fellowship understood in the context of Jewish piety is a religious event as well as a social occasion.

We note first that the Pharisee asked Jesus to such an occasion—a not inconsiderable concession and honor—and Jesus accepted. This is consistent with the "love/hate" dimension in Luke's portrayal of Jesus' attitude toward the Pharisees. On the one hand, Jesus was captivated by their rigorous commitment to take their religious convictions seriously. On the other hand, he was deeply disappointed and highly critical that their well-intentioned reform became so misdirected that the program diverted attention away from the very essence of the faith they professed to be purifying and restoring. The cure prescribed by them often seemed worse than the disease!

Occasion for the critique arises in the contrast between what Jesus was offering them by consenting to enter into religious fellowship with them at table, and their fixation on his failure to conform to the purification code (vv. 38–41). The dominance of their agenda prevented them from being open to who he was and what God was offering to them in and through him. To compound the crisis, they were impervious to their own imperceptiveness. It was a characteristic instance of zeal for observance of the law blinding them to the demand of God that they do merciful justice and love God, which was disclosed both in the law and in Jesus' teachings.

(*b*) *Three woes criticizing Pharisaic scrupulosity.* David Tiede (*Luke,* Minneapolis: Augsburg Publising House, 1988, p. 223) describes the three woes which Jesus directed toward the Pharisees (vv. 42–44) as "prophetic denunciations, filled with the extravagance of prophetic indictment." The exaggerated stress on detailed observance of the law they imposed on others became the grounds for their rebuke by Jesus.

Jesus reproached them for:

a) being hyperscrupulous about adherence to the external details of law observance at the expense of distracting themselves (and others) from crucial concerns in the law for justice and love of God (v. 42)—for example, tithing was emphasized in Jewish religious traditions because the income thus generated could be used to benefit the poor;

b) taking themselves far too seriously (v. 43)—and, by implication, not taking God nearly seriously enough;

c) promoting themselves as being the only really dependable guides to correct observance of right religion through ritual purity when, by their own unrighteousness, they are themselves unclean and thereby mislead and ritually contaminate all whom they have influenced to emulate them (v. 44).

(*c*) *Three woes on lawyerly excesses.* "Wait a minute, Jesus," protested one of the lawyers. "When you castigate the Pharisees, you attack us, too." The lawyers were the "scholars" among the Pharisees, those trained as technical, legal experts who interpreted the law. They must have been particularly sensitive to Jesus' verbal assault on the Pharisees for they were the ones who gave guidance, advice, and direction to the Pharisaic attitudes condemned by Jesus in the three previous woes.

"Now that you mention it . . ." and Jesus replied with three more extended woes directed toward correcting them (vv. 46–52):

a) for devoting exaggerated inventiveness in defining additional obligations to impose on people (v. 46) when they could have, and should have, devoted their ingenuity to assist people to discover creative ways past the daunting demands of obligatory behavior so that they came to experience law observance as a way of celebrating conformity with the will of God through the love and justice that permeated their lives;

b) by misdirecting the function of law, they pervert their calling to testify accurately to the will of God revealed in Torah and instead witness to their solidarity (hypocritical "memorial-making" notwithstanding) with those in Israel's past who have consistently fought against God by murdering those agents whom God empowered to announce God's will (vv. 47–51), (and Luke's readers know that some of those ones were instrumental in doing to Jesus what their predecessors did to the [other] prophets);

c) because, although they have been privileged to be entrusted with a more sustained exposure to the law in order that they might make the purpose of the law available to the unschooled, by their preoccupation with expanding the minutia of demands they declared must be kept if obedience to the law was to be complete, they evade the just demands of the law themselves and deny access to the law's real meaning to the very people whom they have been appointed to serve (v. 52).

The Pharisees and the lawyers among them cannot countenance such an assault. With their resolve to show themselves smarter than Jesus by seeking to force him to misspeak (vv. 53f.), they betray through their hostile, adversarial attitude the accuracy of his sharp critique. They will have a part in persecuting and killing (v. 49) him, and they will be held accountable for it (vv. 50f.).

Sermon possibilities on this passage include:

1. The perils of religious pseudo-professionalism. It is important to guard against setting Jesus in absolute opposition to these Pharisees. They are part of a significantly influential segment of Judaism that yearned to recover an intensified, single-minded religious commitment lived out under the discipline of the Mosaic Torah, the holy law of God. That is a laudable initiative, except when performing the requirements of the law becomes an end in itself, rather than the means for honoring God by offering grateful obedience.

We recognize that such a posture is not peculiar to this particular group of Pharisees. It was a perennial problem that repeatedly received attention and correction in both the prophetic and the wisdom traditions. It is just as prominent and requires similar correction in contemporary piety.

The most obvious place for homiletic convergence is with reference to those involved in the formal leadership structures of the church, either locally or beyond. Worship at clergy assemblies, lay leader meetings or retreats, local parish leadership training workshops, and so forth all might provide a context within which profitable reflection on this section might take place. Care should be taken that this section not be abused as license for "pillar-" or "preacher-bashing."

2. *Renouncing the idolatry of rigid devotion to principles.* Invite the general congregation to enter into this passage and to claim its import for them. We all suffer from the almost irresistible urge to reduce the radical claims of God to a definable, manageable, measurable code of religious behavior. Having allowed that to supplant the insecurity of disciplining ourselves to the fluid demands of a dynamic I-Thou relationship with God, we yearn to discover self-confirmation by persuading and even requiring others to accommodate themselves to the same code we have constructed.

When carefully constructed cultic customs are exposed as phony, evasive, and even antithetical to the legitimate expectations of the faith we claim to profess, we, too, are angry. We resist; we become contentious; we may even attack.

When challenges to any of our principles—all of those things by which we live, which we hold to be precious—evoke resentment and even rage within us, we need to do some self-examination. Have "the things by which we live" supplanted the jealous hegemony of the One in whom alone we claim to live? In urging others to submit themselves to our carefully defined, ever-expanding religious/ethical system, are we diverting them away from that very source of life and health we profess to know and on which we claim to depend? Are we building tombs for the prophets? Maybe even striving to reconstruct the sepulchre in Gethsemane? Have we calculated the extent of the accountability we bear?

Anyone who leads the flock to wade in these deep waters will want to be careful to make it vividly evident early on how thoroughly she/he shares in that common indictment. Only then can the invitation to the congregation be made with credibility. It is not bad being a Pharisee (a Methodist, a Presbyterian, an Evangelical, a Charismatic, etc.) as long as that does not get in the way of being Christian.

ADMONITIONS AND WARNINGS (12:1–13:9)

Luke includes at this point in his narrative an extended section of guidance and counsel about what is appropriate behavior in view of the presence of the restoration of God's reign in creation, and what actions and attitudes are unacceptably inconsistent with that presence. The first segment (12:1–53) focuses on the disciples while the latter part (12:54–13:9) is addressed to the multitudes.

Narrative transition is provided in 12:1 from Jesus' harsh critique spoken to a group of the Pharisees. As leaven corrupts the entire mass of dough, so the hypocrisy of the Pharisees, unchecked, will shape and influence people toward preoccupation with law observance and the keeping of cultic regulations at the cost of diverting attention away from God's will.

To the Disciples:
I. Persevere Against Persecution (12:2–12)

Following hard on the heels of Jesus' caution to "Beware of the yeast of the Pharisees, that is, their hypocrisy" (12:1), Jesus in this first section warns the disciples against what Fred Craddock calls "reverse hypocrisy" (*Luke,* Louisville, Ky.: John Knox Press, 1990, p. 160). When facing the prospect of persecution, disciples of Jesus should not pretend *not* to be what they in fact are. They are to be forthright and open about their consecration to God even before hostile interrogation and threat.

What persecuted disciples attempt to conceal in a moment of terror will be disclosed ultimately. Allegiance to God must not be hidden. As much as they may fear physical deprivation and even death, the consequence of renouncing the faith out of fear (which involves renouncing God's right to rule and returning to eternal enslavement to Satan) is infinitely more dreadful.

The only devoted way to withstand the intimidating threat of persecution is to rely utterly on God. God is faithful and trustworthy of our confidence. God will support; God will sustain; God, through the Holy Spirit, will instruct and inspire; God will vindicate! To doubt that about God under the stress and pressure of persecution is to capitulate to the enemies of God. It is to choose solidarity once again with the obdurate, unrelenting opposition to God. It is to repudiate acquiescence to God's purposes, which through Jesus are being established and promoted by the Holy Spirit in the world. Choosing solidarity with such opposition is *unforgivable!*

A sermon suggestion on this passage follows:

The difficulty in preaching this passage stems from the fact that the presumed circumstances, while patently vivid for Luke and his community, are so remote for most of us. We have all heard stories of people who have been deprived, imprisoned, and even executed for their unswerving allegiance to Christ. We admire them and envy the strength of their convictions. Still, for most of us, confessing one's faith against a hostile, established authority is foreign to our experience.

The underlying perspective of "reverse hypocrisy," however—hiding or dissembling about what is fundamental to who one is in the eyes of

God—is something with which we all struggle daily. Motivational mendacity dilutes and even corrupts the testimony God expects us to give with clarity and persuasiveness about the nature of the world and who is in control. Does such duplicity encourage us ultimately to choose solidarity with the Enemy of God and blaspheme the present work of God's Holy Spirit for less comprehensible reasons than the prospect of physical persecution?

Threats against purity of heart in matters of faith are less dramatic for most of us these days but hardly less insidious. It takes considerable discernment and spiritual discipline for us to order our lives with consistency on the conviction that God is faithful and trustworthy of our confidence, too. We struggle with all manner of established, accepted, and even aggressively prosecuted assaults against the integrity of our discipleship. Still, God will support and sustain us; God through the Holy Spirit will instruct and inspire. Like those first-century Christians, we, too, are worth infinitely more to the God for whom remembering sparrows and counting hairs is not impossible.

To the Disciples:
II. Concerning Possessions (12:13–34)

This section resumes Jesus' hortatory instructions, still being addressed primarily to his disciples. It continues to probe the issue of where ultimate trust is to be lodged to guarantee true security. In *Luke*, p. 162, Fred Craddock alerts us to the logical connection with the previous section between fear expressed in silence and denial and fear that finds expression in "greed and a grasping after things as a means of securing one's future." (A good resource for studying the importance of this latter theme throughout the writings of Luke is *Sharing Possessions,* by Luke T. Johnson, Philadelphia: Fortress Press, 1981.)

The occasion with which Luke introduced the theme of material possessions was the demand made on Jesus (v. 13) to function as a technical interpreter of Mosaic law. A man requires Jesus to apply the guidelines for inheritance disputes (see Num. 27:1–11; Deut. 21:15–17) to a specific case. Jesus rejects the role of a lawyer who authoritatively interprets Torah, preferring the role of teacher of wisdom instead. He responds not with a formal, technical judgment but with wisdom aphorisms and a story (vv. 15–21).

(*a*) *The meaning of the aphorisms.* Greed displays misdirected reliance on the security and power vested in material possessions. Such a preoccupation with possessions diverts one's attention, energy and, finally, one's loyalties away from the radical, single-minded obedience that the claim of God's royal right to rule, present in the person and ministry of Jesus, requires.

(*b*) *Who is in charge?* The rich man in the story faithlessly assumes that he has primary control over his future. His preoccupation with comfortably shaping his future ignores the need to conform his aspirations to the purposes of God. The process of amassing wealth is colored by the intent driving it. He accumulates, *not* the better to serve others out of worshipful love for God, but, rather, to finance his own anticipated extravagant leisure.

His foolishness reflects the fact that he controls neither his own longevity nor the ultimate disposal of his accumulated wealth. God controls! God disposes! It is more serious than simply a matter of imbalanced emphasis. Since such trust ought only to be placed in God, covetousness is idolatry—in blatant violation of the Decalogue. The story illustrates that in the saving economy of God, the rich are sent away "empty" (1:53).

(*c*) *Further aphoristic admonitions.* Jesus next encourages his disciples to reflect on useless (and on *useful*) anxiety, using a "from the lesser to the greater" argument. The natural order, discerningly considered, clearly testifies to the unsolicited trustworthiness of God. How much more will God provide for human needs? Anxiety about obtaining life's necessities is divertive, ineffective, and faithless. The fullness of life that God intends for us has so much more to it than what material possessions can supply (v. 15). *Faithful* anxiety consists of seeing to it that daily energies and attention, having been shaped by absolute trust in God's faithfulness, are devoted to promoting the reestablishment of the rule of God in creation (v. 31).

The concluding admonition (vv. 32ff.) urges disciples to let their lifestyle reflect values shaped by kingdom priorities—that is, values defined in faithful response to the encounter with God's restored and restoring reign. Renunciation of greed liberates one from fixated anxiety about the abundance of possessions and frees one for benevolent compassion and devotion. The fundamental choice is whether to serve God. When you have that straightened out then your option—your only option—is to serve God, even with your possessions.

To the Disciples:
III. End-time Concerns (12:35–53)

Luke used this portion of the extended section of admonitions and warnings begun at 12:1 to cluster together several of Jesus' sayings that share the common motifs of alertness, watchfulness, and readiness. Although Jesus ostensibly addressed his remarks to the disciples, Luke expects his community, which is seeking to be faithful in the interim time as it anticipates the return of its Lord, to hear these words addressed to it, too.

Luke emphasizes keeping vigil for Jesus' return by sustaining the quality of one's discipleship rather than by seeking to calculate the most likely moment for his appearance and waiting until then to prepare. Energies expended on computations about the calendar and sequence of end-of-time events are futile and counterproductive. They divert attention from faithful witness through ministry and self-spending service to the believer's devoted anticipation of the certain completion of God's plan.

(*a*) *Be ready for the return of Jesus!* As Jesus and the disciples are on the way to Jerusalem under the sign of the cross, the claim of the royal rule of God is now being disclosed to anyone with a discerning spirit. It is extremely urgent to respond to that regal presence and participate in the restorative program inaugurated by Jesus, whose aim is the reestablishment and acknowledgment of divine rule.

Watch and be ready! Even if Jesus has not yet returned, the anticipation is just as vivid. Those who are faithfully prepared and alert for his coming demonstrate just how vibrant that expectation is. Vigilant watchfulness is not an alternative activity to servant ministry. Being watchfully alert compels Christian service conducted in the confident conviction that there is no doubt—*he is coming!* The only uncertainty is when, and that is not something anyone can find out ahead of time (vv. 39–40).

(*b*) *The integrity of single-minded service.* It is precisely the faithful service of individual discipleship and the corporate fidelity of community ministry, pursued in harmony with a professed anticipation of the return and visible rule of Jesus, that display the disciples' readiness (vv. 35–36). What a reward awaits! The servant Lord serves the servant disciples at table (with both eucharistic and messianic banquet echoes) in celebration of their devoted allegiance in watching alertly for his coming (vv. 37–38).

Verses 41–48 shift the focus to those who exercise community leadership responsibilities. The accountability they bear for faithful service as demonstration of their confident anticipation of the return of the Lord is different not in kind but in intensity. If all disciples of Jesus are "exhibit A" that God's rule is restored, how much more ought the presence of that royal control be reflected in the manner of ministry of those whom God has gifted with the charisms for administrative and instructional authority? Outrageous abuse of such control is particularly damaging testimony that the gospel is a lie. There is, however, reduced culpability for unintentional sins (v. 48).

(*c*) *Extreme accountability requires exclusive devotion.* The last verses in this segment, verses 49–53, concentrate on a different aspect of the end-of-time concern, namely, the divisive effect, even on customary human (familial) relationships, of the radical crisis for decision that

Jesus' presence evokes, and the exclusive claim for allegiance that presence imposes.

Luke has already toyed with the ambiguity evoked by the image of fire in the minds of his listeners (see 3:16f.). The fire of destructive judgment and the baptismal fire of empowerment will receive thorough exploitation in the Pentecost narrative in Acts 2. Here as there they are not mutually exclusive but complementary. *Both* are divisive. Fiery judgment condemns and vindicates. Empowerment with God's Spirit sets one apart even from those with whom one has the closest relationship (see 8:20–21; 11:27–28).

Possibilities (and a problem) when preaching this passage include:

The problem the passage poses is the disparity between the zealous fascination with which the first Christians anticipated an early return of Jesus and the conspicuous absence of that anticipation in contemporary Christian concerns. Those first Christians were overly agitated by the "early" aspect of their expectation. After all, they could sit on the edge of the bench in eager excitement only so long and, when the edge began to cut in and still nothing indicating Jesus' return had happened, inevitable questions about the veracity of what they had been taught loomed large.

Not many people today are convinced that "Jesus is coming soon" (road signs and bumper stickers notwithstanding). Few Christians are inclined to reflect on the second coming of Jesus at all, much less do it with the glad eagerness of edge-of-the-pew postures.

What deprivation! Early Christians were right to abandon their fascination with trying to calculate date, time, and place. Most Christians today, with their studied indifference to the prospect of Christ's return, have thrown the proverbial baby out with the bath water. Turn-of-the-millennium terror trivializes the possibility.

Indifference to the expectation of the end-time return of Jesus siphons that quality of eagerly ready and breathlessly vigilant devotion to the tasks of ministry and service that discipleship commends. Without that conviction, too much Christian action degenerates into unfocused "do-good-ism." Such a vagueness not only obscures the signals given to others about the urgency of recognizing and responding to God's claims for allegiance, it also dilutes the distinctive flavor in Christian lives of vibrant vitality born of eager, vigilant persuasion that the Lord will come and we are in every moment to be found ready and engaged in faithfully executed discipleship.

Christian behavior ("the Christian walk") is not governed by fearful apprehension of being caught unprepared, and thereby confirming our sloth (the "Jesus is coming—look busy!" syndrome). Discipleship is driven by the glad and certain anticipation that just as the Lord Jesus has already come, qualitatively changing every dimension of human existence, so Jesus will return to confirm both the scope and the quality of the eternal in the restored and resumed royal rule of God.

To the Crowds:
I. Seeing Signs of the Times Rightly (12:54–59)

Luke now broadens the audience for Jesus' extended discourse on warnings and admonitions (begun at 12:1) to include the crowds (v. 54). This section continues the exploration of end-of-the-ages concerns occupying Jesus in the previous, concluding section (vv. 35–53) which he had addressed to his disciples (vv. 35–53). Jesus expresses astonishment at people's obtuseness, reluctance, and even refusal to assess accurately the eternal significance of what is occurring among them right then.

(*a*) *Accurate discernment ought not be limited to predicting the weather.* Jesus marvels (vv. 54–56) that these "weather-wise Palestinian farmers" (J. A. Fitzmyer, *The Gospel According to Luke*, [Garden City, N.Y.: Doubleday & Co., 1981], p. 999) were proficient at analyzing advance indications of approaching changes in the weather. But they were dense at comprehending their own spiritual situation at this critical moment of confrontation with the claim of God to control creation.

It was important to well-being in a culture that was primarily agricultural to train oneself to take note of any hints of change in the weather in order to anticipate the impact on crops. It was immensely more important for God's covenant people to discern portents of God's saving activity in the world and in their lives. People had schooled themselves to observe indications in nature and reach correct conclusions about impending occurrences. Yet those events were of only limited, momentary significance. How much more ought people to discipline themselves to perceive discerningly the opportune moment of responding to Jesus' lordly presence and the reign of God he both proclaimed and reestablished.

The contrast here is not between practiced, practical "country" wisdom and sophisticated training in spiritual reflection. Tokens of divine activity, of godly presence and power in Jesus' life and ministry, were plainer than a dark, black funnel cloud bearing down. What was at issue was not their skill but their will. "Jesus is unmasking their attitude; their problem is much more an *unwillingness* to interpret rather than an *inability*" (Fitzmyer, ibid., p. 1000; emphasis added).

(*b*) *Ordering one's life in anticipation of God's judgment.* In verses 57–59, Jesus employed another *ad hominem* argument. People have learned when impending adjudication of civil disputes approaches how to pursue *ad hoc* negotiations to mutual advantage prior to exposing themselves to the often arbitrary, inflexible judgments of legal authorities. How much more should they show the same savvy in response to clear evidences of the approach of impending end-time judgment before God.

People take the initiative to arbitrate disputes and settle accounts, removing any cause for complaint, before formal, official determination occurs. They should exercise more initiative in reordering their lives in response to the inbreaking of God's rule and the approaching judgment the reestablishment of that rule guarantees will occur—and soon. Prudent perception of the meaning of the moment and carefully calculated exploitation of the opportunity it brings—widely recognized common sense in the ordering of human affairs—makes even more sense in response to the present claims of God's royal right to rule. Reordering one's values and priorities is not something to be postponed until the moment of final accountability on the Day of the Lord.

The following reflections invite sermon development:

A lot of negative inertia will need to be overcome if a convergence of this section with current faith concerns is to occur. So many New Testament passages require us to recognize the urgency of the present moment and to order our priorities, attitudes, and behavior with intensity and single-minded integrity in view of the momentous dimensions of this opportune time. Yet, truth be told, there is little discoverable sense of urgency, minimal "at-the-last moment" intensity, and scarcely any undistracted devotion to be found for ordering our lives to conform to the presence and the expectations of God's royal rule.

Even though our culture is not as thoroughly agrarian as first-century Palestine, we do know how to look out of the window, too. We usually can tell what the weather is going to be like. We sometimes, flippantly, commend that methodology to TV weather forecasters who concentrate intently on radar scans, satellite reports, and meteorological analyses to predict a "seventy percent chance of precipitation" when, if they would only shift their gaze from the screen, get out of their chairs, and open the blinds, they would see that it was raining cats and dogs.

We know, too, of the desirability and advantage of getting disputes negotiated to mutual satisfaction if at all possible before they ever get to court. In this age, where the justice system is saturated with "plea-bargains" and "out-of-court" settlements, Jesus' argument in appealing to that analogy is forceful. However, the implications of "under-the table" accommodation and "getting off lightly," exploited by the privileged few but not available to the disenfranchised and marginalized in our culture, requires some carefully crafted qualifications from us if others are going to buy into the movement of the interpretive argument.

It is not that we do not know how to observe clear indications and reach conclusions. It is not that we are oblivious to the obvious advantages of taking the initiative and getting our "house" in order before we are called to accountability. When it comes to responding with urgency to the claim of God, we *choose* not to observe and conclude rightly. At issue with us, too, is the *will* rather than the *skill.* We are disinclined to take seriously the dimension of the eternal with which the faith that we profess invests every moment, every relationship, every decision of our lives.

However, when Jesus gets through to us; when God empowers us with the Spirit to acquiesce to God's claim to rule in us; when that same Spirit conforms our wills to God's, it makes all the difference in the world—and beyond. The urgency and the zeal are there, not because we suddenly are panicked by the prospect of end-time accountability and eternal judgment. There is zeal and urgency because we do not have enough time, strength, or wit to do all that we want to do out of ecstatic appreciation for God's love and for the startlingly astounding realization that God's judgment on us has already been given in Jesus Christ, and, that in Christ, God decrees for us life and love.

To the Crowds:
II. On Repentance (13:1–9)

Jesus issues a clear call to contrition to the crowd in this last portion of the Admonitions and Warnings discourse begun at 12:1. Luke has strategically placed this section directly after two sections that warn of impending end-time judgment (12:35–53, 54–59).

(a) *Two lethal calamaties and divine judgment.* The juxtaposition of the allusions to two recent catastrophes (vv. 1, 4) and the repeated phrase, "unless you repent you will all perish just as they did" (vv. 3, 5) followed by the parable of the unproductive fig tree (vv. 6–9), with its concluding instruction that if fruit continues to be lacking, "you can cut it down" (v. 9), combine to give an intensified impact to the call to repentance. Nevertheless, Luke intends for those listening to hear this as a word of grace. The call to repentance of sins always carries within it not only the threat of divine retribution but, more important, the promise of forgiveness.

The incident of the brutal, bloody suppression by Pilate posed a critical challenge to which Jesus artfully responded. He balanced a rejection of the simplistic equation that all sin inevitably results in suffering and all suffering is consequent to sin with the crucial affirmation that God, whose patience exceeds human comprehension, nonetheless requires righteousness. There looms a day of reckoning, a time of account giving. Unanticipated tragic events remind us that God does inescapably expect results; therefore, repent and reorder your lives to conform to God's expectation.

Vicious political assault and the sudden lethal crush of collapsing towers (vv. 1–5)—that is enough to give anyone pause. What is at stake with the incidents is the persistent quandary of what is the meaning of sudden, extraordinary suffering. If God judges and punishes the unrighteous, and judges and rewards the faithful, does that mean that those who are afflicted by abrupt disaster are the more reprehensible (even unforgivable) sinners? Such events force us to ponder the issue of ultimate justice in human affairs and how God's purposes are served.

(*b*) *Sudden suffering drives us to rely on God's grace.* Jesus' reply did not seek to offer a theological solution to the perennially perplexing and theoretical dilemma about human suffering, but to direct attention to the challenge to make a personal, faithful response. Specific instances of sudden, severe suffering are not to be understood as random, indiscriminate instances of proleptic end-time judgment by a capricious god. Coping with tragedy and cruel persecution teaches us a great deal about God's mercy and compassion but very little about God's justice. It encourages us to act on the conviction that unequivocal trust in God and complete reliance on the saving grace in Christ extends to include our knowledge of sin, our sense of guilt, and our acknowledgement that we have repeatedly, intentionally, and maliciously violated the majestic holiness of God.

(*c*) *The barren fig tree.* Jesus appends a parable of an unproductive fig tree that instructs about divine patience and forbearance. For a farmer, the risk of giving the tree yet another chance in the meager likelihood that it would finally do what it was supposed to do and produce fruit was not worth it. God's mercy, however, counsels far greater risks. Annihilation is not necessarily automatic. The interval of delay before the judgment of the Day of the Lord is cause for gratitude that God graciously forbears for a time that people might yet repent and "bear fruit" (see Luke's summary of John the Baptist's preaching in 3:7–9). There is still time. The forbearance of God, however, expresses God's mercy and is not to be presumed upon.

Preaching possibilities on this section include:

Sudden unanticipated tragedy reminds us not to be too confident that we know the duration of the interval that remains to us before we must make accounting before God (see 12:16–20). The shock of the tragedy alerts us to the urgency with which we must seize the present opportunity to embrace the cause of God's rule. Such events also warn us that when suffering is absent from human life for a season, that does not prove that repentance is unnecessary.

The tower fell and eighteen were crushed—the entire group save for two who had gone over to the well for water, perhaps. Why them? *The Bridge of San Luis Rey* (the Pulitzer Prize winning novel by Thornton Wilder) collapsed and indiscriminately hurled a motley and diverse company of travelers to their deaths. Was there any common cause behind that tragedy? Malignancies grow, transfusion-transmitted AIDS is contracted, five children drown in the stream at a Sunday School picnic together with the adult who tried to help them—if it had been you or yours, would you have felt, deep down in the deepest recesses of your heart, that there was some justice to it? Would you feel rage? Would you consider yourself betrayed by God? Would you become resigned?

Coming to terms with the precarious dimensions of life helps us finally to discover the preciousness of life. The gospel message infinitely intensifies our understanding of how precious life is—to God, and therefore for us. It also confronts us with our responsibility and our accountability to God for using life well as we serve the reign of God.

SABBATH CONTROVERSY
AND DIVINE PRESENCE (13:10–21)

Controversy over what constituted appropriate behavior on the Sabbath was something with which Jesus had to contend more than once in the course of his public ministry. There were multiple anecdotes of similar confrontations in the fund of stories about Jesus that were current in the early church. That reflected a critique with which not only Jesus but also the earliest church had to contend.

Luke had earlier included some comparable stories in his narrative (see 6:1–11, and the especially close similarities with 6:6–11). Apparently for the purposes of his story, Luke considered that this incident now settled the matter, or at least defused the issue as an excuse for those seeking to promote opposition to Jesus (see 14:1ff.).

(*a*) *The anecdotal situation.* The setting for the story places Jesus in a synagogue on the Sabbath, engaged in teaching. A woman with a bent, rigid back was present in the congregation. Luke's description of the situation is as startling as it is simple. There were plenty of breaches of Sabbath decorum in the incident before the actual healing took place. Jesus, a Jewish male, in the act of instructing pious Jews about God in the synagogue on the Sabbath, deigns to take public notice of the woman. He interrupts his teaching and, taking the initiative, summons her to him. Then he has the audacity to touch her, risking cultic defilement either from contact with her illness or because of possible female-related contamination (compare 8:43–47).

We should note, however, that the account is careful to make clear the true nature of the woman's condition. Her problem was not just age-related deterioration or ill health. She was possessed (by a crippling spirit—v. 11); she was "Satan bound" (v. 16).

(*b*) *The spiritually astigmatic synagogue leader.* The leader of the synagogue did not see the woman for what she had become under the power of Satan or for what she was suffering, nor did he see Jesus for who he was or for what God was accomplishing through him. All he saw was that time-honored and religiously validated custom was being flagrantly violated—and he was outraged. The six other days in the week provided more than enough opportunity for such goings-on—as if decorous Sabbath demeanor deserved more attention than God's liberating restoration of this member of creation.

As maintainer and adjudicator of Sabbath restrictions, the synagogue leader seemed to claim, at least derivatively, lordly authority over the Sabbath and over Sabbath behavior. (Notice Luke's deliberate use of "Lord" for Jesus in this story—v. 15, and see 6:5.)

The leader of the synagogue illustrates one who, although exercising cultic leadership, is not alert to the royal presence of the rule of God in the person of Jesus, and is not at all prepared to repent before that presence. He is so distracted by zeal for promoting scrupulous adherence to the legal tenets governing Sabbath observance that he sets himself against the very healing capacity in Jesus indicative of the restoring power of God to which both law and Sabbath were intended to testify. In Jesus' act of healing, God assaults Satan's control and prevails.

(*c*) *Denunciation of imperception in the presence of God's royal rule.* Jesus rails at such spiritual myopia and urges the leader and any others so like-minded to wake up to what is going on. He argues for a reasonable extension by analogy from an example of compassionate Sabbath "work" done to alleviate the physical need of animals that even the strictest interpreters of Sabbath rules allowed. The Sabbath healing of the woman was more than a commendably compassionate act that was unfortunately timed. It displayed God in victorious contention with Satan and wresting control from that inimical power. The miracle points to the mystery of the effective presence of the restorative power of God.

The ruler just did not get it—but the woman does! She knows what has happened to her, and by whom it has been done. In glad recognition she joins company with Mary (1:46ff.), the angels (2:13), the shepherds (2:20), and so many others in offering joyful praise to God (v. 13b). The woman and the ruler represented that messianic division between supporters and "opponents" (v. 17) that Simeon had foretold to Mary (2:34) and that Jesus himself had but recently predicted (12:51ff.). The division followed along the fault line that was defined by how people responded to Jesus and to the royal rule of God being reasserted through him.

(*d*) *Two similitudes about the dynamism of the kingdom.* The two "kingdom similitudes" (vv. 18–21) exploit examples from nature to signify the dynamic of divine presence and power that accomplishes God's purpose in astonishing dimensions and transforms everything it touches. Both the sower (a man) and the baker (a woman) "perform small acts that have expansive consequences" (Fred Craddock, *Luke,* Louisville, Ky.: John Knox Press, 1990, p. 171). The tree resulting from the sower's action not only fulfills the dynamic of its own nature, in contrast to the unproductive fig tree (see 13:6–9), but also provides service to others of God's creation (the birds). The yeast of God's reign in the second similitude offers a corrective and an antidote to the destructive "yeast of the Pharisees" (12:1).

If the healing of the woman seems limited and local—and inopportune to some—Luke wants us to realize that it is being done by one who at the outset was tempted and prevailed, who has healed frequently before, who is even now on the way to the Jerusalem cross. Unimaginable consequences can, and in the economy of God, do result from apparently insignificant beginnings. If the disciples and the crowds can grasp the reality of it here and now, then future crises, even crucifixion, will be experienced from that confident perspective that is anchored in the certain accomplishment of God's saving purposes.

JESUS AGAIN PREDICTS
HIS DEATH IN JERUSALEM (13:22–35)

Jesus had already made explicit mention of his approaching execution in Jerusalem several times (9:22, 44; 12:50). Again in this section, he refers to the fate that awaits him in the holy city of David. Luke's readers are thereby reminded that the entire journey from Galilee to Jerusalem (9:51–19:27) takes place under the sign of the cross. All of those episodes that relate Jesus' mentoring of the disciples, and all of his interactions with the crowds, and all of the confrontations with the increasingly hostile religious leaders acquire additional significance and pathos when they are interpreted from the perspective of the impending passion of Jesus in Jerusalem.

(*a*) *The presence of God's rule requires a faith-response.* The journey is well advanced, the city looms nearer, and the time is menacingly short. An anonymous person, who represents all of those oblivious to both the opportunity and the urgency of the moment, wants to play theological games in the presence of Jesus. It is the quantitative query (v. 23), to the effect, "How many do you guess will make it to heaven?" Jesus evaded the challenge to define with precision what were the limits of God's grace, and instead urged people to respond to the offer of God to take charge over them right at that moment.

The "narrow door" (v. 24) is not to restrict access but to stress the need for zealous, disciplined effort to attain entry. Desire is not enough. "Few" or "many" is beside the point. The critical consideration is that "the door" will soon be shut. If they miss the momentous moment, they not only encounter indifference and exclusion but risk active repudiation. Those who do not "know" who Jesus is and from whom he has come—and "know" with an impact that shatters their arrogant assumption of acceptability as a matter of course—can offer no identifying evidence of origin that compels his attention: "I do not know where you come from" (vv. 25, 27).

(*b*) *Tardy protests justify exclusion.* The protests of the excluded (v. 26) are self-indictments. Neither liturgical proximity to Jesus nor auditory exposure to Jesus' teaching and preaching about the claims of the rule of God suffice. Latecomers, both by their tardiness and by their outraged confusion, betray that when they were in the presence of Jesus, they did not take seriously either him or the reign of God he proclaimed. They did not seize the opportune moment of saving visitation.

Luke repeatedly warned people against counting on ancestry, or relying on either a racial or a familial identity based on that ancestry, to commend them for favorable reception by God (e.g., 3:8–9; 8:19–21; 11:27–28). The harsh words of rejection (v. 27b), exclusion from the company of the patriarchs and the prophets (v. 28), and the specter of the messianic banquet proceeding without their inclusion (v. 29) combine to convince them of the sham of their own religious posturing and of the reality that they lack solidarity with the great heroes of the faith.

It is the moment of transposed expectations. Long-held assumptions are shattered; long-guarded prerogatives are reversed. It is those whose trust in God transcends their birth-heritage who will be seated in table-fellowship at the end-time messianic banquet with Jesus and the faithful of Israel, and be numbered among the righteous of God. The vision extends to encompass the universal dimensions to God's program of redemption. Peoples from the nations of the four corners of the earth will sit at table with him who came to be a "light for revelation to the Gentiles" (2:32). Those whom God welcomes are distinguished by their faithful obedience in response to the summons of God, not by their ethnic lineage.

A sermon on this section might develop around the following:

Luke's point was not simply to bemoan all of those who missed a golden opportunity during Jesus' public ministry. He wants his audience, his own Christian community, to know that even as they read this account it is a moment of golden opportunity for them. That should be our concern, too—no mean task to confront the interpreter who would effect a convergence between the congregation and this text.

There is something deadly dull about hearing the call to decision for the cause of Christ again and again and again. Why take it seriously? It is nothing to get excited about. We will hear the same thing next week, and the month after, and whenever. We heard Christ's call and responded, once, a long time ago, and if there is need for renewal, well, there is always time. Besides, so many other time-constrained invitations seduce our energies and attentions right now. We will give real study to this other matter, later, when things are not so hectic.

"Today is the first day of the rest of your life," so popular wisdom would remind us. All right, but the same thing is true for tomorrow, or next Sunday, or next Christmas.

What if, instead, we heard it phrased, "Today is the last day to change the quality of the rest of your life"? How can we offer this as an alternative without being phony, manipulative, and hyperbolically apocalyptic? What transformations would occur, and how would you "parson" differently, if *you* were first to take this alternate phrasing seriously? How confident are you that your call, your theological eruditeness, your denominational loyalty have reserved for you a spot at the banquet table? How certain are you that you can identify when that moment just before the "moment too late" approaches? What does the congregation understand itself to be saying when it acclaims, "Praise God from whom all blessings flow," or, "Take Thou my life dear Lord," or, "Blessed is he who comes in the name of the Lord"?

(c) *Herod's murderous intent and the lethal role of Jerusalem.* Verse 31 reports that Pharisees(!) warned Jesus of Herod, who had once puzzled over Jesus but who now has assumed the role of lethal adversary, and is resolved to eradicate Jesus' disturbing influence by executing Jesus as he had earlier rid himself of John the Baptist (9:7–9). Jesus will not be harassed or intimidated by the puny malevolence of Herod. His ministry is not yet complete. Herod cannot impede that. Lethal judgment against him awaits, to be sure, but it will be made elsewhere by others at another time, with Herod applauding on the margins. What Herod threatens, Jerusalem will accomplish. Jesus moves on out of the region, but that is not evidence that he is fleeing any putative threat represented by the Herods of this world. The divine constraint governing the course of events is more compelling for Jesus than any anxiety the malevolent authority of Herod can evoke.

As Jesus anticipates the events that await in the city toward which he travels, he laments in anguish over Jerusalem. Although Jesus wills salvation for

Jerusalem, Jerusalem wills destruction for Jesus, and that dooms Jerusalem to destruction. It gives an especially poignant and ironic tone to the anticipated Palm Sunday acclamation, "Blessed is the one who comes in the name of the Lord" (v. 35). Jerusalem, hailing Jesus as king at his "Triumphal Entry," is like those who call, "Lord, open to us" (v. 25). It is a demand that has missed the moment of opportunity. It comes too late.

"The pathos of the lament is caught up in God's passion to save, which is pitted against human determination to resist, even when the results will be tragically destructive" (David L. Tiede, (*Luke,* [Minneapolis: Augsburg Publishing House, 1988], p. 256). Jerusalem habitually has played the role of executioner of the empowered agents of God. That clearly indicates how Israel has become alienated at the very center of its national, political, and cultic identity from the purposes of God, and how reactionary it can become when reminded of that alienation.

TABLE-TALK: ROTE RELIGION
OR GOD'S ROYAL RULE (14:1–24)

Luke now includes four dissimilar anecdotes that share the common motif of "meal" or "banquet." Both the narrative context and the cumulative interaction of the four episodes focus these stories on complementary aspects related to the reassertion of God's reign over creation in the ministry of Jesus.

Sabbath Healing (14:1–6)

In Luke's view, Pharisees related to Jesus as diversely as did people in the crowds. Some Pharisees had just warned Jesus of impending danger (13:31), and now, after a leading Pharisee had extended to Jesus the considerable honor of inviting him to sit at table-fellowship in his home, other Pharisees who were also present as guests were critically dubious.

(*a*) *Some Pharisees are critical of Jesus' behavior.* These Pharisees were there not for religious table-fellowship but to scrutinize Jesus' behavior and activity to trip him up on any deviation or violation of legal strictures. It was a time of testing, a time of trial. What they did not realize was that, as always in Luke's presentation, when critics stand in the presence of Jesus, it is the time of *their* testing, *their* trial. They failed.

The occasion was an opportunity for restorative healing (one of the compelling claims on his time that Jesus had hurled dismissingly in the teeth of Herod's threat— 13:32), the issue was appropriate Sabbath behavior, raised in Luke's narrative now for the fourth time (cf. 6:1–5, 6–11; 13:10–19). Jesus is a quick study. To forestall criticism such as he had caught earlier, he aggressively took the initiative.

(*b*) *Sabbath healing and Torah restraints.* "Does the law allow me to do this on the Sabbath, or not?" (v. 3b paraphrased—we have heard him ask a similar question with effect before, in 6:9). Jesus contends that it is in keeping with the law (in harmony with the revealed will of God) even if it were not lawful (prohibited by the rules governing Sabbath activity). Then he goes on to claim that, as a well-known matter of fact, it is lawful.

Jesus justifies his act of healing with the familiar argument from the lesser to the greater. The Torah allows exceptions in emergency situations. If the law concedes deviation from the Mosaic norm in a crisis when an animal is threatened with injury or loss of life, how much more does this precedent apply to a human, personally suffering the effects from the sinful chaos of a world in rebellion? The crisis arises because of the afflicted person's opportune access to Jesus, the spirit-empowered wonder worker and healer who is charged by God to set such things right in creation, which may well not recur.

(*c*) *Jesus criticizes the critical Pharisees.* As Jesus takes charge and interrogates the lawyers and Pharisees, it is very clear that they are the ones under scrutiny. Note the progression of the dramatic tension in the tale. In verse 1, they stood aloof in critical, hostile, skeptical silence; in verse 4, they chose to be silent rather than enter into debate with him about what the law allows; in verse 6, they were compelled to be silent.

Their final silence testifies that Jesus has won the day. They find his argument irrefutable. That is the most serious dimension to their indictment. They cannot counter Jesus' argument—but *they do not follow through!*

If what Jesus says is right, then also what Jesus does is right. That recognition requires fundamental rethinking not only about Torah and cult in general but also about spiritually acceptable Sabbath observance for each one of them in particular. Even more important, it demands such a radical revision of one's opinion about who Jesus is and what he is doing that one is compelled to capitulate before such persuasively powerful grace in action.

Kingdom Stationing (14:7–11)

Luke calls Jesus' teaching in this section "a parable," but it is not a parable in the technical sense. Rather it seems to be an allusive analogy that wants to draw a "from the lesser to the greater" comparison from social/religious occasions to one's "status" before God. If self-effacing, even exaggerated, modesty makes sense in assumptions about seating protocol at a wedding celebration, even more ought one to show prudent humility before Jesus, the empowered plenipotentiary of God, and the presence of God's royal rule he incarnates.

(*a*) *Humility promotes proper perception.* What is involved is more than a matter of manners. To leave it as an object lesson in social decorum, or as an example of a calculated ploy of social etiquette, is to miss the point. Unpretentious self-assessment is prerequisite both for perceiving the presence of divine power and for proper appreciation of the amazing grace of having been invited and of being present. How much more is one overcome as the awesome majesty of God, in exalting "the lowly" (1:52), receives, embraces, and escorts the humble to the table reserved for family.

It may seem unlikely that lawyers and Pharisees who had just been so thoroughly quelled by Jesus (vv. 1–6) should abruptly erupt in an unseemly scramble for seats of distinction. The narrative dissonance probably reflects the prior career of the two anecdotes as independent, self-contained stories that circulated separately in the fund of Jesus stories early Christians used.

(*b*) *Those judging become the ones judged.* The impact of the narrative context intensifies the characterization of the lawyers and the Pharisees begun in the prior tale. They assume postures and attitudes of power. They are there to judge Jesus. By that myopic arrogance, they expose themselves to judgment and repudiation by the royal power and authority present in the person of Jesus.

Who to Ask? (14:12–14)

With this third anecdote, the "host" responsible for the social/religious occasion comes even more prominently into focus than in the previous passage.

(*a*) *What determines who is to be invited?* What governs the host's decisions about who is to be welcomed? Personal acquaintance and affinities? Then those who are one's friends make up the guest list. Social obligation? Then the guests are those who have previously welcomed us. If it is social convention, then the guests are those who occupy a station comparable to that of the host and his family (or perhaps a tad higher, if social ambition is a factor). If racial solidarity is a governing consideration, then priority of place would go to those of the same tribe, or to those of an untainted lineage going as far back to the patriarchs as possible.

Religious affinity would restrict the assembly to fellow Pharisees, while political considerations might reduce the potential pool of attenders to only those within the Pharisaic party who supported the political program and aspirations with which this particular leader of the Pharisees was identified. In each instance, it is a boundary to the scope of the invitations extended that is defined by "those like us" or "those whom we would like to be like," and is fueled by anticipatory expectations of reciprocal recognition and honor.

(b) *Why was Jesus invited?* In a way, it is a backhanded compliment that Jesus gives, for under any of the possible considerations listed above Jesus would not have been included. That the ruler of the Pharisees had nonetheless invited him raised the possibility that perhaps the invitation had been prompted by recognition of the presence of the revivifying divine presence emanating from Jesus, a presence that radically reformulates all of those concerns out of which social conventions emerge and are defined. What is driving the host to choose whom to include in the invitation—the expectation of social commendation or political advancement by his contemporaries, or end-of-time approbation by God? Or, could it be gratitude for the currently enjoyed blessings from God?

A sermon on this section might explore limits to religious community that we maintain or remove:

A banquet is an occasion for religious fellowship. It offers opportunity for one who, enamored with the conviction of being claimed by God, broadens inclusively the borders of religious community occasioned by the hospitality of table-fellowship. The host has the chance to do for others what God through Jesus offers to do for the host. God has "filled the hungry with good things," (1:53; cf. 4:18–21; 7:22). Jesus invites the poor, the lame, the maimed, the blind, and the Pharisee, among others, which is why we, too, are there. Knowing this, we can do no other than to emulate his uncalculatingly glad reception of all kinds of persons into the people of God.

Jesus confronts his host—and the other guests, and us, too—not with a challenge to do charity but with a summons to promote inclusive community. "Come into my house and eat with me," the leader of the Pharisees asked Jesus, and Jesus wondered yearningly if he really knew what he was doing. "Come into my heart, Lord Jesus," we sing, and Jesus yearningly wonders about us, too.

When Asked, Who Comes? (14:15–24)

(a) *A banquet guest's pious exclamation.* The blurted beatitude (v. 15) voices a banal truism conforming to the messianic expectation current in popular piety. As the scene has been cast by Luke, it is offered in support of Jesus' immediately prior pronouncement (v. 14). (There is a catchword connection. The "blessed" of the verse 15 beatitude echoes the promise of Jesus in verse 14 that hospitality of the poor and disabled will result in "blessed"-ness.)

If the guest seated at table with Jesus really knew what he was saying and to whom he was saying it, that would have been something! Right there, at that very moment, he could experience what he was hoping for, if only he had the eyes to see perceptively. Luke expects us to conclude that he did not have a clue, as was implied by Jesus' response to his outburst. The parable illustrates Jesus' admonition of verse 13.

(b) *The peril of compromised priorities.* As the story goes, between the preparatory announcement that the planner of a banquet had sent out to those on his guest list to alert them to the impending occasion, and the second notice that the necessary preparations were complete and the time had arrived, the situations of those who had been invited had altered. It was not that their affairs were unimportant; it was that they had allowed their affairs to distract them, so that they lost interest in being included in the celebrative religious table-fellowship to which they had been summoned. "God's offer has priority not simply over our worst but also our best agendas" (Fred Craddock, *Luke,* Louisville, Ky.: John Knox Press, 1990, p. 179).

Preaching on the passage might develop along these lines:
The story makes a dramatic appeal for alertly aware, single-minded, focused devotion to serving the presence of divinely sovereign power. Luke commended such qualitative discipleship to his community even when they were less clear (as are we, too) about when the return of Jesus and the end-of-the-ages messianic feast on the Day of the Lord would occur.

God invites to the banquet those who know clearly, whatever their worldly situation, that their well-being depends entirely on God. For them, no change of circumstances can divert their devotion to the cause of God that Jesus is proclaiming. Jesus "cat-scanned" the authenticity of that guest's laudatory religious remark by listing as having been invited several categories of people (vv. 21–23) which would not immediately or easily have occurred to the guest offering the blessing exclamation. It was not the type of guest list he would have had in mind, either for the occasion of the feast that day or for the end-of-time heavenly banquet. The acid test for him and for the others at table, as well as for us, is whether we can picture ourselves in such a gathering, whether we can discern the ways we have made ourselves poor and maimed and blind and lame and marginalized on the periphery before God, whether we know with grateful clarity why we nevertheless are there at table with Jesus.

Much more than the matter of charitable, paternalistic inclusiveness is at stake. In the context of the story, the curt remark of verse 24 is contemptuous dismissal. When heard in the narrative context of the mission of Jesus and the occasion of his travel toward Jerusalem under the sign of the cross, it becomes an announcement both of the present urgency and of the impending dimensions of God's invitation for intimate religious fellowship. Disinterested reception of such an invitation with reference to the presence of the royal rule of God earns repudiating judgment.

UNEQUIVOCAL COMMITMENT (14:25–35)

In this section Luke reports a considerable qualification to the sweeping scope of the invitation that God through Jesus extends to people. Although the summons is offered widely, although the invitation is inclusive (vv. 13, 16, 21, 23), incorporation in the end-of-the-ages people of God is not automatic. Certain conditions and expectations accompany discipleship. Discipleship is demanding, commitment is costly, and Christ's claim tolerates no rival loyalties.

(*a*) *Traveling with Jesus under the sign of the cross is demanding.* Not only the disciples but "large crowds" were "traveling" with Jesus (v. 25). Luke gives us an oblique reminder here that all of this is occurring while Jesus is on the way to Jerusalem under the sign of the cross that looms before him. The hordes of people flocking along, however, did not know that Jesus' way to Jerusalem was under the sign of the cross, nor did they know what it meant, really, for them to accompany him along the way.

Jesus will not let that ambiguity prevail—he never does. Instead, he requires that any fellow travelers, including those already identified as disciples, must come to terms with the realization that if they continue to follow him who has set his face to go to Jerusalem (9:51), they are proceeding as much as is he under the sign of the cross.

(*b*) *Three illustrations of the extreme demands of discipleship.* Jesus cites three instances (vv. 26, 27, 33) that are illustrative, but not exhaustively descriptive, of the drastic demands of discipleship and includes two parabolic analogies (vv. 28–30, 31–32). Jesus pulls no punches. The issue is crucial enough to counsel that he forego a moderate approach to avoid shocking and repelling his listeners.

Desire for discipleship calls for radical single-mindedness, which, by supplanting all other demands for devotion and allegiance, conforms the will of the disciple to harmonious concurrence with the mind of Christ. Three illustrations of such unequivocal single-mindedness are:

1) willing subordination of family responsibilities to the all-consuming claim of Christ, verse 26: It is stated in radical form. To "hate" family members does not suggest that Jesus requires unnatural antipathy toward them. It does assert that the claim of Christ always has priority over all such loyalties, loves, and

commitments. That may well make it appear to others that followers of Jesus have despised family ties. The extreme language
underscores the destructive dimensions of divided loyalties that
can devastate devoted discipleship.

2) radical refocus away from self-service in favor of unqualified
commitment to the service of God, verse 27: "Carry the cross,"
which is reminiscent of the language in 9:23, means denial of
oneself, even to the most extreme measures and consequences.
The poignancy of the statement intensifies with the recognition
that Jesus himself is going steadfastly toward Jerusalem, and in
that intentionality is, already, carrying his own cross.

3) renunciation of reliance on what one has or controls, in order to
rely totally on the resources and the control of God, verse 33: It
is the critical issue raised by the call to faith. Surrender to the
control of Christ's power over us requires that we surrender control over all of that which gives us power over others or even
over our own condition and situation.

For the true disciple, any time the requirements of allegiance to Jesus
collide with the expectations of *any* other loyalties or commitments, God's
royal right to rule always prevails.

(*c*) *Analogies urging realistic assessment.* The two illustrative metaphorical analogies of "building a tower" and "going to war" (vv. 28–32) are typical of the Jewish wisdom tradition. They warn the listeners (the "large
crowds," the disciples, and us) not to follow Jesus on the way to Jerusalem
and Calvary too quickly, glibly, or spontaneously.

Suggestions for homiletical development might include:

We are admonished to engage in a careful, realistic, and anticipatory
self-examination and a preparatory self-testing as to whether we are ready
to embrace the extreme demands and experience the frequently daunting
consequences of devotion to God. We are to discover whether we have it
in us to be disciples of Christ. And the "it" has very little to do with our
religious discipline or spiritual determination. The "it" is the extent to
which we have surrendered to the power of the Spirit at work in us. Traveling with Jesus on the road to Jerusalem under the sign of the cross
requires us first to assess the extent to which we are prepared to depend
on this power to see us all the way through to the end (both the conclusion and the completion), no matter what. That alone sustained Jesus.

Lacking that, give it up! Forget it! Anything lacking the internal
dynamic that makes a thing what it is becomes worthless (vv. 34–35a). It
not only fails in its function, it also fails in its essence. So a double-

mindedly distracted disciple is the embodiment of deteriorated disciple-ship—worthless! Such "disciples" are ineffective in any service rendered to the cause of Christ. Their ambivalence impedes the success of the cause of Christ by giving misleading testimony about the radical cost of commitment, and their equivocacy effectively repudiates the prior decision to become a disciple.

Luke's portrait of Jesus has him express it in the extreme given the urgency of the opportune moment. Pastoral sensitivity may want to moderate the rhetoric out of consideration for any who are "on the way but not yet committed." Such moderation, however, needs to be informed and tempered by a similar sense of urgency and must not obscure the radical, even dangerous, dimensions always implicit in Christian discipleship.

The one with "ears to hear" (v. 35b) is not the one who is paying attention to what is being said. "Ears to hear" is the openness and sensitivity to hear with comprehension and discernment—and the resolution to alter one's life accordingly.

JOY AT FINDING WHAT IS LOST (15:1–32)

In this section Luke recounts three stories Jesus had told, all of which are built around the tremendous relief and exhilarating joy experienced when that which has been lost is restored. He tied the three stories closely together through the use of common motifs: "lost-found" (vv. 4, 6, 8–9, 24, 32), "rejoice, joy" (vv. 6, 7, 9, 10, 21–24, 32), and repentance (vv. 7, 10, 18). The cumulative impact of the three stories, related one after the other with their common emphasis on "joy," intensifies geometrically.

(a) *Criticism raised against Jesus.* Hostile criticism characterizes the narrative context (vv. 1–2). The person and message of Jesus were proving attractive to "tax collectors and sinners." That provoked resentful complaints from "the Pharisees and the scribes" who protested that Jesus was always welcoming people widely regarded as religious pariahs. (See 5:29–30 for an earlier instance of similar criticism.) The contrast of their pique with the acclaim of those "tax collectors and sinners" who were "coming near to listen to him" illustrates the admonition of 14:35: The Pharisees and the scribes simply did not have "ears to hear." In the Jewish scriptural narrative, when Jews "grumbled" it was an indication of their faithless opposition to the often startling ways God chose to provide for their most fundamental needs (Num. 11:1ff.; 14:27ff.; etc.).

The Pharisees and the scribes protested that Jesus' behavior flaunted his impiety. He not only consorted with those whom the Jewish authorities defined as irreligious, he actually entered into religious table-fellowship with them.

(b) *Three stories that answer the criticism.* Luke presented the three-story sequence as Jesus' response to counteract that charge and to defend his ministry to the outcast tax collectors and sinners. Associating in table-fellowship with tax collectors and sinners does not taint the integrity of Jesus' spirituality. Rather, Jesus sits at table with them to benefit *their* spiritual condition.

"Religious" Jews may reject them out of hand, but God had not rejected them. God missed them. God yearned for their repentance and return. When they were restored, God was glad and celebrated, and God invited others to celebrate that, too. If "religious" Jews were oblivious—or, worse, hostile to this clearly disclosed will of God—it simply demonstrated that they were also lost. However, they did not recognize, much less acknowledge and repent of, their lostness.

The common application appended to the first two stories (vv. 7, 10) extends over and impacts the third. The actual joy of the father over the penitent return and restoration of the younger son and the father's potential joy should the elder son also repent are analogous to God's joy when, through Jesus, someone who had renounced God's sovereignty is restored to a lovingly obedient and trusting relationship with God.

Note that the motif of the interest of God in those who are popularly regarded as "the despised of God," so prominent in the three stories in this chapter, recurs repeatedly throughout the remainder of the travel narrative. The repetition intensifies our anticipation of the events pending in Jerusalem by which God through Jesus welcomes all of those "lost ones" who yearn to be found.

We will consider the first two stories together because they are so similar, and the third separately because it is so famous.

Finding the Lost Sheep and Coin (15:3–10)

Both "The Lost Sheep" (vv. 3–7) and "The Lost Coin" (vv. 8–10), exploit the common human experience of losing and finding—the sense of apprehensive anxiety over that which has been lost and the contrasting rush of relief when it is found. Luke moderates that contrast somewhat because, for him and for his community, the man and the woman who search for what has been lost are so suggestive of Jesus and his mission (compare with the use of the shepherd image in Ezek. 34:12, Isa. 40:11, etc.) that doubt about the lost being found is out of the question. (Note "*until* he/she finds it," vv. 4c, 8c, and "and *when* he/she has found it," vv. 5a, 9a, and compare the Matthean counterpart to the first parable: "*if* he finds it," Matt. 18:13, where the finding is less certain.)

(a) *Celebration upon recovery of the lost.* Because Luke wanted his community to see clearly that both stories are making the same point he imposed the same structure on both stories. So we find the man, having found the lost sheep, not returning it to the flock, but instead carrying it back to the village for a restoration celebration (vv. 5f). That matches the similar celebration in the second story (v. 9)—and in the third story, too, see verses 22ff.—but at the expense of implying that the rest of the flock are abandoned unattended out "in the wilderness" (v. 4), an exceedingly precarious and dangerous place for sheep to be left to fend for themselves. Not only is the wilderness a harsh and hostile environment, the wilderness is that part of creation most visibly under the control of the devil (see 4:1ff.).

(b) *The "one to ninety-nine" contrast.* Another interesting modification Luke made to his version of the lost sheep story is that he moved the hyperbolic contrast of "one" and "ninety-nine" away from the experience of intense relief at the moment of finding (comp. Matt. 18:13) and into the application external to the story proper (v. 7, and, by implication, v. 10). There it is asserted that God is more pleased over one transgressor who mends her or his ways than over ninety-nine pious persons who never have transgressed. That sounds like "bad theology" until we remember that the narrative context has Jesus telling these stories to critical Pharisees and scribes who know how serious the transgressions of "tax collectors and sinners" (and, by association, of Jesus himself) are, but who are oblivious to how distant, how "lost," they themselves are. They are those "ninety-nine" who smugly and arrogantly think that they are already righteous (cf. 10:29; 16:15; also see 11:37–52), and thereby, to stretch the analogy, have chosen to remain by themselves, vulnerable, in the wilderness without even imagining, much less taking part in, the restoration celebration.

(c) *The divine initiative.* What should we make of the connection between the initiative motif (the man "goes after," v. 4c; the woman "searches carefully," v. 8c) and the response of "joy in heaven," (v. 7), and "joy in the presence of the angels of God," (v. 10), over one repentant sinner? The argument is from the lesser to the greater. Such human concern over potential economic disaster is completely understandable. How much more is God concerned, and eager through Jesus, to seek out all tax collectors and sinners, *and* all Pharisees and scribes? (The motif will recur in the third story, too—see v. 20.) The intensity with which God seeks the lost has been the burden of Luke's entire narrative, and is being prophetically enacted even as Jesus determinedly travels toward the Jerusalem cross. But one must, through repentance, choose to benefit from being thus found.

The critical issue raised by both of these parables was not whether Jesus will modify his methods to conform to "acceptable" behavior as defined by religious authority and custom. The crucial question was whether the Pharisees and the scribes—who previously had grumbled about Jesus' behavior—could be moved to participate in the joyous celebration over the restoration of a tax collector and sinner. Even more to the point, what was at stake was whether they could recognize themselves in the symbol of that which had been lost but was now found. By their obdurate criticism of Jesus—and, even more, by their refusal to respond to his person and message in common cause with those whom they had schooled themselves to despise—they demonstrated their solidarity with those opposed to God, and showed themselves to be "at home" in the devil's wilderness.

The Loving Father (15:11–32)

This third parable of "the lost being sought and found" builds on the two previous stories (see the preceding section) and dramatically advances the perspective they present. Historically dubbed "The Prodigal Son," it is one of the most treasured stories from the public ministry of Jesus and ranks with the birth narrative (2:1ff.) and "The Good Samaritan" (10:30ff.) among the most widely known stories from Luke's Gospel.

(a) *Central emphasis on the father's love.* The traditional title notwithstanding (there are really two lost sons mentioned in the parable), the story's main focus is not on either of the sons but on the father. That recognition prevents us from considering the story to be a rare form of parable that has two points instead of the more common one point. Rather, the one point of the parable—the durative quality of the father's love no matter what—is viewed from two perspectives.

The father loved both sons. He took the initiative to reach out to both (vv. 20, 28). Love so motivated his single-minded action toward each that he acted without consideration of public opinion or cultural restraint.

Out of love for the younger son, the father hitched up his robe above his knees, ignoring the inclination to maintain his own public dignity, and galloped down the lane in full sight of his neighbors as the son deferentially came through the village toward him.

Out of love for the elder son, the father left the festivities, deferring his social responsibilities as host of the celebration, to try to negotiate the elder son's participatory inclusion. He offered his sons, equally, his compassion and generosity, not as evidence or proof of his love but as the fruits of his love (vv. 12, 22, 31).

(*c*) *Both sons are shocked.* We should be hesitant about regarding the moment when the younger son "came to himself" in the pig sty in the far country as an instance of instant spiritual insight. He simply became realistic about his situation and what the options for improving his condition really were. His calculations and fantasized pleading were not at all informed by a grateful grasp of the inexhaustible depth of his father's love. He was as stunned as the rest at the precipitously boisterous way his father cut his self-serving pleading short to embrace him and restore him and designate his return the occasion for a feast honoring him.

The elder son was equally shocked at his father's behavior—and outraged at the imbalanced immoderation of the father's love. It had never occurred to him that he would even see his younger brother again, much less have to endure his restoration as an honored family member. He had written him off completely. As far as he was concerned, when the younger son abandoned the family, the family membership was reduced by one.

Once he learned what was happening, he could not bring himself even to name the younger son "brother." In sharp contrast to the father's generous response, the elder son complained bitterly against the younger son—*and* against the father's injustice (vv. 27–30). That is more than just griping. People do that when they cannot stand to come to terms with the ways in which God chooses to deal graciously with human alienation. It was the kind of activity (v. 2) that had occasioned the relating of this collection of stories in the first place. (Note that in v. 27 the servant gave accurate testimony concerning the grace event that was being celebrated but left out the altar call!)

If the younger son is a symbol for the "tax collectors and sinners" whom Jesus sought out for God, the elder son stands for the Pharisees and the scribes, then and now, who murmur. He is like those who are so preoccupied with guarding the boundaries of God's grace they do not notice that with the very act of line-drawing they exclude themselves. The extent to which one shares God's joy discloses the presence of glad, loving, gratefully obedient service—or its absence.

Sermon suggestions on these "lost and found" stories include:

1. Being lost within the faith community. Try to help others understand that, by means of this section of the narrative, Luke expected his community not simply to see itself on Jesus' side, making common cause with him against all those who are viciously imperceptive. Rather, the community is also to consider what in its corporate life corresponds to the Pharisaic attitudes and scribal perspectives that caused them to become belligerent to the cause of Christ at the service of religion. When do we resent God's undeserved goodness toward others instead of being joyfully celebrative? What makes us hostile rather than open to the option of being embraced by and embracing that loving, restorative presence?

Only when the community of the Easter faith comes to grips with those faithless dimensions in its communal life will we correctly see ourselves in the lost sheep, the lost coin, and *both* lost brothers—that is, among the tax collectors and sinners of our day whom Jesus continues to welcome and to invite for religious table-fellowship, and among those who disdain them.

2. Being interpreted by the stories. Do you know that God and the angels rejoiced like that father over you when you were "found"? And so did others of God's faithful people?

Do you rejoice like that over another who returns to God? No matter who that one is or how that one is regarded by others, even perhaps has been regarded by you?

Are you sullen and resentful, constructing barriers between yourself and those whom God would give to you to bless you and to be blessed by you? Even perhaps resentful toward God, holding God to account, and requiring God to set things right?

Are you—as one who has been received, welcomed, kissed with forgiveness and restored—as exuberantly eager to emulate the initiative of God, announcing to brothers and sisters even while they are still in the far country not yet come to themselves that God grieves for their grief and yearns to kiss them with forgiveness, too?

Are you more inclined to share joy over the restoration of a lost sheep or the recovery of a lost coin, the location of missing car keys or the discovery of a banking error in your favor, than you are to share joy over renewed fellowship with a notoriously degenerate human being, perhaps even one of your own kin?

And who is it who, through his stories, forces you to raise these questions about yourself? How does what you make of him affect how you answer this entire series of questions?

USE OF WEALTH AS A PARADIGM FOR DISCIPLESHIP (16:1–31)

Luke now describes Jesus addressing the issue of the faithful use of wealth in service to God, prompted perhaps by the negative example of the younger son in the previous parable (15:13), which certainly was not the way to employ one's assets in the service of God's royal rule.

The chapter divides easily into two subsections (vv. 1–13, 14–31), both of which contain stories that begin "There was a rich man . . ." (vv. 1, 19) and include applications that extend beyond the primary topic of the faithful use of money (vv. 8b–13, 14–18). Jesus addressed the first section to his disciples (v. 1); the second he directed toward the Pharisees (v. 14).

Discipleship demands singular devotion to God and exclusive commitment to Jesus and to the cause of God that Jesus serves. Such genuine devotion and commitment tolerates no rivals, no alternative loyalties, no distractions. That principle excludes moderating considerations dictated by religion, ethnic origins, and heritage; it excludes family, tribal, regional, and national loyalties; it excludes cultic and cultural custom; it certainly excludes being possessed by one's possessions. This is a motif that occurs frequently in Luke's Gospel (cf. 1:53; 3:11, 13f.; 4:18; 6:20f., 29, 33–35; 12:15–31, 33f.; 14:12–14; etc.).

Parable of the Manipulative Manager (16:1–13)

The primary concern of this story is the well-considered uses the disciple makes of material possessions to advance instead of impede growth in fidelity to God. But there is also a *carpe diem* extended application of this principle to cover all of the moral decisions confronting the disciple, decisions to be made solely under the governance of the One whom the disciple embraces as the legitimate object of loyalty.

(a) The story of the resourceful manager. Take the example of the suspect manager (vv. 1–8). Jesus commends the manager's method, not the solution. The manager was prudently practical in a crisis situation. It is not the manager's fiscal manipulations Jesus commends to his disciples to imitate, but his astuteness, his cleverness. The manager realistically grasped the extreme character of the crisis into which he suddenly and unexpectedly was plunged. He shrewdly assessed and exploited his best option for seeing the crisis through not merely to survival but to his best advantage. The manager's timely, ingenious program provided an alternative to a suddenly uncertain but vividly longed for future.

The master was impressed at the manager's "eleventh hour" resourcefulness. Jesus hoped that his disciples were at least that resourceful, too. It is another instance of the familiar analogical argument from the lesser to the greater. If the manager could so cunningly provide for his next several years' maintenance, how much more should disciples school themselves to order their affairs and relationships to conform to their convictions about a life that partakes of the quality of the eternal as Jesus was disclosing that life to them?

Luke accumulated additional independently circulated sayings of Jesus about the faithful stewardship of material possessions and appended them as extended applications to the story (vv. 9–13). In yet another display of his extraordinary literary skill, he wove these appended sayings together with an intricate pattern of multiple catchwords (which is, unfortunately, more visible in the Greek text than in any of the English versions.)

(*b*) *Three exhortations to use wealth for advancing God's purposes.* Verse 9 urges us to use wealth in such a way as not to compromise or destroy our participation in the future of God that Jesus opens to us, but rather to intensify our dedication to serving that future. The crux of the faith challenge is one of accurately discerning and affirming precisely in what it is that your future truly consists.

Wealth ("dishonest" is an unfortunate translation—the phrase means "worldly possessions," not illegal gain) is not the proper object of your devotion but is a convincing medium with which you may demonstrate and live out "what it is to which," or, better, "who it is to whom," your devotion is truly offered. From that perspective, "make friends for yourselves" does not mean that you are to buy the approbation of your contemporaries or the loyalty of those whom you help by generous charity. God and Jesus are the only friends you are to need or to know. Out of love for them, use your wealth to serve the love they reveal for you.

There is a congruity to a person's life (vv. 10f.). Whom you really serve—yourself, Satan, God, whomever—defines your operative values and determines your choices. What are the "true riches?" The "true riches" are the "friends" who long to "welcome you into the eternal homes" (v. 9); "true riches" is "what is your own" (v. 12); "true riches" is the absolutely exclusive option to "serve God" (v. 13).

Verse 12 is particularly interesting. One would expect it to say the opposite of what it does. After all, if you cannot arrange your own affairs wisely or manage your own resources prudently and profitably, who is likely to entrust what they value to your control? Jesus asks the opposite, however, which we can understand only if we look beyond the example of material wealth.

In the context of all that is represented by the journey to Jerusalem, "what belongs to another" alludes to the need for the sustained fidelity of the disciples to the cause of Christ down the stretch as the really tough times loom ahead. "What is your own" refers to their subsequent participation in or exclusion from the completion of the eternal purposes of God as that is to occur in the triumphant resurrection.

The message of verse 13—that how you use material possessions is a clear indication of whom it is that you devotedly serve—seems redundant and anti-climactic, but not if we probe the underlying perspective.

A stewardship presentation might consider the following:

For what is "wealth" a metaphor? Leverage, power, influence, reputation, abilities and skills, creativity, any and everything "the children of this age" value, admire, respect, and reward? As a disciple, you have access to and participate in those. Use them well—gospel-defined well! Exploit the full opportunities for service of God in each moment, no matter how "worldly" and materialistic, no matter how mundane or seemingly insignificant. Each moment requires consecration or threatens disaster.

Be self-serving as cleverly as was the shrewd steward, only take a great deal more care to understand from the perspective of God's eternity in what way you serve yourself best. That understanding is finally grasped in the paradoxical surrender of the desire to best serve yourself in order that you may be liberated to serve God alone. It is not dissimilar to what was at stake for Jesus in the wilderness as he, too, contended with Satan (4:3–13).

Righteousness and Misdirected Trust (16:14–31)

Luke shifts the narrative focus away from the disciples. Jesus' remarks now are directed toward a group of sneering Pharisees (v. 14). They were not impressed with the radical contrast he had just drawn between "serving God" and "serving wealth" (v. 13). In the Jewish scriptures that the Pharisees took great delight both in repeating and conforming to, it was a widely affirmed spiritual teaching that prosperity was visible confirmation of the favor in which God held the observant righteous (cf. Deut. 28:1–14).

(a) *Jesus deplores Pharisaic self-confidence.* Jesus responded by sharply indicting the Pharisees for being far too selective in their Bible reading. Wealth does not necessarily indicate righteousness. The testimony of prosperity is ambiguous at best. True valuation concerning one's righteousness before God is demonstrated far more persuasively by other evidence—say, compassionate and generous charity and single-minded devotion to God no matter what occurred, Job-like, to one's fortunes.

In the moment of kingdom crisis, the money-loving Pharisees, unlike the dishonest steward (at the chapter's beginning), are not shrewd. Their preference for self-service over selfless service of God's royal rule is displayed by their hypocritical use of money to enhance the esteem in which they were held by others. They were so eager to appear upright that they neglected what was necessary for them to be held upright (to be justified) by God.

The rich man in the story Jesus told (vv. 19ff.) would have agreed with the Pharisees. Success and the prosperity it produced were convincingly calming indications of being sheltered by God's good favor.

Jesus saw that such an opinion, by misperceiving the ethical and religious ambiguity of wealth, was really an insidious sign of impious trust in one's own sufficiency. It self-servingly promoted a reliance so inappropriate and so demonically deceptive that only the indigent, the "have-nots" (such as Lazarus), were liberated from its tangled web and free to live in absolute reliance on God alone. That was not callously to praise poverty. Rather, Jesus wants us to acknowledge that the less you have control over, the less encumbered and impeded you are when discerning who it is to whom you are to surrender the right of control over you.

A sermon on this part of the passage might consider:

Luke did not include the story to encourage his community (or us, either, for that matter) to sit in the grandstand watching Jesus trouncing those self-righteous, hypocritical Pharisees and cheering him on in his assault against them. Rather than promoting Pharisee bashing (whomever our particularly favorite "Pharisee target" might be), the passage requires us to discern the "Pharisee within." What is there within us that responds with sneers rather than with remorse and that compels us to employ religious arguments, even scripture quotations, to justify idol-loyalties that compete with the exclusive allegiance we owe to God alone?

(*b*) *Jesus' ministry does not negate the law and the prophets.* The inner logic of verse 16 juxtaposing "the law and the prophets" with "the good news . . . is proclaimed" is not one of contrast but of complement. "The law and the prophets" (the latter of whom, John the Baptist, was not only "the last" but also among the greatest—see 7:26–28) is not being supplanted by Jesus' preaching about God's rule, but rather is thereby being extended and enhanced.

Those who are truly attuned to the law and the prophets will know who Jesus is and will recognize that what God is accomplishing through Jesus is precisely that to which both law and prophets pointed in anticipation. Jesus' invitation to participate in the restoration of God's royal rule is a compelling summons that requires great effort to resist. (Several English versions, including the NRSV, distractingly distort the passive form "is constrained, forced, compelled" into an active "everyone tries to enter it by force.")

The hyperbolic impact of verse 17 builds on the observation that gospel does not contradict law; law serves gospel. The realm of God is not limited to those who have been taught to observe the law of Moses. Still, for those law observers for whom the will of God is clearly discerned in the context of Jewish religious practice, Torah observance continues in force as disciplined testimony to experienced grace. That is as its rightful role with reference to God's covenant with Abraham always had been.

The legal example in verse 18 illustrates verse 17 and reinforces what has already been said in the chapter. *Any* infidelity, whether in marriage relationships (v. 18), or in divided and therefore compromised loyalties (v. 13), or in phony, ostentatious religious posturing (vv. 14f.), is outright rejection of the constraining claim of the presence of divine regal power.

(*c*) *The first part of the story of the rich man and Lazarus.* The first portion (vv. 19–26) of the story Jesus told about a drastic reversal of fortunes in the afterlife (vv. 19–31) is strikingly similar to stories told in other cultures and locales of the Mediterranean world. It is the kind of story designed to reconcile people to their lot in life who have gotten the short end of the stick.

However, Luke gained considerably more mileage out of the first part of the story simply by setting it in the narrative context at this particular place. The rich man was not shrewd (v. 8), did not make the right friends (v. 9), was not faithful in a very little (v. 10), nor over what belongs to another (v. 12). He served wealth and despised God (v. 13), and so, after his death, found himself to be an abomination in the sight of God who knew his heart (v. 15). The story echoes a perspective often expressed by Jesus earlier in Luke's narrative (see 6:20, 24).

It is striking that the rich man who had such extravagantly abundant possessions in this life asked so little of Father Abraham (and of Lazarus, too). Yet they would not and could not do even the little he requested. The reversal of fortunes in the afterlife has to do with more than just material possessions and physical comfort/torment. He who had relied on wealth in place of relying on God found himself in a situation for eternity where he had no one on whom to rely—not God, not himself, not even Father Abraham, the founding patriarch of Israel, though that one does know him as a "child." This first part of the story dramatizes the exchange of verses 14f.

(*d*) *Part 2: The rich man's awakened concern.* With verses 27–31, the story takes a new turn. The plight of this self-preoccupied person stirred him to concern for others—in this instance, his brothers—who were entangled in the same self-delusion as he had been. "For pity's sake, send Lazarus to warn them. Let him testify to them that God is dead serious about people's obedience. Let Lazarus bear witness to them that God is not fooling around!" This now provides a dramatized commentary on verses 16f.

The request is refused. The rich man's brothers, like him, already have the warning, the witness, the testimony of Moses (law), and the prophets. Moses and the prophets make it quite clear that the righteous are to rely only on God. Not even the testimony of a messenger risen from the dead will be any more persuasive to someone already deaf to the will of God revealed in law and prophets. Having heard Moses and the prophets, if you cannot get it there you are not likely ever to get it.

A sermon on the story might expand on what follows:

Luke surely expected his community to connect the conclusion of this story with the church's proclamation of Jesus' death and resurrection. The testimony of the Jewish scriptures was still true, yet Luke's colleagues in the faith had experienced people who would believe neither the testimony of scripture nor the witness of Christians to the good news that God has raised One from the dead who not only in his words but by his life demonstrated that God was dead serious about human obedience. Even more pointedly, the story converged with their own inclinations to equivocate. They, too, had Moses and the prophets; they even had the witness of the greatest of them all, John the Baptist; they had the testimony of Jesus' preaching of the good news of the restored rule of God; they had the Easter proclamation of him raised by God from the dead. How thoroughly had it "taken"? How single-minded were they in their willingness to place their trust exclusively in God? How consistent were they in relying on God alone, wherever they were, whatever happened, no matter what? How about us?

DISCIPLINED DISCIPLESHIP (17:1–10)

Luke redirects Jesus' attention back to the disciples who have been the primary audience for the prolonged interval of intensified instruction extending over the entirety of the journey from Galilee to Jerusalem (9:51–19:27). He grouped four sayings together that surely circulated as independent *logia* of Jesus in the oral tradition of early Christianity.

The grouping is not casual or haphazard but rather displays subtle movement in the process of nurturing for effective discipleship. The first two sayings (vv. 1–2; 3–4) are about what the true disciple is to do. The third saying (vv. 5–6) exposes the disciples' feelings of inadequacy to do their duty as disciples, which Jesus sets aside as unreal. In the concluding saying (vv. 7–10), Jesus indicates that whenever disciples did what they were supposed to do but did not think they were able to do, that is no reason for self-congratulation. Serving others on behalf of the renewing reign of God is what faithful discipleship is all about.

(*a*) *Undisciple-like behavior.* The first saying has a pronounced reverse spin to it. The designation "little ones" was a term that early Christians often used as a special label for recent converts. We should suspect that this meaning may be intended anytime we encounter the term in early Christian literature, as we do here in verse 2. The phrase in verse 1 which the NRSV translates "occasions for stumbling" ("temptations to sin" in the RSV) is a more vivid expression that carries the idea of traps deliberately set with the intent to beguile or deceive and thereby ensnare.

The first saying speaks, then, of activity that is exactly the opposite from what one would expect of a true disciple. A person who with malicious intent deliberately causes a new and therefore especially vulnerable believer to be lured into sin is a person who serves those powers and authorities who have usurped God's right to rule in human lives. That recognition accounts for the savage severity of the consequences of such hostile activity. It is the dark, obverse side to that mutual responsibility Christians who are given to each other by God bear for one another within the faith community. Faithful disciples must act in exactly the opposite way.

(*b*) *True disciples act to restore.* The first saying sets up the contrast to the second saying (vv. 3–4). Rather than serving as agents through whom new converts succumb to the entrapping snares of sin and thereby violate the new, life-giving relationship God has just established with them, disciples are to exercise pastoral oversight, support, and nurture. The scope of forgiveness of the true servant of God reflects the unlimited forgiveness of God that servant has experienced. To violate such pastoral responsibility betrays solidarity with those who would intentionally entrap believers (which gives force to the "be on your guard" admonition in v. 3a).

The "rebuke" the disciples are to address to the sinning "disciple" is more than just corrective reproach. It is that act of supernatural power that repudiates and expels those forces which have sought to wrest control of creation from God. Luke uses the same term often for the verbal act of cleansing exorcism in preparation for the restoration of the rule of God (cf. 4:35, 39, 41, etc.). As such, it is already a summons to repentance. So disciples are to maintain discipline in the church, as agents for admonition to repentance, mirroring in their manner of conduct toward new converts and, by extension, all believers that same inexhaustibility of forgiveness which, in Jesus, they experience from God themselves. If God does not keep tally of forgiven human transgression, how much less ought we?

(*c*) *The quality of one's faith is critical.* As what Jesus has just had to say to the disciples about their responsibilities and their accountability sank in, Luke imagines them awed by the enormity of it all and not at all sure that they had enough of what it took within them to bring it off. (Luke used "apostles" to refer to the inner circle of disciples in verse 5 as he did frequently elsewhere in his narrative, but it is particularly appropriate here since he had the post-Easter community so clearly in mind.) "Increase our faith," they pleaded.

Jesus responded that even if their faith were less than it actually was, the unimaginable was possible when they trustingly and confidently acted on it. The minutest amount of authentic faith makes possible results that a dependence on any other resource would discover to be out of the question. That has already come to expression in the real requirement of forgiveness of the repentant sinner in verses 3–4.

A sermon suggestion on this saying follows:

The issue is not the quantity or extent of a person's faith. The need is not for *more* faith but for actions consistent with that faith with which one has already been blessed by God. The confident implementation of activity engendered by the faith we have deserves greater priority than the dismay we experience at our incomprehension, our lack of conviction, our resistance to rely absolutely on the One who has given us the faith we have. We have not begun to exhaust the potential for advancing God's intended good for creation for which the faith we own now empowers us, as imperfect, inadequate, and unreliable as it may sometimes seem.

Do not underestimate and therefore worry about the extent of the faith resources available to equip and empower you to meet the difficult demands of discipleship. Faith that issues in faithful action and informs it has far greater potential than you can imagine. Through the faith you already have (by which God has led you to become disciples and continues to maintain you in your discipleship), God can accomplish extravagant, unbelievable wonders. If faith, put to work, is capable of accomplishing the most unlikely, even absurd things, how much more should one vigorously and confidently exploit its potential for the advancement of God's saving purposes?

(*d*) *Discipleship and the master/servant relationship.* The fourth and final, more extended saying puts the extravagant demands of faithful discipleship—and the implied rewards that such extreme efforts on behalf of the saving program of God might lead one to anticipate—back into perspective. The inappropriateness of exaggerated underestimations of one's faith potential are balanced by equally inappropriate expectations of rewards for faithful obedience. Serving God is its own reward. Being called by God to such service is already so rich, so great, so fundamental and comprehensive a gift that nothing else is either needed or proper.

Jesus exploits the analogy of the master/slave relationship by offering a reversal of roles that could only be heard as ridiculous. In the economic/cultural institution of slavery, the lord does not wait on the slave at table; the master does not serve the servant. A servant is a servant, whether out in the fields or in the house, or both, whether such indenture would seem just in another context or not. Servants serve rather than expecting to be served. There is no virtue or merit in doing that, not even in doing that well. That is simply what a slave does.

A homiletical application of this saying might emerge from the following:

Consider the analogy of the master/slave relationship. That is particularly difficult for us to grasp as a positive model. It is difficult not simply because of the historical distance we have to the economic institution, and the uneasiness we feel because the attitudes engendered back then still haunt and corrode the quality of our culture. It is also difficult because liberation from oppression at every level receives so much emphasis these days.

In the first century C.E., people believed that any master could rightly expect absolute obedience from a slave-servant. Jesus urged that a similar view should shape our understanding of discipleship. When the efforts of diligent discipleship, even while accomplishing the impossible, are measured against what God has done for us in Jesus Christ, then disciple duty is doing only what is due. More than that, discipling is done not because God deserves it but because God rules and the disciple is God's slave. Fidelity in the duties of discipleship provides no ground for triumphalism, or for feelings of moral superiority, or for anticipation of special appreciation or future reward owed by God because the disciple has discipled so well.

A servant serves the master; that is what a servant does. It does not deserve special notice. Nor would one expect the roles to be reversed. It is, ironically, only in the context of the divine economy of God's rule that such a role reversal is thinkable, even reverent (cf. 22:17–19). Our astonished comprehension of the servanthood of Jesus, who came not to be served (although he was master) but to serve, shapes the self-understanding by his servant disciples of that servanthood to which God calls us in Jesus Christ.

TEN LEPERS CLEANSED, ONE THANKFUL (17:11–19)

Luke prefaces this story about Jesus' healing of the ten lepers by reminding his readers that Jesus and the disciples were "on the way to Jerusalem" (v. 11, cf. 9:51; 13:22). He expects us to recall that the trip was undertaken and continues to be shaped by the impending threat of the cross (cf. 9:31, 44; also see 18:31–33). That perspective, which casts the theological presupposition against which all of the stories related in the "journey account" are to be understood, controls this account, too.

(a) *The "literary geography" of the account.* If you have a Bible atlas open, you may be puzzled to discover that Luke's reference to their route progressing "between Samaria and Galilee" simply does not compute. Surely they should have gotten farther than that by now (see 9:51–52, 56; 10:1, 38, etc.)

We need to remember that the journey motif, while certainly having theological significance, is primarily a literary device Luke used to tie together into a sequential narrative an impressive array of independent stories about Jesus in addition to those Mark had used in his Gospel. The phrase "between Samaria and Galilee" is literary geography that provides an appropriate narrative context to introduce this story.

Scholars rightly alert us that echoes of the story of Elisha healing the Syrian general, Naaman, of leprosy (2 Kings 5:10–14) helped to shape this story. Luke would expect his community to recall that Jesus had referred to that story from the Jewish scriptures in the sermon he preached in the synagogue at Nazareth to inaugurate his public ministry (4:27).

(*b*) *The lepers accost Jesus.* People were scared to death of leprosy in those days. They knew less about it and had less control over it than we do over AIDS today. There were detailed and complex regulations defined for protecting the community (see Lev. 13–14).

These ten lepers knew the regulations and prohibitions, and they observed them. Isolated from participating in the social life of the village, they properly kept their distance at the entrance to the village and shouted to warn the unwary not to come too near, but also (no law that said they could not) to solicit alms from any who were moved by religious charity or human compassion.

Still, their cry as Jesus approached, "Have mercy on us!" had a different tone than was usually there. There was the inflection of a faint glimmer of spiritual perception. They knew something of who Jesus was. When they saw him, they called him by name; further, they named him "Master" (v. 13). Their imploring for alms resulted in *so much more* than a few coppers. They received instead unexpected and unhoped for cleansing and healing. One of them at least gained inclusion and solidarity right then with the end-time people sustained under the royal rule of God.

(*c*) *The lepers follow Jesus' directive.* Well, not exactly "right then." They all had to make their move in response to the initiative of God. When Jesus "saw" them, he discerned the true cause and extent of their polluted isolation with a perceptive clarity that far surpassed their own. But all he told them to do was to go and get themselves examined by a priest. (The religious inconsistency to the story, namely that Jesus would be so insensitive as to send a Samaritan for Levitical examination to Jewish priests instead of a Samaritan priest, or that the Samaritan would have gone without protest, is beside the point.) Jesus had not given them alms as they had hoped. Still, the only purpose in going to the priests was for them to get certified, according to Levitical regulation, that they were no longer contaminated with the dread disease and that they were therefore eligible for restoration to full community participation.

"As they went they were made clean" (v. 14b), which was a considerably different and far profounder "mercy" than that for which they had asked. We should note, without necessarily assigning it to Luke's intent, that the transforming experience of cleansing "as they went" parallels the deeper theological significance of Jesus' "on the way to Jerusalem" (v. 11—the two verbs are variant forms of the same verbal root).

Nor should we overlook Luke's implied critique on any exclusive devotion to ritual observance, even for all the "right" religious reasons, that obscures accurate perception of the presence of the saving Messiah. All ten had asked for mercy, and all ten received mercy in the form of healing—far more than they had asked. Only one out of the ten received mercy beyond mercy.

That one out of the ten, having been seen by Jesus, "saw" the real significance of the cleansing and returned to confirm the blessing, and he received the full extent of the mercy Jesus was offering. The Samaritan saw with spiritual perception and, turning back, was converted and came to Jesus praising God, thereby joining those who, from the beginning, praised God for Jesus (cf. 2:13f., 20; etc.).

(*d*) *Solidarity of suffering and solidarity of faith.* There were ten lepers. But one of them, (the thankful one—v. 15b), was a Samaritan (v. 16b), a "foreigner" (v. 18b), not one of their own at all, not one who "belonged." The other nine were Jews, who, ordinarily, would have avoided all contact with a despised Samaritan.

It must have been really tough to be both a Samaritan in the company of Jews and a leper. Still, the dread disease that severed them all from social intercourse with their own brought them together into a fellowship of similar suffering with one whom their religious and social prejudices would otherwise have counseled them to ostracize and avoid. Misery does indeed love company, and necessity does make for strange bedfellows.

Ten were lepers; one was additionally Samaritan. It is another instance where those most frequently judged peripheral and even despicable by human standards are central to the saving purposes of God. (See the Good Samaritan—10:30ff.; Dives and Lazarus—16:19ff. Luke has testified previously to the precedence of a non-Jew over Jews in the perception of the presence of divine, royal power—see 7:2ff.)

Nine *Jewish* lepers and one *Samaritan* leper. In extreme adversity, those distinctions were no longer important. What the ten shared in common misery dissolved those considerations that ordinarily would have kept them estranged. Surprisingly, the same is true at times of extreme opportunity also—such as the opportune moment of encounter with the presence of the restoring and renewing power of God.

The Samaritan "saw" and returned to be included. That could have been true for all ten. If those nine cleansed Jews had been more sensitive to their solidarity in suffering with the Samaritan, they might have been led back by him in a solidarity of thankfulness. They and he could arrive together in high expectation to prostrate themselves at Jesus' feet and to call him "Master" with much deeper meaning. Then they, together with the Samaritan, would have been given access to saving solidarity with God, a solidarity that was Jesus' to broker for those with gratefully perceptive faith (v. 19).

It was not that the other nine were not grateful. We may imagine them praising God all the way to the priests, and beyond. So exhilarated were they at how the encounter with Jesus had improved their health, their physical condition, their future prospects, they overlooked the far greater miracle of who Jesus was and what God was accomplishing for the entire creation through him.

The nine Jews probably did not even notice that the Samaritan was no longer with them. Restored to health and therefore once again acceptable in Jewish society, they would have been just as glad to see him gone. He was no longer their companion either in suffering or in blessing. He was, once again, one of those estranged and marginalized others—a Samaritan.

A sermon suggestion on the story follows:

We must be careful not to trivialize the story by reducing it to an instance when only one out of ten was polite enough to come back and say "Thank you." More is at stake than commending the attitude of polite gratitude for blessings and mercies received. The story is about perceptively discerning what really is taking place in such a restorative encounter. It is an instance of being touched by the creative power of the God who is bringing order out of chaos and wholeness out of all that is disgustingly defective and contaminatingly deteriorated.

God is eager to renew creation. God yearns for us to wake up to what is going on, to return to intimate trusting fellowship, and to claim common cause with God's grand and glorious restoration program.

So great is the divine zeal that God takes the initiative. God sends Jesus in whose person and preaching and activity one may clearly see God's saving intent in operation if one only has eyes to see, and ears to hear, and an open and receptive spirit to perceive with discernment.

According to this story, the odds are about nine to one that we will get it—which is a pretty optimistic, gracious, and generous estimate, when you think about it. The church would be in a lot better shape if that ratio held true.

When healing touches our lives and relationships, the story challenges us not to abbreviate our perception of grace gained, or to limit our offering of glory given, or to encompass only our glad recognition that the distortions that had troubled us before were now straightened out. Spiritual healing compels us to search for and acknowledge the Healer, and to discern the vast cosmic scope of the reclamation initiative of which our restoration is but a small part. Having found and discerned, we are to make common cause with that saving enterprise.

The Samaritan, on returning, was interrogated by Jesus (vv. 17–18). Jesus was not seeking information with those three questions. He was offering sharp criticism of the imperceptiveness of nine Israelites whose greatest hope should have been focused on longing for the coming of the Day of the Lord and the disclosure of God's royal rule.

An encounter with Jesus that both transforms one's physical and spiritual circumstance, and also evokes comprehension of who Jesus is, produces glad glory offered to God, not just for cleansing but also for Jesus and for what God is doing through Jesus. Whereas all ten, having been touched by kingdom power, were miraculously healed of leprosy, only one—the Samaritan—had the wit to give himself over gladly to the restored rule of God thereby revealed.

"Your faith has made you well" (v. 19) refers to more than the cleansing. It encompasses the discernment of the presence of the rule of God that brought the Samaritan back in glad and joyful celebration as a kingdom participant. "Rise" means more than "get up." It alludes to participation in resurrection life. "Go on your way" could lead him to the priests, it could lead him back to the Samaritan community, it could lead him to search out the nine who were oblivious. Whichever resulted, from now on, his way coincided with God's way.

PRESENCE OF GOD'S RULE
AND THE COMING SON OF MAN (17:20–37)

When you think back over the vast stretches of human history, so much has gone wrong in God's created order. How do we know that God is even aware of all of the pain and suffering in the world, all of the injustice and oppression, all of the diabolical self-seeking and self-serving? How can we tell when God has begun to do something about it? What are the indications, the "signs," that will alert us and convince us of the presence of God's creative restoration and saving renewal? Is it going on right here, right now? If not now, when? If not here, where?

The restoration of God's royal rule. Jewish religious sensibilities had been coached in the conviction that God's renewal of creation was surely to come, but not until sometime in the distant future, on the Day of the

Lord. At that time God would reestablish royal rule on Mount Zion and restore creation to its original perfection. Gruesome wars, appalling natural disasters, and horrible human calamities would presage the presence of that awesome power. The end-of-the-ages prophet would foretell it and give due warning; the Messiah would announce it and inaugurate it; the Spirit of God, bestowed once again on God's people after such a long absence, would confirm it and equip people to participate in it.

The commanding way in which Jesus taught and preached, the mighty acts he did, and who people were to conclude he was, seemed disturbingly ambiguous to some (see 11:14–16). To others, the significance was crystal clear. For them, it was by the presence and power of God's Spirit active in God's Servant Messiah that those deeds could be done with such authority.

Early Christians were further convinced that the same renewing and re-creating Spirit had been conferred on them by the risen Lord Jesus. They were the spirit-endowed, end-time people of God living in the interval of the initial unfolding of the end of the ages. But whether people resisted the possibility of the presence of God's regal power in the person and work of Jesus in the belief that it all was still in the distant future, or ardently believed that Jesus disclosed none other than messianic presence, the dynamics of the present moment held in tension with anticipated events, distant or near, evoked for all alike the persistent pondering: If not now, when? If not here, where?

Luke was anxious for his community to recognize that both of those questions exposed fundamental misunderstandings about the nature of God's rule. Present belief, attitude, and behavior did not depend on *if* God's reign was now beginning anew. The true parameters of the present time for perceptive believers were forged by the conviction that God is sovereign ruler over all creation. That certainty absolutely controls the quality of the present moment as a summons to faith no matter when or where God chooses to make the divine order more evident. Luke organized this section of his narrative so that through these words of Jesus both the presence of the rule of God and the future coming of the Son of man are held in tension in the person of Jesus himself, who incarnates the presence of divine dominion and for whose triumphant return the church looks longingly.

By placing these anecdotes directly after the story of the healing of the ten lepers (17:11–19), Luke's narrative sequence obliges us to recognize that the issue underlying all of this material is the same: Are you discerning enough to know when you are confronted by the powerful presence of the claim of God's royal rule? In the present section, the Evangelist binds the originally independent stories together both by the use of catchwords ("coming," vv. 20, 22; "Look here/there," vv. 21, 23) and by the contrast between being preoccupied with apprehensive anticipation and being oblivious to the present reality vis à vis the presence of God's realm.

Sermon possibilities from this section include:

1. Making the reign of God apparent. In verses 20–21, the critical question was not the calendar calculation about which the Pharisees queried Jesus. Far more momentous was who they thought it was whom they were asking. If they could get that second concern rightly resolved in their heads and in their hearts, the former question would fall into the proper perspective and take care of itself.

The above assertion is true for the present life of the church. Many Christians lament the loss in today's spirituality of a sense of that vibrant, electric expectancy of the impending return of Christ that energized early Christians. Yet God's rule is already effectively present. "The kingdom of God is among/within you (pl.)" (v. 21).

Perceptive involvement in the worship and work of the church and participation in the Christian fellowship makes the present reality of God's regal authority vivid. It does more than simply disclose to us the presence of God's royal rule. We are claimed for that rule and called to take part in it.

David Tiede (*Luke,* [Minneapolis: Augsburg Publishing House, 1988], p. 299) cautions that the phrase "things that can be observed" (v. 20) may be technical vocabulary referring to precise adherence to cultic rites and ritual practices. Could there be an allusion here to counterfeit religious vigilance that is on the alert for indications of the coming of the impending end as a signal for when it is high time to get serious about "what the Lord requires"—whether that be Torah observance, and/or gospel preaching, and/or commitment to establishing peace and justice?

2. The coming of God's royal rule will be recognized by its effects. Verses 22–37 remind us that living in the interval when the saving promises of God are "already fulfilled but not yet completed" entails an opposite hazard. Appreciative, faith-evoking recognition of the presence of God's power to create and rule in the person of Jesus must not make us suspect that the realm of God in all its completed splendor and magnificence has already been fully established.

The error of exaggerated overconfidence has frequently attracted Christians during those times when their current situation was so critical and threatening that the community of faith yearned for concrete confirmation, even realization of their ultimate hope in God's triumph over all the forces of evil. The narrative time of Luke's Gospel requires him to remind his readers that when Jesus is saying this to his disciples, his passion in Jerusalem still looms ahead (v. 25).

The future return of Jesus is couched in "days of the Son of Man" language (v. 22, etc.). (For detailed information about this complex and obscure first-century term, together with careful definition of the limits to its significance within earliest Christianity, see Douglas R. A. Hare, *The Son of Man Tradition*, Minneapolis: Fortress Press, 1990.) The image is of spectacular, instantaneous judgment. There will be no tell-tale advance notice. Ordinary events will continue as they always have. Then, suddenly, disaster or salvation occurs—decisive, ineluctable, final, and from a human perspective, inexplicably arbitrary.

The biblical analogies offered to clarify the critical character of the moment include the stories of Noah and of Lot. Both traditions described protracted intervals when the impending divine judgment seemed remote, vague, unlikely, even unreal to the imperceptive. Only Lot and Noah had a clue as to what was looming just over the horizon. Even then, one instant of unfaithful nostalgic hesitation caused saline disaster.

It is not unlike the times of the wilderness wanderings when the children of Israel loudly and repeatedly resented God for luring them into present hardship. Current privations reminded them of how much they missed the predictable though minuscule comforts that had been theirs during Egyptian slavery. Those preoccupations prevented them from praising God for the future hope of the promise that was infusing the present.

By what indication or advanced warning will we know of the return of Christ and the fulfillment of the end-of-the-ages judgment of God? Not by calendar calculations, not by scrutiny of sequences of supposed anticipatory events, not by legacied or conjured convictions of "the Holy Place," whether on Mount Gerizim or on the Temple Mount in Jerusalem, or wherever. Inquiring as to the place is no more fruitful than striving to cipher the time.

The completion of God's purposes will be so sudden and so unexpected that it will be recognizable not by its approach but by its consequences. Flash floods do not announce their approach but leave stark evidence of their having passed through. We first recognize death in the desert by the vultures circling overhead. The completion of the realm of God is known not by its coming but by its effects. As before, God's footprints first disclose divine presence only after God has walked by.

What you are doing when God reestablishes domain does not matter as long as whatever it is harmonizes with who you know yourself to be before God. To bring this perspective home with as much force as possible, Luke repeated a phrase he had first found and presented in his own narrative (9:24) as forged in the context of Jesus' own passion prediction (9:22). The difference between those destroyed and those saved is measured by self-denial for the sake of the cause of Christ (v. 33).

PARABLE OF THE PERSISTENT WIDOW (18:1–8)

(a) *End-time expectation in the early church.* It is God who alone grants justice and vindicates. God is faithful and will not let the elect down. That is the point of this parable. Luke included it here in his narrative to counteract any inclination to discouragement in his community because the final judgment had not occurred. Since that judgment was still pending, their vindication before the entire world—but especially before those who were aggressively opposing them and their mission—was not evident.

The story continues the theme of the preceding section of instruction by Jesus to his disciples concerning the anticipated consummation of time at the end of days and the final judgment. Luke's community also "longs to see" (17:22) the return of the Messiah as the coming Son of man, and the completion of God's design to save. The story seeks to confirm their anticipation of that pending occurrence.

Christians were experiencing increased resistance to their preaching and teaching, and even suffered from overt hostility during times of persecution. They yearned for the inbreaking of the Day of the Lord when their vindication by the divine judgment of God would be made plain, and those who were impeding their labors for the cause of Christ would be called to account.

The fact that the Day-to-End-All-Days had not arrived did not mean that God is unaware of or indifferent to the sufferings of the elect. The parable offered encouragement to them not to give in to their despair but to remain confident that the triumph of God on the Day of the Lord would bring the total vindication of the faithful with little delay. The gist of the story is similar to that of the story of the insistent friend, which Luke had already related in 11:5–8.

(b) *Interaction between the widow and the judge.* For full appreciation of the story, we should devote specific attention to both of the characters. Widows were recognized as especially powerless and vulnerable in the Near-Eastern Mediterranean cultures of the first century. The Jewish scriptures described them as particularly precious to God since they were solely dependent on God, and commended them to the pious for compassionate consideration and assistance. (Luke is especially supportive of such specific concern.)

The judge is portrayed in the worst possible light. The nature of the office of judge in the Jewish system of religious law was to serve as a servant of God who makes God's will known through Torah. The judge's function is to declare the wronged party innocent and the guilty party a transgressor, and thereby vindicate the righteousness and holiness of God to which Torah testifies. This judge, however, "has no fear of God" (v. 4), nor does he respect anyone else. The only person whose interests he serves is himself. By definition, therefore, he is a bad judge from whom one would not expect to obtain justice.

The judge is not simply defective in the quality and focus of his judicial functioning, he is fundamentally hostile to the religious nature of Torah and therefore despises his office. He actively serves unrighteousness. That is, he has aligned himself with those supernatural powers and principalities who, in their opposition toward God, have usurped God's exclusive role as both ruler and judge.

The impotent widow accosts the judge. So the story dramatically graphs the unlikely odds that the interplay between the two personified extreme situations can result in justice. What a surprise, then, that the powerless woman badgered the judge who was indifferent to the woman's cause into doing justice. She exploits his commitment to serve himself absolutely. The judge is more quickly moved to "grant justice" by irritation at the loss of peace her nagging inflicts than he is by awe before the Mosaic law or fear for what God expects from him.

After exploring the story with the congregation in the first part of the sermon, it might move in the following direction:

The story intends to work by contrast to bring us to a new and deepened insight into the justice of God. God is not indifferent to the cause of justice. God cares greatly to maintain divine righteousness and to vindicate the innocent. Nor is God wearied, or hassled, or irritated by repeated, devout, prayerful petitions. So the story confronts us with

> "the tremendous suggestion that every word of prayer must penetrate to a depth of the heart that can be reached only by unceasing iteration. Is this not an indication that prayer is not a matter of pouring out the human heart once and for all in need or joy, but of unbroken, constant learning, accepting, and impressing upon the mind of God's will in Jesus Christ?" (Dietrich Bonhoeffer, *Life Together*, [New York: Harper & Brothers, 1954], p. 49).

The value of repeated prayer is not that God is thereby coerced to engage more speedily in vindicating action, but that those who are God's chosen are sustained in their fidelity. God welcomes such importunity from God's elect.

Then comes the startling assertion: God "will quickly grant justice to them" (v. 8a). Two considerations help to make sense out of what otherwise must have only aggravated the discouraged impatience troubling Luke's community.

1) "Quickly" was accurate only when time was viewed from God's perspective. That may not seem so quick if we lose sight of that perspective and measure the interim in terms of our brief history.
2) The promise alludes to the passion of Jesus toward which Jesus and the disciples even now are traveling. After the ignominious and unjust crucifixion, God vindicates Jesus by raising him from the dead. With the vindication of Jesus and the saving participation believers have in that event, the justification of God's elect begins. That reality lies not ahead for Luke's community but in the past. That is quick!

Verse 8b catches us up short and reminds us that the critical issue is not the fidelity of God but human faithfulness. Will the God who is absolutely dependable meet with similar constancy from those who have been called? Before Christians indict God for apparent indifference to their predicament as the delay of the climactic Day of the Lord seems to imply, they had better be as concerned about the quality and consistency of their fidelity to God.

When the God who is faithful is ready, will God find the faithful ready? It is more likely if they consistently align themselves through persistent prayer to God's cause and Jesus' approaching return to rule. In the event that our faithfulness does not measure up to God's (and it never will), the sure mark of God's patient long-suffering is that "when the Son of man comes" God will grant justice—and more! God will grant mercy in Christ, as God already grants justice and mercy, even though scant faith be found.

WHOM DOES GOD ACCEPT? (18:9–17)

Luke placed the two anecdotes, the story about the Pharisee and the tax collector, and the incident concerning the little children, next to each other for a purpose. Both traditions report what appears to be governing and even definitive circumstances with respect to one's relationship to God, which are reversed dramatically when they are viewed from God's perspective.

What is at stake is more than the contrast between pious lip service and heartfelt religion. By placing the two anecdotes together, Luke suggests that the disciples are not unlike the Pharisee in the story. The initial surprised exhilaration the disciples had felt at being themselves included into the most intimate circle of Jesus' associates had blunted. Now they, too, were susceptible to an attitude of arrogant self-assurance, as demonstrated by their peremptory dismissal of the children as if they were insignificant and of no interest to Jesus.

We should note that the introduction to the section (v. 9) makes it clear that Jesus did not tell the story of the Pharisee and the tax collector either in response to criticism of his ministry by hostile Pharisees or as a direct assault on the Pharisaic movement. He was speaking, rather, to those who, having perhaps been impressed by the Pharisaic reform, had come to rely on their own religious efforts.

(a) *The contrast between the Pharisee and the tax collector.* The effectiveness of the story depends on our appreciative recovery of the dramatic contrast between the two figures in the story. Remember that the Pharisaic reform movement was dedicated to acknowledging how God's call for human obedience and worship pervaded the entirety of the human experience.

Luke had already portrayed Jesus as at the same time attracted and repelled by Pharisaic Judaism. He was fascinated by the promise of their call for fundamental religious integrity that permeated the entirety of one's life. But he was repelled when their attention was too often devoted to measuring the scope of their religious integrity at the expense of ignoring the radical trust and love the Jewish religion was created to express.

Pharisees were serious about their religion and they encouraged other Jews to do the same. By contrast, when tested by the well-known principles of Jewish orthodoxy, the tax collector was dishonest, exploitive, oppressive, and cultically unclean, none of which commended him to favorable divine regard. The Pharisee really was religious, and the tax collector really was despicable.

(b) *The Pharisee's self-assessment.* The Pharisee has carefully and confidently crafted his self-description, and there in the Temple now reports it to God for confirmation and endorsement. He has examined himself and he likes what he sees. He has measured himself in comparison with the negative examples of those who clearly demonstrate their transgressing lack of righteousness. He is proud of what he has become, and by most standards of decency he should be.

The Pharisee has, out of love for God, schooled himself habitually to conduct himself with behavior that is consistent with what God has disclosed as characteristic of a pious, righteous, and holy life. That is no inconsiderable accomplishment considering all the other enticing options clamoring for attention and allegiance.

Furthermore, the Pharisee is confident that he will be able to continue such behavior. He knows himself to be dependably observant to a measure beyond what Torah (the Jewish law) requires, and he is persuaded that he can rely on himself to continue to live in that manner. He presumes that God can be counted on to recognize the excellence of his life's walk and will reward him accordingly.

He modeled those "who trusted in themselves that they were righteous and regarded others with contempt" (v. 9). Such a brazen initiative before the divine presence vividly disclosed the extreme distance that still existed between the Pharisee and the realm of God's royal rule.

(c) *The idea of "distance" in the anecdote.* Distance—a crucial concern in the story—is reflected in the posture of the two. Both distanced themselves from the worshiping assembly. The Pharisee (the word means "one who is separate") was "standing by himself," aloof and judgmentally arrogant. The rest of them were not in his religious league. The tax collector, "standing by himself" humbly, with eyes downcast, knew that through his transgressions he had forfeited his right to inclusion in the assembled community and that he stood guilty and vulnerable before the wrath of a righteous God. The Pharisee trusted in himself and in what he did; the tax collector trusted in God and in what God would do.

The Pharisee distanced himself not only from the gathering of worshipers, and, through critical comparison, from the tax collector, he also unintentionally distanced himself from God. Unlike the tax collector, the Pharisee underestimated both the extent of his continuing unrighteousness and the stringent severity of God's justice. He thereby deprived himself of the two perspectives necessary for him to perceive and appreciate the scope, depth, and extent of God's mercy.

There was no sense of solidarity within him. The Pharisee shows no awareness of having responsibility for or participation with the tax collector, either in his transgressions or in his confessing agony, his penitential remorse. To "regard others with contempt" and reject them for their unrighteousness is to usurp God's prerogative to judge. When people "trust in themselves," they "exalt themselves" (v. 14). Yet only God exalts, and God chooses to do so for God's reasons, which are not the considerations that compel humans to categorize one another. Judging and exalting are both activities that rightly belong solely to God.

Suggestions for a sermon on this portion of the passage:

The tough task for us is to retrieve the emotions surrounding these two characters of Pharisee and tax collector with the vividness and the sharpness they would have carried for those to whom Jesus was telling the story. Try "your favorite Sunday school teacher" and "a streetwise drug pusher," perhaps. Only then do we hear the surprised "aha" the story evokes as we are encountered by 1) the radical claims of a gospel that devalues even the best-intended religious efforts, and 2) the totally unexpected "gracing" of the contemptible.

It is such an insidious thing, this creeping craving to confirm our acceptability before God by comparing ourselves with all of those others whom we are sure will never have access to fellowship with God's royal presence. We do not mean for that to happen. It is just that we have, ourselves, come so far from where we were when God first laid claim upon us. It has not been an easy pilgrimage. We have known fits and starts, lurches ahead, backsliding, divertive side trips which seemed harmless enough at the time but which, only retroactively, we have come to label demonic. Still, with God's help, and with lots of effort, struggle, determination, and discipline, we have come along a significant distance—especially when you think of that one/those ones over there!

What an insidious temptation it is for us, having studied the story carefully, to come away from our consideration thinking, "God, I thank you that I am not like other people: thieves, rogues, adulterers, or even like this arrogantly self-sufficient Pharisee."

(*d*) *The "Pharisaic" disciples.* The verses following the story of the Pharisee and the tax collector, verses 15–17, pan over to focus on the disciples (and therefore, as always, on us Christians, precisely in terms of our relationship to Jesus and how that shapes our understanding of who we are before God and how we may best serve Christ). The incident tries the attitudinal posture of the self-satisfied Pharisee on the disciples for size.

Because they are Jesus' disciples, because they have left all to follow after him, they not only assume they have first right of approach to Jesus, they presume to control the access others have to him. They were disdainful about all the hubbub and chaos that resulted from adults seeking to present their small children to Jesus for tactile blessing. That demand seemed so trivial in comparison with Jesus' momentous mighty acts and authoritative teaching they had been observing. Jesus interested in little children? Please!

(*e*) *Jesus' passionate preference for the little child in us all.* Of course Jesus was interested in little children, more than the disciples knew. Their inability even to imagine that he might be interested said more about their relationship to Jesus than did their pompous posturing. Not only did Jesus countermand the disciples' ill-considered prohibitions and summon the small children to his side, he affirmed how eagerly he looked for the "little child" in all who would follow him and participate in the reassertion of God's royal rule. He held the little children before the eyes of condescending adults as models for any who would be included in God's realm. Kingdom people were people who knew and rejoiced in their complete dependency on the merciful goodwill and love of God.

That anecdote had a special "bite" for Luke and his community for, by then, the terms "little children" and "little ones" had acquired a technical meaning referring to new or recent converts to the gospel faith. They were those who were immature in the faith rather than simply the chronologically immature. Consequently, the story voiced sharp criticism for those in the Christian community who were condescending toward the naiveté and the lack of theological and ethical sophistication of new converts.

A sermon on this part of the passage might take shape along these lines:

1. Complete trust and reliance on God. We, too, may take it for granted that our considerable pilgrimage toward deepened discipleship qualifies us to function as gatekeepers who control access to God's attention. Those whom we deem worthy are welcomed and passed through, whereas we protect God from being pestered by others—the immature, those just beginning their pilgrim way, and especially those who are obviously impious, decadent, and depraved.

Self-assurance concerning one's acceptability before God inclines toward arrogantly limited recognition of the wide-ranging scope of backgrounds and conditions among humanity that God wills to enfold under God's divine rule. The self-assured arrogantly tend to imagine God as being interested primarily in people who are precisely like them.

Perception of one's sinfulness requires recognition of one's vulnerability before divine justice. Precisely that recognition, and the accompanying realization that there is nothing to be done to rectify the situation, compels the self-acknowledged sinner to abandon any pretense of self-commendation and to rely absolutely on the mercy of God.

God does not prefer scrupulous religious behavior done as an end in itself. What moves God, what gladdens the divine heart, is realistic, accurate assessment of one's inadequacies and of one's predilection for those choices that renounce the claim of God for loving obedience. God welcomes such recognition, for then such a person is open once again to know that there is no help other than the sovereign mercy of God.

The difference between saints and sinners cannot be determined by the contrast in active cultic participation, measurable ethical behavior, or duration of association with Jesus. Saints are sinners who know themselves always to be in need of vindication and who are serenely confident in their conviction that God will not let them down.

2. *Consider preaching the entire section, as the above treatment suggests.*

ON BEING RICH TOWARD GOD (18:18–30)

"How can I be a better Christian?" Sometimes when people ask the question they are yearning for intensified discipleship and enriched service, which makes it an appropriately devout query. But it can be a diabolically dangerous question, too, not unlike the question of the rich ruler who wanted Jesus to clarify for him how he might more engagingly commend himself to the favorable attention of God.

If one is serious in asking a question like that (Jesus assumed that the ruler was—he always does), one announces spiritual vulnerability. The cost of discipleship amounts to the renunciation of precisely that on which one places greatest store, of that on which one prefers to rely for stability and status in place of relying solely on God. Such alternate trust and dependence must be surrendered, whether it is in material wealth, or in the role of beloved family man or as honored town elder, or whatever *quid pro quo* bargains one assumes to have struck with God, even if only by implication.

The kingdom vocabulary in the section is richly varied: "eternal life" (v. 18) = "treasure in heaven" (v. 22) = "be saved" (v. 26) = "enter the kingdom of God" (vv. 24, 25) = "follow Jesus" (v. 28) = "age to come" (v. 30).

(*a*) ***The rich ruler's initial query.*** The ruler addressed Jesus as "Good Teacher." Although Jesus' reply seems to be an apparent rejection of such an acclamation, it offered the key to accurate perception which Luke and his community would affirm. The response intends neither a corrective to a mistaken judgment nor humble demurral to extravagant praise. The goodness the ruler ascribed to Jesus is the goodness of God made plainly visible in the work Jesus was doing. The irony of the exchange is almost Johannine in flavor.

The *question* he put to the "Good Teacher" disclosed how unaware the ruler was of whom he was addressing. "What must I do?" he asked. His eye was so firmly fixed on the future and how he could get it all to turn out right that he was oblivious to the possibility that the "Good Teacher" from whom he sought sage spiritual advice could admit him to eternal life right now—and would offer to do so shortly (v. 22).

Was the ruler only looking for approbation of his pious behavior? Wealth and abundance were popularly regarded by many as evidence of divine favor (with biblical support). Jesus did not contradict that. For everything in the way of proper religious behavior the ruler had done, he knew that he still had not done enough. What more could he, should he, do?

There is a logical inconsistency to the ruler's question that indicates the fragility of his piety. What one does *earns* something; to *inherit* is the consequence of an effective relational gift. Furthermore, the sequence is reversed. One is embraced by the claim of God's rule (to inherit eternal life) and then is empowered to act consistently with the logical service of that divine authority. "What I must do?" to merit salvation is a scary thing to ask. It is an inquiry that makes demands so radical and unrealistic that one finally abandons the quest for adequate performance in despair—or, for faith.

(*b*) *Jesus' response.* Jesus' first answer (v. 20) must have struck the ruler as reassuringly likely. It was the standard response of Jewish piety to such a question, listing that portion of the law of Moses that addressed the quality of a person's relationships to other humans. The commandments listed the accepted demands governing religiously commendable interpersonal behavior. The ruler's acknowledgement of accomplishment to such an obvious truism (v. 21) may well have been tinged with condescension and pride of piety.

Jesus' second rejoinder (v. 22) cut to the core of the ruler's problem. Scrupulously and faithfully practiced piety does not mean that you have arrived. Rather, it prepares one for a deeper level of commitment and service: 1) care for others more than for yourself, and 2) assume the position of dedicated disciple. The ruler may even have been expecting some similar response, at least of the first measure. Charity (see Luke T. Johnson, *Sharing Possessions: Mandate and Symbol of Faith,* Philadelphia: Fortress Press, 1981) was a widely acknowledged and highly regarded religious act of Jewish piety. There were, though, rabbinical prohibitions against excess in charitable works lest one become an additional burden to the community.

For Jesus, the claim of God's royal rule focused not just on what the ruler had and therefore could afford to give, but on how the ruler evaluated what he had as a resource to be employed in devoted service of God. Radical charity was not the prelude to discipleship. In the very act of self-spending, the ruler-turned-disciple already would emulate this Master/Good Teacher/Messiah who even now was on the way to Jerusalem impelled by radical, self-spending love.

Jesus' advice commended consistency in commitment to sacrificial other-directedness to the point of renunciation. The challenge to radical charity unto the extreme of self-impoverishment was not in the hope that what was devoted to charity would be returned later multiplied.

(*c*) **Worldly treasure and the treasure of God's rule.** The contrast is not chronological, between treasure disbursed charitably now that would result in reception of more treasure later. The contrast is qualitative, between treasure which was assigned its worth by the world's values, and treasure defined by kingdom concerns (see 12:33 for a similar use of the phrase "treasure in heaven").

Eternal life is not a greater treasure, or even the greatest treasure, on the value continuum of material possessions, or of religious observance. It is the paradox of God's right to rule. Only by making himself poor could the ruler become rich toward God by being enriched by God. "Blessed are you who are poor for yours is the kingdom of God" (6:20). Elaborately scrupulous religious behavior and law observance is not required. A little child's faith can grasp that (cf. 18:16–17). If obedience is a matter of degree, God demands it all—absolutely all.

If the emphasis stayed on "What must I do?" the only level of engagement for the divine/human encounter is that of law observance. The "one thing lacking" discloses a compelling challenge to renounce that which gives one status and power in exchange for the reflected status and the imputed power of the reign of God. Beyond that, it requires that we abandon the delusion that "what I do" has anything whatsoever to do with our controlling our access to that quality of life that partakes of the eternal.

Jesus took the ruler's inquiry (and the ruler himself) more seriously than the ruler was prepared to expect. In the exchange, he discovered that, although the ruler supposedly "kept the commandments," he violated the first and greatest commandment, which controlled the integrity of all the others (see 10:25–28). Jesus claimed on behalf of God control over that in which the ruler placed ultimate trust, in order that he might give up the inclination to ask "What must I do?" and be liberated to love God and to trust in God. Jesus does that with us all.

The first of the next section (vv. 31–34) offers a dramatically contrasting description of what *God* will "do" to secure eternal life for all who trust God rather than trusting what they themselves have done or can do. It reminds all of us who are participants in Luke's narrative of the shadow of the cross looming over the entire journey to Jerusalem.

(*d*) *The ruler's response to Jesus' challenge.* "He became sad" (v. 23) is one of the more understated and tragic phrases in the Christian Testament. The choice was where one vested one's ultimate absolute reliance; the option offered was that of faithful, obedient trust.

The ruler refused the opportunity to be an instrument of God's restored rule through whom the One who blesses was blessing others. He missed the chance to be the locus of that which Mary celebrated in the Magnificat (1:53): "He has filled the hungry with good things," so he became the locus of the judgment: "[He has] sent the rich away empty." By depending on the blessing rather than upon the One who blesses, the ruler chose to be possessed by his possessions rather than to be ruled by God. He chose to value the gift above the Giver who was prepared and eager to give so much more.

The sadness of the ruler leads Jesus to reflect mournfully through exaggerated hyperbole on the defeated struggle (vv. 24f.). This sets up the contrast drawn in the subsection between realistic acknowledgement of what is humanly impossible and the affirmation that with God nothing is impossible (vv. 26f.).

Peter (speaking for the other disciples, too) memorializes the dimensions of renunciation that all of the disciples experienced when they chose their choosing by Jesus. What a venture costs not only is measured by what one must contribute and invest but also includes what one must give up. Closing out old options is just as critical an exercise of discipling as is the seizing of new opportunities.

Luke does not portray Peter as petulantly pondering out loud whether he and the other disciples have made a sucker's bargain. Peter's concern is not whether the *quid* of his current status before God as a disciple of Jesus is not worth the *quo* of those sacrificial renunciations discipleship always requires. Peter's observation queries whether "following Jesus" really fulfills the challenge in Jesus' exchange with the rich man to "leave it to God." Jesus replies, "Yes!"

Preaching on the anecdote might explore:

It is not that the rich are inherently worse off before God than are the poor (though the ethical questions of how wealth was gained and at what cost to whom, and to what extent acquiescence to and even participation in exploitive, oppressive forces was involved must be carefully considered). Luke's bias is that the rich are far less likely to acknowledge how completely dependent on God they also are. They have come to depend for so long a time on their own capabilities and competence, and on the supporting and coercive power that wealth, once acquired, controls.

Such self-sufficiency does not have to defeat God's purpose. Leave it to God, and that camel will slide right through the needle's eye. Leave it to God, and even the richest person will be embraced by God's royal rule, which *is* to inherit eternal life. The critical issue becomes our comprehension and affirmation, informed by the gospel, of all that is involved, of all that is implied when we "leave it to God."

But for the merciful love of God it is impossible for the rich to enter the reign of God. Who are the rich? Let us not define that too narrowly (so that we clearly are not included). The first sentence of this paragraph is true for all of us, no matter of what we consider our particular "richness" to consist—family man, influential citizen, feminist, or whatever.

Let us not define the "poor" too narrowly, either. The ruler's main trouble was that it simply never occurred to him that, before God, he was as poor as anyone alive, and considerably poorer than most of those with Jesus on the road to Jerusalem.

Every time we read a biblical or ecclesial admonition about the mandate to minister to the poor and those in need, we must first carefully consider in what ways we recognize ourselves to be poor, in what lackings our self-unsatisfiable needs consist, and how God meets our impoverishment with God's richness. Only after such reflection can we ready ourselves to be agents of ministry to the needs and to the poverty of others, in whatever ways that poverty may present itself.

Of what does our God-denying richness consist? Could that be why Luke added the next two verses (v. 29f.) at this point in his narrative? At first, hearing Peter's interjection sounds strikingly similar to the ruler's initial inquiry. Going through the figurative eye of the needle is impossible even for those who have renounced that which is most precious—say, their homes with all that implied—as long as invocative emphasis is on the first person plural: "*we* have left . . . , *we* have followed. . ."

Hearing with Understanding; Seeing with Perception (18:31–43)

Standing in the presence of Jesus is an occasion charged with enormous potential. At that moment the assertion of God's right to rule is personally at issue. At that precise instant, God's claim to reign can become intimately, personally compelling. Who is likely to realize that? Who will probably get it right?

In the story immediately preceding, the rich ruler for all of his yearning does not get it right (18:18–26). In this section the crowds who have been attracted to Jesus by his astounding activity, his astonishing teaching, and his electrifying presence do not realize it (though they make some progress—vv. 37, 43). The disciples who have responded at considerable personal cost (vv. 28–30) to Jesus' summons to be intimate colleagues cannot hear it (v. 34). But a blind man does! Who would have predicted that? In the next section a puny and despised tax collector does (19:1–10)! Who would think of such a thing?

It calls to mind the terrible enigma in the message given to Isaiah:

> 'Keep listening, but do not comprehend;
> keep looking, but do not understand.'
> Make the mind of this people dull,
> and stop their ears, and shut their eyes,
> so that they may not look with their eyes,

> and listen with their ears,
> and comprehend with their minds,
> and turn and be healed.
>
> Isa. 6:9–10

(*a*) *Prediction of the passion (18:31–34).* As the extended trek from Galilee to Jerusalem (begun at 9:51) approaches its conclusion, Luke used this additional passion prediction to remind his readers/hearers explicitly that the entire journey was shadowed by the sign of the cross betokening what awaited them at the trip's conclusion. In contrast to the ruler's inquiry as to what he must "do" to clinch access to eternal life (v. 18), Jesus detailed for the Twelve what God was about to do to reestablish God's reign over all creation. It is the "exodus" event of deliverance that had been anticipatorially discussed on the Mount of Transfiguration (9:31).

Although delineated more fully in its particulars here, still the gist of the announcement was not a new disclosure. The disciples had heard essentially the same thing just prior to beginning the journey (9:22), and allusions to the passion were scattered throughout the trip's duration as Jesus instructed the disciples. In spite of all of that, the disciples understood nothing about it—they were even *kept* by God from comprehending its import (v. 34).

With the threefold assertion of the disciples' lack of comprehension, Luke stressed that at this stage in their relationship with Jesus they were still without a clue as to what they were to make of this forebodingly enigmatic pronouncement by Jesus. It echoes the threefold assertion of their lack of understanding to a similar declaration by Jesus at the journey's inception (9:44–45).

This passion prediction announced one of the "mysteries of the kingdom" that Jesus had declared ultimately would be revealed to the disciples (8:10) but for which they were not yet prepared—indeed, were prevented by God from grasping (cf. 8:17–18). Only after experiencing the empty tomb (24:12), the eucharistic presence (24:25–31), and the illuminating intervention of the resurrected Jesus (24:44–47) would the disciples be empowered to "look with their eyes . . . listen with their ears . . . comprehend with their minds . . . and be healed."

(*b*) *Healing of the blind man (18:35–43).* Luke now describes Jesus as nearing Jericho, the last major town before beginning the ascent to Jerusalem. He thereby alerts his audience that the extended journey of Jesus and his disciples from Galilee to Jerusalem, begun at 9:51, is nearing completion. The narrative anticipation of what will transpire in and around Jerusalem intensifies.

Not only are the disciples accompanying Jesus on this last leg of the trip, but also a large crowd streams behind and before. There on the outskirts of the settlement of Jericho was a blind beggar. A rapid exchange occurred: The beggar asks for information, the crowd replies, he calls out to Jesus, the crowd rebukes him, he calls louder, Jesus responds. With the story, Luke wants us to recall that Jesus used the words of Isaiah at the very beginning of his ministry to assert that one of his messianic tasks was to broker "recovery of sight to the blind" (4:18). This story invites us to compare the disciples and the crowd who can "see" (but not perceive) with a man who, not "seeing," perceives. "Jesus opens the eyes of a man who can already see." (Fred B. Craddock, *Luke,* Louisville, Ky.: John Knox Press, 1990, p. 217.)

(*c*) *The different reactions of the crowd and of the blind man to Jesus.* Luke documents a significant variation between the term of identification used by the crowd in response to the blind man's query: "Jesus of Nazareth" (v. 37) and the blind man's form of direct address: "Jesus, Son of David" (vv. 38, 39). They knew Jesus by his accent; he knew Jesus by his power. They saw him only as someone from Nazareth; the blind man "saw" him as Davidic Messiah. (Luke registered repeatedly in the early stages of his narrative how tremendously significant the motif of Davidic Messiah was for an accurate identification of Jesus—1:32, 69; 2:4, 11; 3:31; 6:3.)

Next we note that in between the repeated cries with which the blind man tried to bring himself to the attention of Jesus the crowd accompanying Jesus "rebuked" the blind man. Overly confident of his insignificance, and perhaps a bit piqued by his temerity, they sought to marginalize and dismiss him. But they were thereby ignoring the marvelous testimony to the identity of Jesus he was offering if they only had "ears to hear."

Instead of learning from him, they "rebuked" him. In Luke's vocabulary, that term means considerably more than simply "scolding him to be silent." Elsewhere Luke used that term when Jesus exorcised demons (4:35, 41; 9:42, etc.) or restored other aspects of creation that evidenced it was defective, defiled, and under the chaotic control of supernatural forces opposed to the reign of God (4:39; 8:24, etc.). Even those near to Jesus, those attracted to Jesus and accompanying him toward Jerusalem, if their ears are "stopped" and do not "listen," it shows that they yet resist the rule of God within them.

The blind man's begging cry, "Have mercy on me" (vv. 38, 39), like that of the ten lepers (17:13), is both a plea for charitable alms and something significantly more, as indicated in both instances by the forms of address used (ten lepers — "Master"; blind man — "Son of David"). Jesus met and maximized that "something more."

There is a progression in the blind man's perceptive appreciation of what Jesus has to offer him. The ordinary solicitation of alms escalates to a plea for divine restoration (healing of blindness — v. 41) by the Davidic Messiah. That need having been met and his physical sight restored increases the acuity of his spiritual perception and impels him to assume the posture of disciple (he "followed him" — v. 43a).

This sequence implies an intensification in the perception of need, beginning with the hope of receiving compassionate alms through the recovery of the sense of sight to entrance into the saving fellowship of believer with the Messiah of God. The man, with physical sight restored corresponding to his spiritual perception, joins with the expanding numbers of those who are "glorifying and praising God for all they had heard and seen" (2:20).

A sermon on this section will want to take the following into account:

"Have mercy on me" (vv. 38, 39) might seem self-centered and self-serving in the extreme. Many of our petitions may sound like that to others. But what must capture our attention in this story — and any time we hear similar pleas addressed to Jesus — is not the theological defensibility of what is being asked but the asking person's transparently trustful testimony as to who Jesus is and what extraordinary things the person believes God can and does do through him.

The blind man's response to Jesus and to what Jesus did for him "opened the eyes" of the observing crowd. What they witnessed healed their spiritual blindness and restored perception. Whereas they had earlier rebuked him for acknowledging Jesus as Davidic Messiah, now as they "saw" his transformation, they, too, are transformed and join with him and all those others in praising God, stretching back to the shepherds returning from Bethlehem. And thereby the "crowd" (v. 36) becomes a "people" (v. 43) — God's people.

From the perspective of the development of the narrative, introducing the motifs of the crowds, praising and glorifying, enabled Luke in this section to continue to build toward the soon-to-be-related triumphal entry into Jerusalem.

ZACCHAEUS (19:1–10)

Luke had set the stage for including this story at this juncture in his narrative by mentioning in the preceding anecdote that Jesus encountered the blind man "as he approached Jericho" (18:35). Now (v. 1) Jesus enters the city of Jericho accompanied by the crowd, which presumably had increased in size. The imagination enhances the congestion of the scene further by picturing many inhabitants of Jericho lining the way as Jesus passed through. The expanding crowd accompanying Jesus into the city, the mixed returns on what was taking place—the pejorative criticism on the one hand, the happy welcome at the saving presence on the other—all these features anticipate the approaching triumphal entry into Jerusalem and prelude the events of Holy Week.

(a) *Zacchaeus seems an unlikely person to perceive who Jesus is.* Zacchaeus is introduced, presented in the worst possible light, at least from the perspective of the crowd. He was physically unimpressive. Furthermore, he was rich when most of those making up the crowds accompanying and waiting on the appearance of Jesus were poor, some of them desperately so.

In addition, Zacchaeus was a tax collector, an agent for the hated power of Imperial Rome and its system of oppressive taxation, whom Jewish religious instruction has taught them to hate even more. A tax collector was to be regarded as an apostate, someone to be excluded from the fellowship of the people of Israel whose community he was deemed to have renounced when he aligned himself with those charged with accumulating the brutal Roman tariffs. Worse than this Zacchaeus was a *chief* tax collector who supervised a team of tax-collecting extortionists.

Then appears the *startling surprise* in the story. Only Zacchaeus, of all of those who were assembling there, was ready and responsive to who Jesus was and to the glad urgency of the opportune moment to respond to that which Jesus alone could offer. Once again the story explores a theme Luke believed to be crucial: the eternal consequences of "seeing" and of "not seeing."

Zacchaeus was frantically eager to see Jesus. He took extraordinary measures to compensate for his physical deficiency, in order that nothing might hinder him from "seeing Jesus" as plainly and as clearly as possible. He dismissed considerations of maintaining the dignity of rank and status as insignificant to the promise of the moment at hand; he scrambled up a tree like any curious adolescent (v. 4). Luke had repeatedly portrayed Jesus as interpreting similar unusual efforts to attain access to him as a welcome sign of unusually perceptive faith (5:19f.; 8:44; 18:37f.).

(b) *Jesus responds with saving recognition.* Zacchaeus's single-minded eagerness to see Jesus was met by the response of Jesus who looked at him (v. 5a) with greater clarity, perception, and understanding than Zacchaeus had ever been regarded by anyone before. That Jesus inexplicably addressed by name the man who was unceremoniously stuck up in the tree underscores the clarity of perceptive recognition between the two.

The necessity of Jesus' staying with Zacchaeus, the need for haste (v. 5b), the requirement that such fellowship occur "today," all reflect an urgency that permeated the ministry of Jesus throughout but that intensified as he neared Jerusalem. It was the necessity of kingdom opportunity in response to anyone who demonstrated openness to the claim of God to rule in human lives.

Zacchaeus's happy, joyous welcome (v. 6) is the obverse of the sadness with which the rich ruler had demurred when faced with the claims of the sovereignty of God (18:23). It also contrasts sharply with those multiple incidents related earlier in the narrative where Pharisees received Jesus with critical reservation, suspicion, and hostility (7:36–50; 11:37–54, etc.). Zacchaeus responded with joyful welcome to Jesus' request, and the fellowship that followed signaled the approbation of verse 9 was a reality that both of them recognized, even if the crowd did not (v. 7). The crowd's response is the dark, murky backdrop that throws the brilliance of the encounter between Zacchaeus and Jesus in sharper focus. The crowds observed everything that transpired but watched it without perception, and therefore only the scandalous incongruity of it all made an impression on them.

(c) *Zacchaeus was atypical of the popular view of tax collectors.* To understand verse 8 as a sudden reversal of behavior for Zacchaeus obscures the central thrust of the story. "Zacchaeus is presented in this episode as an exemplary rich person who has understood something of Jesus' ministry and message and concern for the poor and the cheated" (J. A. Fitzmyer, *The Gospel According to Luke,* [Anchor Bible], New York: Doubleday, vol. 2, 1985, p. 1,222).

Zacchaeus affirms that he habitually has conducted himself at variance with popular Jewish religious opinion concerning tax collectors. (The verbs are iterative present tenses, the present tense of repeated action.) Zacchaeus reports that he regularly devotes one half of his wealth to the relief of the poor. Whenever one of the tax collectors under his supervision deals fraudulently with someone, he routinely makes generous restitution beyond what the law requires. The crowd's disparaging judgment of him is wrong. They are no more adept at seeing him for who he really is than they are at seeing Jesus for who he is. Jesus' identification of Zacchaeus as a "son of Abraham" (v. 9) repudiates the opinion popular in Jewish piety that tax collectors were to be lumped together without exception with sinners who have transgressed the holy will of God and who are therefore to be excluded from the children of Abraham, the people of God.

The story dramatically reiterates a point that Luke has made frequently before. God does not judge as humans judge. It was not the popular opinion about Zacchaeus's occupation that determined how God received him. How he received Jesus and whether he perceived the royal rule of God Jesus was reestablishing determined that. If "God is able from . . . stones to raise up children to Abraham" (3:8), surely God welcomes allegiance from a compassionate tax collector who, by way of exception and out of love for God, scrupulously maintains integrity in his fiscal dealings. God gladly conveys such a camel through the needle's eye (18:25, 27).

Verse 10, "For the Son of Man came to seek out and to save the lost," does not contradict the above interpretation. The observation applies to multiple disclosures throughout the journey to Jerusalem section, and indeed is an apt summary of Luke's presentation of the entire thrust of Jesus' ministry. It is the crowd that is indicted by this story. They were so put off by their suppositions concerning Zacchaeus that they failed to "see" that in terms of the righteousness of God they were as "lost" as anyone, and they were diverted from "seeing" Jesus and gladly welcoming him to their salvation.

A sermon suggestion on the story follows:

Direct people's attention to the contrast between Zacchaeus and the crowd, and the disparity disclosed concerning both their self-perceptions and the quality of the manner with which they received Jesus. We do not need additional encouragement to cultivate our skills in perceiving those attributes in others that confirm our disparaging evaluations of their presentability before God. We have all become far too adept at that already.

"The Son of Man (*did*) come to save the lost" (v. 10): lost sheep, lost coins, lost sons (ch. 15), rich rulers (ch. 18), superficially enthusiastic and spiritually myopic crowds, and lifetime Christians who have sat in the pew for so long a time we have lost the sense of the awesome marvel of it all. What we require to know, what we need to anticipate is, when Jesus comes will we be free to concentrate on who he is and on what God wills to accomplish through him for us, or will we be so distracted by the itch to disparage others and even to complain if it seems that such a person thinks to be included that we, too, will miss the "acceptable hour of the Lord?"

PARABLE OF THE POUNDS (19:11–27)

Coming as it does at the conclusion of Luke's extensive narrative of the journey from Galilee to Jerusalem, this story poses a sharp query to the disciples (and to Luke's hearers—then and now). During that journey,

Jesus repeatedly instructed his followers about the nature of discipleship devoted to the royal rule of God. What do they intend to do with the gospel instruction with which they are being entrusted? The story further serves to remind us that Jesus' sojourn in Jerusalem will not culminate with a crescendo of universal acclamation greeting the dawning of the end-of-time Day of the Lord with its full display of God's royal rule on Mount Zion. Jerusalem instead means crucifixion.

(*a*) *A probable conflation of two stories.* Luke appears to have blended two stories into one. The first story concerned a nobleman who journeyed away in the quest to be confirmed by some unmentioned higher royal authority in his aspirations to serve as king over his own region. He was opposed in his intentions by a deputation of his enemies. Upon his return, having been successful in his mission, he executed those who had opposed him. (Both Herod and his son, Archelaus, traveled to Italy to secure the right to rule from Imperial Rome, and, on returning, had a number of rivals executed.)

The second story is a variation of the story we have come to know in its Matthean form as "the parable of the talents" (Matt. 25:14–30). By combining them, Luke was able to speak both a word of encouragement and a word of consolation to his community.

The following assertions describe the gist of the story:

a) Those forces opposing God have not yet been completely quelled into submissive silence. (Verse 14 may allude to the hostile reception Jesus had received from some of those whom he encountered during the course of his public ministry, and, by extension, to the resistance and rejection members of Luke's own community were encountering as they sought to preach the gospel.) An extended interval yet remains before the full reestablishment of the rule of God is accomplished. Tremendously significant events will occur during this interval of anticipation.

b) The servant disciples of the reign of God have tasks entrusted to them in the interim that require obedience, risk taking, and unequivocal trust.

c) When God's rule is again fully in place, the divine judgment on those hostile powers and their agents will be both thorough and devastatingly destructive, and the faithful servants of God whom they have opposed will be vindicated and rewarded.

(*b*) *Human expectations are at variance with the saving purposes of God.* The phrases "near Jerusalem" and "because they supposed that the kingdom of God was to appear immediately" in verse 11 record the ambiguity of the moment. In one sense, the rule of God had appeared in the person and work of the one who was speaking to them, a reality they had difficulty discerning and could detect only dimly, and moment by moment. Their expectations were shaped by Day of the Lord suppositions current in their traditions that looked to the complete restoration throughout creation of the rule of God and the eradication of all other powers, authorities, and spiritual beings who claimed to rule in God's stead.

Although Jesus is inaugurating the restoration of divine rule in creation, there will be an interval before the reign of God is completely established everywhere and over everything. What was about to appear in the next interval in Jerusalem was not the realm of God in all its awesome majesty, power, and perfection (although, paradoxically, to the perceptive eyes of faith, it *was*). Instead, the apparent triumph of all of those supernatural forces opposing God and seeking to supplant God was about to unfold.

(*c*) *Faithful and unfaithful servanthood.* The impact of the story depends on the recognition that inherent to what it means to be a "good" servant/slave is such selfless devotion that one is willing to take intimidating personal risks for the sake of being faithfully obedient to the advancement of the master/owner's interests. The contrast (vv. 16–19) between the comparatively insignificant amount of money deposited with the slaves (about three months' wages for a laborer) and the impressive reward for faithful productivity (authority over five to ten cities) indicates the high premium that faithful obedience, especially when it is risky, carries in the realm of God.

By contrast, the caution dictated by the third slave's disobedient timidity at the potential ruin inherent in the risk (vv. 20–23) led him unwittingly into the graver danger of having defied the royal nobleman's clear command, "Do business with these" (v. 13). His behavior was at cross purposes with his own assessment of what the master expected of him. He allowed his terror to counsel him to dodge the mandate he had received. He worked against his own conviction of impending, inescapable accountability. So the third slave incarnates failure as measured by kingdom criteria to any response other than glad, total dedication to the claim of God's royal rule.

The interval extends between Jesus' announcement of the presence of the realm of God and the obvious manifestation of the restored rule of

God over all creation. The function of believers during that interval continues to be not solely or even primarily one of watching and waiting impatiently for God to get on with it. God entrusts us with something exceedingly precious of God's resources, and God expects us to "do business"—God's business—with it, and thereby produce results for the royal realm of God. We will be held accountable for how we have carried out that mandate, and we know it.

Helpful considerations when preaching on this passage include:

Christians today need to hear the word of encouragement and admonition as much as did the early Christians in Luke's community and beyond. Our zeal for the work of spreading the rule of God through our living and telling the gospel is too little evident.

The second thrust of the passage impacts us differently, for the enemies of Jesus (and of the church of God) do not fear and despise that kingdom presence. They ignore him, or they dismiss him. They are not even persuaded that there is such a noble person. And even if there might be, he will never pull off the goal of coming back and wielding effective royal authority and power. He is gone, never to return.

How have people become convinced of that? When Jesus goes into Jerusalem, the royal presence is so compelling it cannot be ignored or dismissed. Why is it not equally as compelling and inescapable in the community of faith today? Could it be that the church has succumbed to the lure of the culture's presuppositions and goals—that it has become market driven rather than kingdom compelled?

Too often the church wraps the gospel in the smothering fabric of profane values and objectives. It is "doing business" with the power and resources of God. But too often that business is not in response to the clear mandate of God but is business done in pursuit of the objectives and guided by the values of those forces seeking to rule in God's stead. The "Lord" it serves, the "Lord" it proclaims, the "Lord" to whom it is answerable is no threat to the powers of this age.

The story requires us to recover what it is that we know about God. What does the Lord require? How consistently is the ministry that we support and in which we engage molded to be responsive to the expectations we know that God has graciously lodged in us?

Ministry in Jerusalem

Luke 19:28–21:38

In this section, Luke recounts those events that propel Jesus to the culminating consequences of his entire public ministry. Indeed, what looms before him and his disciples is the reason why he was born in Bethlehem. The impending tragic-triumphant climax was pointedly anticipated throughout the extended journey from Galilee. That journey has now been concluded as Jesus enters Jerusalem.

The crescendo of opposition that rushes Jesus rapidly to trial and execution seems to indicate that, out of his zeal for advancing the dominion of God, Jesus has made some tragic miscalculation in strategy. However, the Evangelist counts on our recalling that, time and again, the narrative has alerted us to what was to occur—indeed, in terms of the divine program for salvation, *had* to occur (cf. 2:34f.; 9:22, 31, 44; 18:32f.).

JESUS' ROYAL ENTRY
INTO JERUSALEM (19:28–40)

(*a*) *The crowd acclaims King Jesus.* Luke, by shaping the narrative transition that marked the conclusion of Jesus' extended journey from Galilee to Jerusalem with the phrase "After he had said this" (v. 28), compels the hearers of his narrative story to relate the anecdote that follows to the parable of the pounds that Jesus had just told (19:12ff.). From that perspective, Jesus was not entering Jerusalem after having acquired kingly power (as the audience to whom the story was told had thought—19:11). The events about to unfold in Jerusalem would inaugurate the journey that would take Jesus away, after which he would return with royal authority. In the interval, he was entrusting the dissemination of the good news of the gospel to the disciples.

We encounter another equivocal feature of the Lukan narrative in the multitude that accompanied Jesus into Jerusalem. Luke had recently referred to the larger crowds who were accompanying Jesus as he drew near to Jerusalem (18:36; 19:3). Still, it is the disciples of Jesus who are involved with him during the entry into Jerusalem (vv. 29, 35f., 37, 39). They personify obedience, dedication, and joyful commitment. As subsequent occurrences rush toward a tragic, inescapable climax, their loyalty will erode, their devotion dissolve. But now they know themselves to be disciples/servants of the Messiah/King. Only, suddenly, at verse 39, the larger crowd, extending beyond the circle of the disciples and holding a broader spectrum of opinions, inexplicably reappears. This crowd includes Pharisees who require Jesus to suppress the behavior of the disciples.

A sermon on these aspects of the passage might explore:

The alert reader will recall that in Luke's narrative Jesus has *always* been king (cf. 1:32f.). Luke does not presume at this point in his Gospel to determine an issue that can be resolved within the human heart, and even then, only moment by tentative, ambivalent moment.

It is enough to sharpen our awareness, however, at how poorly we distinguish those who truly belong to Jesus. Overestimating, underestimating, misjudging, reproving—we do that badly, and it is none of our business anyway. Luke will insist that it belongs to the initiative of the resurrected Jesus to rehabilitate and empower disciples for effective work in the service of the dominion of God (24:13–52).

(*b*) *Jesus' "royal" entry.* Luke anchored his version of the entry into Jerusalem firmly in the traditions of the holy history of Israel. Features in 2 Kings 9:13 and in Zechariah (especially chapters 9 and 14) were interwoven into the fabric of the story. At the same time, masterful literary craftsman that he is, Luke used the details of the story both to heighten the dramatic impact and to anticipate coming events.

- The Mount of Olives, mentioned twice (vv. 29, 37), provides narrative anticipation of the agony, betrayal, and arrest to come (22:39–53, cf. 21:37).
- Detailed information about the location of the colt (v. 30) and anticipation of the owners' query (v. 31) affirm the all-knowing prophetic perceptiveness of Jesus.
- That the colt never had been ridden (v. 30) made it particularly suitable for cultic service.
- The owners' (lords') compliance to the needs of the Lord (vv. 33f.) indicates expected acquiescence to greater lordly authority.

Especially striking is the emphasis Luke placed on the royal motif in the account.

- Luke's use of the name "Jesus" twice in verse 35 reminds us that it was in the context of affirming his kingly authority and power that this name was assigned to him by the angel Gabriel (1:31–33).
- The disciples set Jesus on the colt of royalty (v. 35; cf. Zech. 9:9); he did not assume that posture on his own.
- The people spread their cloaks on the road (v. 36) in recognition of Jesus' kingly identity.
- Only in Luke's version of the story do the disciples embellish the quotation from Psalm 118:26, the use of which was anticipated by Jesus earlier during the journey (cf. 13:35), with the explicit acclamation "the king," and blends with it the praise motifs voiced by the angels at Jesus' birth (cf. 2:14).

Two observations are critical for our understanding of this story at the beginning of the Jerusalem segment of Luke's account. First, the disciples thrust the title of "king" upon Jesus, when royal power was not theirs to award. Their role was to support and extend his ministry and thereby to serve the royal rule of God.

Second, acclaiming Jesus as "king" was both premature and for the wrong (or, better, insufficient) reasons. The "deeds of power that they had seen" (v. 37) witnessed to the fulfillment of that which Jesus, using the words of Isaiah, had announced in the synagogue at Nazareth at the beginning of his public ministry (4:16–21), and which he had repeated in response to the query of John the Baptist (7:18–23).

Jesus' mighty acts were only part of what disclosed Jesus' identity as Messiah. His humiliation, crucifixion, and death, compatible to the prophetic anticipation in scripture, filled out that picture (cf. 24:25ff., 44ff.). His return in the fullness of royal power, in anticipation of which the disciples are to work diligently and faithfully in expanding the absent king's holdings, has not yet occurred (see Acts 1:6–8).

(c) *The Pharisees demand that Jesus calm things down.* Verses 39–40 put before us an additional aspect of ambiguity concerning the crowds of disciples who surround Jesus with joyous acclamation. Pharisees are in the crowd of disciples, but apparently, instead of taking part in the praise of God, require Jesus to suppress the demonstration. Who are they? Disciples of Jesus? They call him "Teacher," as if they were, yet refer to "your disciples" as ones who were other than they.

Throughout the Lukan narrative, the Pharisees respond variously to Jesus. Unlike the hostile role they play in Mark's Gospel, Luke portrays them as sometimes critical, sometimes confused, sometimes receptive and hospitable. They criticized Jesus' behavior (15:2) and ridiculed him (16:14), yet at other times they sought to be instructed by him (17:20) or warned him of danger (13:31).

Here they appear to have Jesus' best interests in view as they counsel caution. A low profile was better than such a highly visible public demonstration, lest Jesus and his followers come to the attention of the suppressive coalition forged between the established interests of jealous Temple-centered religion and the merciless political might of Imperial Rome.

These Pharisees overlooked or forgot that Jesus repeatedly had confronted powers far more viciously violent and hostile—and had prevailed every time. The events that were about to occur would not disclose his vulnerability, but would make plainly evident the ultimate impotency of all powers and authorities that resist the restoration of the rule of God. That was why he had set his face to go to Jerusalem and would not be turned aside.

Jesus' response insisted that, even if the Pharisees were loath to recall what was at stake, the rest of creation remembered. All of creation was affected by the significance of this event. All creation joined with disciples, shepherds, the heavenly host, and all others who perceptively encountered in Jesus the presence of the power of God. Such acclaim must come to expression, and the stones of Jerusalem metaphorically were creation's mouthpiece. Even those rocks were more responsively aware of the transforming power of the presence of the reign of God in the person of Jesus than were the Pharisees who called him "Teacher."

The Pharisees are that part of the crowd which, as anticipated in Isaiah 6:9–10, "does not comprehend . . . does not understand." When the Pharisee-disciples demanded that Jesus rebuke the other celebrating disciples, they betrayed and confessed their own lack of perception at the import of the moment. This causes us to notice that the word they used in their demand on Jesus, "*rebuke* your disciples," is the same word Luke used repeatedly when telling of a clash between the rule of God and those supernatural powers that opposed God (see 4:35, 39, 41; 8:24; 9:42, etc.).

Such lack of perception is not just myopic, it is demonic. Jesus' response is surely more than a corrective, it is a "*rebuke*" directed now toward them rather than toward the disciples. On this discordant note, the Pharisees disappear from the Lukan narrative not to reappear until the second volume of his work, the book of Acts.

Another preaching perspective on the passage follows:

The entire processional episode is saturated with ambiguity. Is Jesus "king" or not? And if he is, what does that mean? Has he returned having obtained his royal power, or is he departing to secure kingly authority? Does the joyously welcoming crowd support him and what his mission is intended to accomplish without exception or qualification, or not? If so, what does that mean for their future activity and well-being? If not, then what are they doing there at all?

Such ambivalence certainly must feel very familiar to us as we reflect on the mixed motives and the cautionary convictions that accompany our own spiritual journeys and have us producing equivocal responses and ambivalent behavior even at "kairos" moments of opportunity and crisis.

This dramatically moving story compels us to reflect on all the inadequate Palm Sunday-like accolades we have felt moved to offer. The ambivalence with which we hail Jesus' right to rule, the compromised loyalties that impel our yells, the selective obedience we offer to one whom we will know as Lord only under certain strictly held conditions—we know all of these, and we are ashamed and embarrassed, and spiritually humiliated.

Even as we sink into that posture of penitence, we feel the paving beneath our feet begin to move and stony mouths yawning open to voice praises. From such stones as these God is able to "raise up children to Abraham" (see 3:8) who burst out in adorational hallelujahs. How much more is God able, how much more does God want, to raise up children to Abraham out of our stoned hearts? Praise God—even if we use the wrong terms, or say the right thing for all the wrong (or inadequate) reasons, or show ourselves uncontrollably joyful at what others find to be painfully and even dangerously awkward moments. Jesus forgives and corrects, empowers and commissions us, as he did the disciples (Luke 24 and Acts 1).

PROPHETIC LAMENT AND PROPHETIC ACT (19:41–48)

Luke's narrative of the life and ministry of Jesus began in the Temple in Jerusalem (1:5–23; see also 2:22–38). He now brings the story full circle and returns to the same locale for the concluding stage of Jesus' teaching and preaching ministry (through 21:38), just prior to his arrest, trial, and execution. In Luke's version, this is the first time that Jesus has returned to the Temple since he was an adolescent (2:41ff.). This section relates both a prophetic lament (vv. 41–44) and a prophetic act (vv. 45–48).

(a) *The contrast between the crowd's cheers and Jesus' sorrow.* The passage presents a dramatically vivid contrast to the scene just sketched. The disciples were cheering, the Pharisees were sanctimoniously "shushing"—

and Jesus' heart is breaking over Jerusalem's (*and* the disciples', *and* the Pharisees', *and* our) spiritual sightlessness.

Each audience is blind in its own way. The disciples think that they have it all worked out, and confidently expect God to conform to their projected timetable. The Pharisees counsel caution, oblivious to the fact that Jesus, far from being helplessly vulnerable, carries an authority such that those Imperial Roman powers before which they are cowed owe accountability to the authority of the one whom they are trying to suppress. Jerusalem, the City of David, is oblivious to the advent of precisely that Davidic Messiah it claims to be watching for so longingly. The Temple crowd, putatively devoted to obedient service of the God whose presence is acknowledged both in the Holy of Holies and in the Mosaic Torah, is awash in homicidal hostility to that very divine presence incarnate in Jesus' person, and prophetically disclosed in his actions and in his teachings.

A sermonic 'spin-off' on this aspect follows:

That is just amazing, when you think about it. What a caution to admonish us in our smug satisfaction that we know all about God's plan to set right and restore creation, and in our naive confidence that we know 1) when the successive stages in that plan for recovery will occur, 2) how God will bring it off, and 3) what the dominion of God will ultimately look like.

(*b*) *The prophetic lament.* In the first subsection of this passage, verses 41–44, Jesus voices a *prophetic lament* over imperceptive Jerusalem. Fred Craddock reminds us that such a prophetic lament is:

> ". . . a voice of love and profound caring, of vision of what could have been and of grief over its loss, of tough hope painfully releasing the object of its hope, of personal responsibility and frustration, of sorrow and anger mixed, of accepted loss but with energy enough to go on." (*Luke*, Louisville, Ky.: John Knox Press, 1990, p. 229.)

Jesus grieved over Jerusalem's imperceptiveness, and the grief is just as profound and intense as was the joy in heaven over the return of the lost (cf. chapter 15). The "time of your visitation" (v. 44), which should be the time of Jerusalem's salvation is, instead, the time of Jerusalem's judgment and destruction because of the city's about-to-emerge determination to kill the bringer of that salvation. The account of this incident may have been shaped to echo the fate of Jerusalem as Isaiah 29:3 and Jeremiah 6:15 had anticipated it.

Jesus' entire ministry up until now had been devoted to stimulating a response of perceptive recognition and glad subjection to the presence of divine dominion. Not knowing the true nature of the moment was something Jesus had already warned his hearers that they often did (cf. 12:56).

"The things that make for peace" (v. 42) may be a play on the Salem/shalom motifs related to the etymology of the name of the city: Jeru-*salem*. It corresponds to the "peace in heaven" that the disciples had just been celebrating with Jesus' approach to the city (v. 38; cf. 1:79; 2:14) and is God's gift to Jerusalem (and the rest of creation), too, if it only was perceptive enough to recognize who and what was coming into its midst.

The city's hostile indifference represented all of those whom Jesus had encountered during his public ministry who had resisted "seeing" (acknowledging and embracing) the rule of God he announced and offered. Because of their stubborn, rebellious resistance, their hearts had been hardened. God prevented them from grasping the eternal dimensions of this moment and this person.

Both Luke as he wrote and his community as they were hearing this narrative were convinced that the destruction of Jerusalem by Rome, which had actually occurred just in the recent past, was God's punishment of Jerusalem for its rejection of Jesus. Jerusalem, demonically hostile to the moment when its salvation stood within its gates, was shortly to go against the legions of Rome with disastrously fatal results both for the city and for the people. Their fanatic zeal—fueled by the counterfeit conviction that God was inspiring them to rise up against Roman rule and was empowering them to prevail against Caesar's legions—confirmed how myopically impervious to God's presence and purposes they had become. It was Jerusalem's experience of the judgment pronounced in verse 26, "from those who have nothing, even what they have will be taken away."

(*c*) *Jesus cleanses the Temple.* The *prophetic act* (vv. 45–47) at the Temple was done by one who knew full well that Jerusalem habitually killed its prophets (13:33–35). Echoes of Jewish prophetic traditions may again be heard here (cf. especially Isa. 56:7; Jer. 7:11; Zech. 14:21). Jesus expelled from the Temple area what Luke presented as corrupting mercantile operations.

Luke regarded the Jerusalem Temple in a positive light. The "cleansing" is not the beginning of the Temple's destruction but a purifying act whereby cultically defiling practices are evicted by the restoring and renewing power of the reasserted rule of God. Jesus thereby transformed it into a fit and proper location for his teaching concerning the inbreaking realm of God.

What has happened to the Temple is what has happened to the people of Israel, indeed to all of fallen creation. The Temple was the place where the dominion of God should be most clearly and winsomely visible.

Because God's rule has even here been supplanted, the resulting corruption and hostile resistance testifies to their repudiation of God's rule.

The "den of robbers" (cf. Jer. 7:11) is not just the crowd of kiosk hucksters who were exploiting the pious. The "chief priests and scribes and leaders of the people" deserve to be included, too. These religious functionaries who supposedly broker the interaction of Israel with the God of life, have, instead, formed a coalition of conspiracy that seeks to destroy that life and to deprive the people of that presence.

As the twelve-year-old Jesus had debated and been nurtured there (2:41ff.), so the adult Jesus, moving toward the climax of his ministry, was making the Temple the locus for the last major period of his teaching ministry (19:47; cf. 20:1; 21:1, 5, 37f.; 22:53) and setting his classroom in order. The effective teaching concerning God's will and God's rule was what the chief priests, scribes, and leaders of the people should have been doing there themselves. So demonically possessed are they that when Jesus prepared to do what they should have been doing, they, instead of being inspired by his example, conspired to kill him.

A sermon suggestion on this account follows:

These verses pose some tough but necessary questions. They make us consider how rapidly we conclude that we know what God requires, how quickly we think we perceive what God is about, how certain we are that we are clear as to what constitutes an adequate and appropriate response.

There are also implied warnings to curb our tendency to give short shrift to any who claim to have been entrusted with a new direction for ministry in which God would have the church move. "Testing the spirit" is not exhausted by assessing conformity to what we have always done. Discerning requires a much more open, reflective, searching, and prayerful process.

In another direction, we must hear the strong caution raised against the possessively protective and jealous way we sometimes act toward projects, procedures, and programs we have imported into the holy space of the life of the community of faith. Whatever good intentions and goals may have led us to their introduction—even, for instance, the accomplishment of religious needs and purposes—we must be ruthless in our assessments of the extent to which they advance or detract from (and maybe even impede) our glad obedience to where God would have us invest energy, resources, and presence at the service of God's royal rule.

Finally, for all of the fierce critique these verses may generate, we must not neglect the word of grace God offers here. God yearns for us Jerusalemites to be moved by Jesus' tears, to have our blind eyes opened, and to at last know and embrace the things that make for peace in the time of our visitation. God longs for us to renounce divertive and even corrupting practices, and to repudiate our murderous and destructive intentions. God wants us to recover why we have been appointed "chief priests, scribes, leaders of the people," or whatever contemporary functions and offices correspond to those first-century roles, and then God desires us to devote ourselves with single-mindedness to service in those roles conforming to God's will, God's purposes, God's rule for the advancement, rather than the impediment, of the gospel summons.

ATTEMPTS TO DISCREDIT JESUS (20:1–19)

"Who do you think you are?" "What do you think you are doing?" "To whom are you accountable?" That is what the religious leaders wanted to know when they demanded (v. 2) that Jesus identify the one authorizing his activity.

It was not only that he had recently caused chaos in the Temple area by disrupting with his iconoclastic, purifying zeal the established commercial ventures that had become accepted there (19:45f.). More than that, he was returning regularly to the Temple (19:47f.; 20:1), regarding it as the fit locale for teaching concerning his views of the will and purposes of God. And the religious leaders *did not like it.* (Luke's community knew exactly why, and so do we. Luke has prepared us to expect it almost from the beginning—cf. 2:41–50.)

With this section Luke begins a series of stories extending through 21:4 about controversies between Jesus and the religious leaders that accumulate and intensify the crescendo of antipathy with which they had come to regard him. Included are three incidents they initiated by asking questions designed to ensnare him. It provides the darkly stained backdrop for their coagulating plot to kill him (22:1ff.; cf. 19:47).

(a) Religious leaders challenge Jesus' authority. The ones challenging Jesus—chief priests, scribes, elders—knew a great deal about authority and accountability. They were constrained by Temple and cult regulations; they were accountable to the religious establishment; they embodied the authority of Moses as they provided definitive interpretation, expansion, and application of Torah for the contemporary needs of pious Jews.

Now, as they indignantly observed, this Jesus, who had not paid his dues to the guild, who was neither priest, certified scribe, or acknowledged elder, had invaded their turf and was teaching God's good news with insidiously captivating conviction. The people were giving him a much more attentive hearing and were finding a persuasive credibility in his teachings far beyond what they, the established authorities, had ever received.

"Who gave you this authority?" they demanded to know. That is the right question! It is the one we, too, must ask of Jesus. If we have been following Luke's Gospel narrative carefully, we already know the answer: God gave Jesus this authority! The religious leaders were asking the right question—but for all the wrong reasons. Jesus was understandably dubious about their ability to hear and accept the answer. So his reply, while not responding directly to their query, provided an implied affirmation to the people in the Temple who heard it, and to us, too.

Perception of the presence of God is what is at stake here. God's presence had always been acknowledged in religious Judaism with particular reference to the Holy of Holies of the Temple cult, to the Mosaic law, and with the people of the Covenant, all of which the religious leaders were dedicated to serve. Jesus probed their perceptiveness by asking how they assessed the source of the authority with which another person, John the Baptist, had performed cultic acts purportedly in the service of God. He was asking them in essence, "Can you discern and affirm divine authority when it is present anywhere else besides the Temple protocols and the scribal interpretation of Mosaic law?" Luke has taken care to ensure that we are very clear about the correct answer concerning John the Baptist (1:14f., 66ff.; 3:2ff.; 7:26ff.).

Jesus was not being strategically evasive. The question he put to his interrogators was not asking after their personal opinions about John the Baptist. It tested the quality of discernment operative in the authority they claimed and exercised as religious leaders. The lack of such discernment posed serious questions about the quality of their ability to recognize God's presence and will in Temple and Torah.

If the religious leaders had accurately discerned the nature and source of John's authority, perhaps they might be open to acknowledging Jesus' authority, too. By the Baptist's own testimony (3:16), Jesus' authority was similar in source but vastly more powerful than his. If, then, they affirmed John's exercise of divinely originated prophetic power as from God, as a considerable number of "the people" did (v. 6), they already by extension had their answer concerning the source of Jesus' authority.

Jesus was eager for them to arrive at such a recognition. He yearned for that to occur, even at this late date when their schemings unequivocally advertised their malevolent intent (19:47).

As Luke has prepared us to expect, the religious leaders were not up to the challenge. Their cagey calculations (vv. 5f.) displayed political caution rather than discerning conviction. They feared people more than they feared God. The people were in a better position both to ask the question the religious leaders had asked and to respond with perception to the counter question posed by Jesus.

When the religious leaders equivocated in their response, they neutralized any last vestige of hope that they might embrace the claims of God's royal rule. They also nullified any claim *their* authority had to compel a response from Jesus. Jesus recognized their malevolent duplicity (v. 8) and would have none of it.

The exchange between the religious leaders and Jesus involved more than professional jealousy and competitive resentment. The Temple was the traditional locus for the exercise of the authority of the chief priests, scribes, and elders. The locale originally had symbolized that their authority was derived from the authority of the God whose presence among the people was focused in the Holy of Holies. When they had to inquire concerning the source of Jesus' authority, it indicated the degree of rebellious and sinful imperception with which they were afflicted. They who had devoted themselves in lifelong service to the God of the Presence should have been keenly aware of the presence, power, and authority of God at work in Jesus.

The adamant opposition of these functionaries to the presence and authority of Jesus was not born of jealous competition over who was best empowered to serve more adequately the God of Presence in the Temple. Their vicious resistance to Jesus and their assaults on Jesus' credibility disclosed that their authority actually was derived from, and was accountable to, the supernatural forces opposing the royal rule of God. Those forces sought to supplant God's dominion with a realm hostile to God's purposes for creation. The assault by the religious establishment against Jesus was not the consequence of professional pique but of demonic subjugation.

(*b*) *Jesus tells the parable of the wicked tenants.* At this point, Luke invests his narrative with a little noted yet severe literary transition. Jesus turned and told a story to the people (v. 9), but it was told about the religious leaders (v. 19). Jesus' shift in attention is harsh, with apocalyptic overtones of eternal condemnation and dismissal.

The story of the wicked tenants had undergone development in the oral tradition prior to its inclusion in our written Gospels. Although all parables by reason of their analogical nature imply allegorical appropriations, Christians by Luke's time had already developed this story into a complex parabolic allegory. The vineyard = Israel (cf. Isa. 5:1ff.), the owner (lord) of the vineyard = God, tenants = religious leaders, slaves = prophets, *beloved son* = Jesus (cf. 3:22), "others" = those worldwide who have supplanted the Jerusalem religious leaders, the apostles, and their successors, the church. For Luke and his community, it is an allegory that unfolds the turbulent, marvelous mystery of the course of salvation-history and the role God had assigned to them in it.

The allegorized parable indicts the religious leaders for their myopic inability to recognize the source, and therefore the nature and character, of the authority with which Jesus taught. The story also charges them with accurately surmising Jesus' authority and identity but refusing to honor it for fear that their authority as religious leaders would be negated. To reject the empowered agent of God is to reject God.

Sermon considerations on this section follow:

The section reminds us that the kinds of questions we address to Jesus and to God may tell a whole lot more than we realize about where we are in the light of God's saving purposes. How one responds to Jesus, his mighty acts, his wise and insightful teaching, his compassionate and commanding person, and whether one responds with impassive indifference, active opposition, or exhilarated joy is indicative of one's relationship to the presence and claim of the authority of the royal rule of God.

Furthermore, we are reminded that a story told by Jesus informs and addresses us in vastly different ways depending on whether we hear it as a story about others or as our story. It is not enough for us to interpret the text. We must be open to allowing the text to interpret us—individually and in all our corporate relationships. On the one hand, it offers stern warning to us when we are so seduced by our allegiance to religion that we are not only insensitive but even destructively adversarial to that which God is accomplishing in the world through God's spirit-empowered people—the church. Then it offers strong affirmation and encouragement to us to listen faithfully and receptively—to *hang on* to God's word—and be obediently responsive to God's commission to us.

TAXES TO CAESAR (20:20–26)

(a) *Religious leaders send counterfeit inquirers to bait Jesus.* The religious leaders had just been roundly trounced in exchanges with Jesus (19:39–40, 47–48; 20:1–8, 19) and have sent substitutes who pretended to be earnest inquirers. "Teacher" they called him (v. 21), but they did not really believe it for a minute. With the description of them as "spies who pretended to be honest, in order to trap him" (v. 20), Luke warns us that they were using the title as a dissembling expression of pseudo-respect designed to disarm Jesus so that they might more easily catch him in a political indiscretion.

Luke says that the spies "pretended to be honest" (literally, *righteous*). They demonstrated their duplicity when they asked Jesus, "Is it lawful . . ?" *Lawful* meant in accord with Mosaic law. They misused Mosaic law to advance the particular political program of the religious leaders. Yet, those leaders' sole reason for being was to guard and advance the righteous fulfillment of Mosaic law. Although the "spies" and the religious leaders who had sent them were unsuccessful in manipulating Jesus into making a seditious statement, Luke will portray them later as acting for all the world as if they had succeeded (cf. 23:2).

If they "pretended to be honest/righteous," they surely must have been inept, for the story documents that they would not know a righteous person if they were to see one. The righteous person, the spiritually empowered agent of God, stood right there before them. That reality did not even register with them.

The spies were only concerned with satisfying the religious leaders who had sent them to snare Jesus in his words through duplicity and thereby render him vulnerable to Roman judgment. Luke counted on his hearers noting the tremendous irony of it, for Jesus *did* "teach the way of God in accordance with truth" (v. 21) without deferring to them or to anyone else in any significant way. They had it exactly right if they only knew, if they only had ears to hear and eyes to see.

(b) *Jesus saw through the spies' subterfuge.* If they did not recognize Jesus, Jesus knew them. He saw them with perception, discerning their insidious intent, and he nailed them. Jesus' method of responding to a question with a counter question (he had used the same strategy in verse 3, and frequently elsewhere) forced those who would entrap him onto the defensive. The interrogators become the interrogated. That seems to happen often when we address questions to Jesus.

"Whose head (literally, "image") and whose title does (the denarius) bear?" (v. 24). Only governmental rulers had the right to produce coinage, on which their name and likeness was stamped. The coinage produced was held to be the property of the ruler whose image and name it bore. Jesus' question inquired after the inscribed identity of the legitimate owner of the object, and to whom it was therefore to be returned on demand. Upon their response, Jesus' pronouncement (v. 25) urges upon them and us a subtle appeal to the "from the lesser to the greater" argument. The saying demands consideration of what it is according to the teaching of Moses that corresponds in the righteous person's life under the rule of God to the image of Caesar on the coin of the Roman realm.

A contemporary historical event lent special vividness to the story for Luke and Luke's community of faith. With the fall of Jerusalem in 70 C.E., the Temple in Jerusalem was destroyed and the offering of sacrifices on the Temple mount ceased. In retaliation for the Zealot-incited Jewish uprising, the Emperor Vespasian confiscated the Jewish Temple tax (which Jews had considered so holy that it could not be paid with the coin of the realm that bore Caesar's image) and converted it into the *Fiscus Judaicus,* the "Jew Tax." Caesar poached that which was God's. Even worse, the Emperor diverted the funds thus collected to the upkeep of a temple dedicated to the worship of Jupiter. The "Jew Tax" went to support a pagan temple. One can imagine how odious it was to any religious Jew, including the Jewish Christians in Luke's own community, to be forced to pay such an assessment.

A possible direction for sermon development follows:

There are those who have found in this anecdote a capsule summary of Jesus' political philosophy. We Christians, they say, are caught in a time of tension as we strive to live as responsible citizens both of this age and of the age to come. Our human allegiances are divided between two arenas, the sacred and the secular, the religious and the political, the holy and the profane. The task with which we continually are challenged is to discern which of our loyalties are appropriate to this age and the secular affairs of Caesar, and which are appropriate to the new age and the spiritual rule of God. So the story serves, they hold, as the charter text for a doctrine of a balanced, judicious separation between church and state.

Others have found in the narrative dominical verification for a theory of God's dual operation whereby God—sometimes directly, at other times through delegated and accountable political functionaries—accomplishes God's purposes in human affairs. Often the church is distressingly unsure whether God's right hand knows what God's left hand is doing, much less whether they reasonably complement each other.

Then there are those who see the story as an illustration of how cleverly Jesus disposed of insidious opposition. The devious adversaries who tried to trap him were just no match for him. They posed for him a conundrum designed to impale him on one or the other points of an insoluble dilemma. But Jesus was just too cagey for them, and by his ambiguous reply astutely eluded their trap. (Surely, we are reading the text far too superficially if we only find in it an example of clever first-century Messianic gamesmanship.)

All of these readings miss the impact this story had for Luke and for other early Christians as well. In this exchange Jesus is not giving practical advice for how the truly religious person may honor his/her lawful obligations to the secular government without compromising the integrity of obedient devotion to God. Nor does the narrative underestimate the legitimate requirements of civil authority in contrast to the quality and scope of what is required by one's obedience to the royal rule of God. Finally, the anecdote does not want to illustrate the adroitness with which Jesus astutely avoided the political snares his adversaries set for him. Its concern is focused in a different direction.

Jesus' question about the image on the coin, and his resulting pronouncement, pushed the issue way beyond what the counterfeit interrogators had in mind. If one can identify so readily through recognition of the imprinted image precisely what it is that belongs to Caesar, what then are the things that are God's? What bears God's image? What carries God's name? *We do* (cf. Gen. 1:27)!

Once we identify with consenting recognition just whose image it is that we bear, and, therefore, to whom we belong, and once we order all of the priorities in our lives to conform to the legitimate ownership we acknowledge, the claims and demands of all of the Caesars in this world will be ordered in proper perspective. Let Caesar have what he wants. He'll never own you. You bear the image of God; God graciously allows you to bear God's name.

CONTROVERSY WITH SADDUCEES (20:27–44)

You might say Jesus was asking for it by intruding into the heart of the religious leaders' turf when he set up his soapbox podium right there in the sacred Temple area. First, "the chief priests and the scribes with the elders" (v. 1) had accosted him, then their fraudulent "spies" tried verbally to entangle him (v. 20), and now the Sadducees put a ridiculous riddle to him. They posed one of those highly theoretical, enigmatic puzzles which, from a human perspective, defies satisfactory or persuasive resolution.

(a) *The riddle posed by the Sadducees.* It was one of those exaggerated Bible questions (cf. "Moses wrote"—v. 28) that people employ primarily to humiliate, ridicule, and discredit someone while they themselves maintain the guise of being innocently earnest religious inquirers. Jesus was asked the question not out of honest perplexity and interest but because those interrogators wanted to embarrass him. We have all met someone like them at one time or another; perhaps at times we have been like them ourselves. It is a ploy of religious gamesmanship at its worst.

The Sadducees summoned Jesus' attention by addressing him as "Teacher" (v. 28). Although that was a very respectful form of address, they were using it insincerely. They pretended to need help in understanding an issue related to the widely held belief in a general resurrection on the Day of the Lord. But the Sadducees did not even believe in a general resurrection.

We know very little about the Sadducees. From the few times contemporary authors made mention of them, we gain the impression that they were a conservative, aristocratic religio-political Jewish party with some claim to special access and functions in the Jerusalem Temple. There are several references in first-century literature to their categorical denial of belief in a doctrine of general resurrection. It was one of the distinctive convictions of this disputatious minority sect within Judaism. That they nevertheless formulated their question to Jesus on the presumption of acceptance of the idea of resurrection betrays the insincerity they brought to the encounter.

The theoretical conundrum they put before Jesus played off the ancient custom of levirate marriage (the duty of a dead husband's brother to the widow) described in Deuteronomy 25:5–10. The situation they proposed was ridiculously improbable, but they were not interested in being believable, just in being unbelievably difficult. If there were seven brothers, and if they all were successively married to the same woman, and if they all died childless, and she died, too, whose wife would she be in heaven? The Sadducees did not really care. What they did care to do was to diminish the high regard and esteem in which Jesus was held by those people who came to hear his teaching in the Temple area.

(*b*) *Jesus' response to the Sadducees' verbal assault.* Jesus counterattacked from two different trajectories. In the first place, anyone who does not believe in something is more than likely to be ill informed about it. That was patently the case with the Sadducees with regard to the character of resurrection life, as their convoluted and exaggerated hypothetical case amply disclosed.

Jesus sought to disabuse these critics of their misinformation. Resurrection life is not simply end-of-the-ages resuscitation followed by resumption of the life previously lived with all of its relationships intact and continuing. General resurrection presumes radical discontinuity with life in the present age. (Luke reinforced the concept of resurrection discontinuity for his own community of faith through the post-resurrection appearance stories he included toward the end of his Gospel and in the first part of Acts.)

Jesus proceeded to correct the perspective of the Sadducees from a second, different slant. Lying behind their ignorance of the character of resurrection life was their error in denying general resurrection. Since they only accepted the books of Moses (the Pentateuch) as authoritative scriptures, Jesus responded from within the limits of that presumption. Moses testified (v. 37) to the reality of resurrection by referring to the God of Abraham, Isaac, and Jacob as the God of the living, even though all three patriarchs had long since died. Therefore, they were not dead but alive before God with resurrection life. Jesus used an argument based on a passage in the Sadducees' scripture to set aside the Sadducees' appeal to scripture as an authoritative basis for the artificial problem they had posed.

"Some of the scribes," overhearing, expressed grudging admiration of Jesus' lucid and aggressive response. Their calling him "Teacher" had more substance and integrity than that title had as it was used either by the Sadducees or by the religious leaders' spies in the preceding section. They signaled recognition that the tactic of attempting to trap Jesus into making pronouncements that would make him vulnerable to formal judicial process before either the religious leaders or the empowered agents of Imperial Rome had aborted.

(c) *Jesus countered with a riddle of his own.* Jesus was not impressed with the scribes' reluctant respect, nor was he yet done with them. Having dealt with the Sadducees' riddle, Jesus posed a scriptural riddle of his own to the scribes (vv. 41–44). "David's son is David's Lord, and David himself knew it. How is that?"

In the strong patriarchal society of David's time, no one, least of all a king, would logically refer to a descendant of his as his *Lord.* The descendant should call the ancestor "Lord," and not the opposite. If, however, it has been supernaturally revealed to the king that the descendant is to be Messiah, then a king speaking of that one of his progeny as "Lord" made profoundly pious sense. (Luke gives a detailed solution to the riddle in Acts 2:24–36.) That the scribes had no answer at all to Jesus' probing counteroffensive clearly disclosed just how sterile their vaunted wisdom and talent for the authoritative interpretation of scripture had become.

BEWARE OF THE SCRIBES! (20:45–21:4)

This section contains two contrasting parts: scathing indictment by Jesus of the negative model of the scribes' ostentatious religious duplicity (20:45–47), and the consequential neglect of the service to which God's covenant people are called. The incident of the widow's gift (21:1–4) is a pitiful example of excessive religious fervor going unchecked even though it was the clearly disclosed and well-known will of God that such a one be the recipient of compassionate ministry. This is the concluding section to the collection of stories of conflict in the Temple area, begun at 19:45, a heaping together of incidents provoked by the Jewish religious functionaries in reaction to what they considered to be the scandalously radical teachings of Jesus.

(*a*) *Jesus attacked the phony religiosity of the scribes.* Although in the beginning of this section Luke portrayed Jesus as directing his remarks primarily to the disciples (v. 45), "the people" were within earshot, and of course so are Luke's hearers/readers, then and now. The target of attention is the scribes, some of whom had just expressed grudging admiration when Jesus had adroitly deflected the Sadducees' transparent trap (v. 39). Luke will not have Jesus' scorn diluted by scant approbation. His denunciation and warning is similar in tone to the earlier tirade against "lawyers" (cf. 11:45–52).

Jesus scored the scribes for the disparity between their fake pious appearance and their actual motivations, and for indulging in sham religion rather than striving for disciplined integrity between inner spirituality and visible style of behavior. Their self-commending preoccupation with pretense and display, with attracting social and religious recognition, with pretentious public prayer is exposed as counterfeit.

Primary evidence was the scribes' merciless exploitation of widows (cf. 18:1ff., and the comments above on that section) whom God had commended to the people of the covenant for special care and protection (cf. Deut. 10:18; Isa. 1:17, 23; 10:2–3, etc.—the concern is expressed often in Jewish scriptures). The reference to "widows' houses" (v. 47) as well as to the "poor widow" (21:2f.) permit us to think of the scribes' "long prayers" (v. 47) as hypocritical public intercessions to God for special care for the very same widows whom the scribes themselves are exploiting.

(*b*) *The offering of an indigent widow.* The second part to the section relates the story of the poor widow's offering (21:1–4). We trivialize this story if we hear it only as a narrative admonition for Christians to cultivate sacrificially generous stewardship of material possessions. The story may have circulated earlier in the oral tradition as an individual, self-contained anecdote of exemplary, self-sacrificing piety. Already in Luke's source, however, (the Gospel of Mark), the story of the poor widow's excessive offering had been appended by the catchword method ("widow"—20:47; 21:2–3) to Jesus' prior warning about scribes.

Luke's narrative context gives it a different spin. "In this context Jesus is more lamenting the injustice which the scene reveals than commending the virtue of generosity" (David L. Tiede, *Luke,* [Minneapolis: Augsburg Publishing House, 1988], p. 354).

The scribes had exploited rather than protected widows, and the rich people had gotten the message the scribes' example commended. Although scripture claimed it to be God's will, attentive care for widows and orphans really did not matter to them. The wealthy, out of devotion to God, obeyed the law that encouraged lavish contributions to the Temple treasury—contributions, however, that hardly diminished the excessive level of their wealth. Yet, they routinely ignored the needs of the poor widow whom God through Moses had especially commended to their compassionate generosity and care.

The poor widow, from profound piety and, perhaps, from religious ignorance, gave to the extent that it increased her already precarious vulnerability ("all she had to live on," v. 4), an excess explicitly forbidden by Jewish law. Rabbinical literature transmits ancient scribal prohibitions that proscribed acts of excessive philanthropy that left the enthusiast destitute and consequently a greater burden on the community's charity.

While such a proscribed act was occurring, neither the scribes, nor the Pharisees, nor the chief priests—*none* of the religious leaders—made protest or offered restraint to the poor widow. Neither did they address remonstrance and admonition to the wealthy. Nor did they serve as God's agents of mercy to minister to the poor widow's need. Yet they, more than most, knew that God willed for Israel to serve God by caring for widows. So she becomes a concrete case, a living testimony of God-protected vulnerability being devoured by the religious establishment.

Here is a possible direction for sermon development:

The chief priests, the Pharisees, or, as in this case, the scribes often appear to be such artificial figures in the narratives of the Gospels. They are depicted in what almost seems to us to be caricatures of hypocrisy, deceit, and duplicity. None of us resemble them—or have any inclination to be like them. Then we realize it is only a difference of degree. We engage in spiritual mendacity, too, but we seldom are that blatant about it.

For many of us, the social and cultural settings in which we are most at home would consider flagrant hostility about religious conviction or condescending indifference to the idea of deity as simply too gauche. Our hypocrisies are more veiled, more subtle, more oblique—and we all engage in them. We are just not so obvious.

It is precisely in such cautiously contrived and veiled dissemblings that we make common cause with the scribal mentality. With every mendacious act or posture, we assert solidarity with those who assume the trappings of religious fervor not for reasons of devotion or conviction, but for purposes of moral masquerade and phony self-aggrandizement.

That is what makes all such stories about Jesus in Luke so tough for us to read. It is also why we read through them so quickly and so superficially without taking the time to enter and participate in the anecdote, to ponder, to immerse ourselves in humiliating self-examination, and to be thereby transformed.

What is at stake is more serious than simply embarrassed recognition of our immature, insincere, pompous posturings. We distort, deform, and pervert the legitimate claim of the saving love of God. We prostitute God's call to service in response to God's rule, distorting discipleship into religiously disguised service to ourselves. We deflect our energies and attentions so that what God calls us to do goes undone and those to whom God would minister through us are neglected.

We cannot simply pass this off by making condescending reference to the hucksters of phony religious enthusiasm who prey on the poor and the gullible, and to the con artists of the religious media who with flagrantly manipulative deception dupe the naive in the name of devotion to God. There is no question that they have plenty for which they will be held accountable. Even more at risk of "the greater condemnation" (20:47) are the leaders, the influential and affluent members of communities of faith who pretend to piety for personal aggrandizement, and who, for their own benefit, mislead or even exploit the gullible, the unwary, the immature, and the vulnerable.

JESUS TALKS ABOUT
THE END TIME (21:5–24)

This section is the first part of a prolonged discourse by Jesus concerning events and experiences associated with the inbreaking of the end of the ages, which extends over the rest of chapter 21. All of the events Jesus describes in this section are presented not as end-of-time events per se but as events that are preliminary to the arrival of the end time and the total supplanting of this present age by the eternal rule of God.

Luke artfully balanced a sense of the immediacy of end-time vividness and drama while at the same time urging his hearers to moderate their frenzied yearning for the climactic culmination of "this age" to approach rapidly. He was not interested in providing a schedule of events to come that would enable his community to chart the progressive approach of the time of the end. He wanted to provoke from within his community confidence and assurance for faithful obedience in the face of the tough demands both of the present and of the future.

Luke wished to move fellow believers to resolve to endure with unswerving faith and vigilant composure whatever tribulations, distress, and hardships would come to them in the course of their obedient service to the call and commission of Christ. He wanted them to depend on the confident conviction that the purposes of God that Jesus revealed would be triumphantly and completely accomplished.

(a) Questions evoked by Jesus' prediction of the destruction of the Temple. "Some" (v. 5) from among "all the people" (cf. v. 38) who regularly were coming to hear Jesus' teaching in the Temple was how Luke described those who provoked the discourse. They expressed awestruck appreciation of the magnificence of the building and the rich grandeur of its decor. However, in Luke's version Jesus directed his discourse to all who were there.

Their effusive outburst at the Temple's beauty evoked from Jesus a prophetic pronouncement concerning the razing of the Temple. He hastened to disabuse them of any inclination to put too much store in the significance of the opulence of the edifice. Architectural ostentation could be just as two-faced and deceptive an indication of the quality and authenticity of devotion to God as was the public, pseudo-pious behavior of the scribes (see the previous section, 20:45ff.). Impressive as it was, the Temple was not to be equated with the realm of God. It only pointed symbolically to that eternal reality. It was an artifact of this age and would not endure.

Such an assertion understandably evoked two questions: When will the end time come and how will we recognize its presence (v. 7)? They were assuming that such a catastrophe could only be one of the end-time events when everything belonging to this present age would be destroyed. (For Luke's community, as for most Christians toward the latter part of the first century, the recent fall of Jerusalem to the Roman legions commanded by Titus in 70 C.E., together with the accompanying destruction of the Temple, ratified their conviction that they were living in the "last days." That reinforced the identity they held of themselves as the end-time people of God, which they saw confirmed also by the outpouring of the Holy Spirit upon Christians right from the beginning of the post-Easter church's existence.)

(b) Cataclysmic events presaging the end. Jesus responded to their questions with descriptions of a list of occurrences that would precede the events heralding the climactic culmination of this age, implying that the Temple's destruction was just such a preliminary occurrence. These precursory events included the appearance of those making phony "Messiah" claims who would give false and misleading alerts (v. 8), the emergence of massive political unrest and international conflicts (vv. 9–10), and the occurrence of worldwide natural disasters accompanied by cosmological forewarnings (v. 11).

The extent of the events preluding the end of the ages indicates the scope of all that is to be embraced by the transforming reassertion of God's royal rule—greater than the limits of cultic Judaism God's purposes have worldwide, even cosmological dimensions.

Preceding and accompanying all of these events preliminary to the end will be an extended interval of particularly severe, brutal, and intensely isolating persecutions directed against Christians (vv. 12–19). How they fare in response to the call of God, the commission of Christ, and the empowering of the Holy Spirit even in the most adverse circumstances should be of far greater concern to them than speculation over "when" and "by what sign." Their fidelity is persuasive evidence that the triumphant consummation of God's intent to restore all of the created order to God's rule approaches.

Vicious persecution is not to be dreaded, abhorred, and avoided. Such hostile aggression gives rise to unparalleled opportunities to announce the restoration of the realm of God in places and to persons the deformed values of "this age" count as significant. During such persecution Christians who are brought before civil or religious authorities to be interrogated and judged will, by their testimony, be agents through whom the persecutors' exercise of authority is judged by the truth of God. This is very similar to the consequence on the numerous occasions in Luke's narrative when opponents who sought to interrogate and examine Jesus found themselves, in the course of the exchange, being examined by the truth of God present in the person and words of Jesus.

The effectiveness of the testimony of Christians under such tense and hostile circumstances was not limited to their perceptive insight, wisdom, and argumentative skill (vv. 14–15). Through them Jesus will be testifying and continuing to judge in the light of the eternal rule of God those who have presumed to pass judgment on his faithful servants. (These verses reiterate the promise Jesus had already given to the disciples in 12:11–12.)

Vulnerable to hostile religious and political power, Christians know clearly that Jesus is their only necessary resource for support, sustenance, and inspiration. Subjected to rejection and treachery by friends and even family, Christians know clearly that their only necessary true family and society is the community of faith.

(c) *Where the destruction of the Jerusalem fits in.* Luke's community knew of concrete cases when all of the manifestations of persecution described in verses 12–19 had occurred. Indeed, in the Acts of the Apostles continuing his Gospel narrative, Luke detailed a number of such specific anecdotes that already had become a precious part of the church's heritage.

A particularly illuminating case in point was the destruction of Jerusalem (vv. 20–24), which included the demolition of the Temple, the allusion to which in verse 6 gave impetus to the entire extended discussion. From the time-perspective of Luke's narrative, that event still lay in the future, but from the time-perspective of Luke's composition and of his community's hearing his account, the event had occurred recently.

Luke shaped this section to counteract any lingering assumptions in his community that the destruction of Jerusalem was the final, climactic end-of-the-ages event. In Jewish scriptures Jerusalem repeatedly was identified as the focal point for the end-time restoration of the realm of God over all creation. Christians needed help in rethinking that expectation, which they found in their Bibles, in the light of the leveling of Jerusalem by the Roman army.

Luke insisted that the fall of Jerusalem and the destruction of the Temple was merely one component (though a very significant component) that paralleled a much broader worldwide, even cosmos-wide, pattern of expanded primordial chaos in the natural, the human, and the heavenly spheres. It conformed to "the falling . . . of many in Israel" which Simeon had anticipated at the time of the dedication of the infant Jesus (2:34). The Jerusalem event was a calamity that reflected the intensity of God's wrath on Jewish imperceptive unresponsiveness to the presence and claim of God's right to rule—the obverse to the initiative that God through the Christian mission was taking to summon the Gentiles for inclusion.

Inclusion of the Gentiles was a startling assertion. Jewish writings indicate that Judaism had come to expect that, as God reestablished divine rule on Mount Zion at the end of time, all of those Gentile nations that had oppressed Israel would become recipients of divine retribution (cf. Dan. 2:44; Bar. 4:24–25, 30–35). God would vindicate Israel and restore it to its divinely appointed place and function in God's saving economy.

In his teachings Jesus reversed that late Jewish expectation of the obliteration of oppressing Gentiles in favor of the earlier Jewish conviction that God called Israel into covenant in order that they might be agents through whom the Gentiles would be recruited for inclusion in the salvation of God. The completion of that wider initiative of God—the fulfilling of "the times of the Gentiles" (v. 24) which was a large part of the mission entrusted to Luke's community (v. 24:47; Acts 1:8)—was a more dependable indication that the interval preliminary to the end times had been spanned.

A direction to pursue for preaching purposes follows:

Revisit Luke 17:20–37 (and the comments made above on that section) for earlier Lukan assertions of end-of-time events and expectations.

Complex as this sequence and all of these issues are, the toughest task will be to get people to take the concerns of the section seriously. There is little anticipation or zeal evident in most communities of faith today concerning the inbreaking of the end time and the supplanting of the powers and values of this present age. There is little apprehension that Christians aggressively engaged in mission will encounter severe and hostile opposition, much less formal persecution by civil and religious authorities. Usually the worst one encounters from family and friends is indifference and apathy mixed with condescending tolerance and ridicule.

Early Christians surely were misguided in their attempts to put together a sequence of end-time events that would serve them as a dependable indicator of the return of the Messiah and the beginning of the end of this present age. We do not need to revive those efforts. But the loss of a sense of confident, vivid expectation of the culminating fulfillment of God's purpose to restore God's rule and to rehabilitate the totality of creation divests us of a certain sense of urgency and deprives us of a particular "edge" to the life of faith.

"When will those times dawn?" and "By what signs will we know them?" are uninterestingly divertive. Confident expectation that God will triumph, however, lends a quality of expectant assurance to the pilgrimage of faith we desperately need to recover. How would such a recovered quality of confident, expectant assurance shape and color the life of faithful discipleship and service?

WHEN THE END OF DAYS DAWNS (21:25–38)

This section completes Jesus' discourse, which Luke had introduced at verses 5ff., on events preliminary to the end of time. The discourse concludes the segment on Jesus' teaching in and around the Temple at Jerusalem (19:47–21:38). Luke prefaced the discourse with an abbreviated account of the cleansing of the Temple (19:45–46), and set it apart with an *inclusio* (using the same summary statement both at the beginning and at the end of a segment): "Every day he was teaching in the temple" (19:47; 21:37).

(a) *Signs signaling the end time.* Up until now, in the discourse proper, which began at verse 8, Jesus had moderated the people's zeal for an early appearance of the end of days. He did not talk about events of the end time but rather of many overwhelming occurrences, several of which his community had already experienced or were experiencing, that he indicated were preliminary to the inbreaking of the end time. He summed up this extended preliminary interval under the phrase "until the times of the Gentiles are fulfilled" (v. 24).

Now, however, using apocalyptic imagery (dramatic, poetic, visionary symbolism for end-time events), Jesus turns to focus on events at the end of the ages, on the Day of the Lord. This is particularly pronounced in verses 25–28. What Jesus is alluding to now are *phenomena* that lie in the future for Luke and his community.

Those who are thrown into terrified consternation by the turbulent signs of the end are in that state because they have chosen not to be chosen. They have chosen not to know what God has been accomplishing in their world and among them all along. They could have "seen" and followed during Jesus' earthly ministry. They should have "seen" the opportune time rather than having supported the adversaries when persecuted Christian disciples gave testimony (v. 13). The destruction of Jerusalem ought to have given them a significant clue as to the tenor of the times. Yet only at the end time, and out of their terror, do they finally, in the returning Jesus, perceive what is occurring—to and for their judgment.

What an extraordinary word of promise and of grace Jesus spoke for the Jews. When "the times of the Gentiles are fulfilled" (v. 24), the cosmic manifestations signaling the arrival of the end will begin to appear, heralding the advent of the Son of man. This will be the time of the approach of the redemption of God for the rest of the Jews (v. 28). What God has allowed to happen—indeed, even caused to happen to Jerusalem (vv. 6, 20–24)—is not God's final word for the Jews. God wills their redemption as God has always maintained. Some had already responded, some were responding during the course of "the times of the Gentiles"; but many will not (as the narrative in Acts repeatedly makes clear).

(*b*) *The analogy of the sprouting fig tree.* As dramatic, startling, and fearful as the signs throughout the cosmos might be to the unbelieving beholder, for faithful disciples the end time will not be a time of dread apprehension but a time of rejoicing, glad anticipation, and hope fulfilled (v. 28). Of all of the good news celebrated accompanying Jesus' birth, of all of the good news he preached and taught during his public ministry, of all of the astonished, delirious, overwhelming jubilation with which dejected disciples heard the Easter message of resurrection and were themselves inundated with power from on high, of all the gospel proclamation that has been announced by the church in his name since, *this* good news of the end-time advent is the most compelling and urgent for both Gentile and Jew.

In the discourse Jesus next appealed to the image of the leafing fig tree, representative of the season of new growth on all of the trees (vv. 29–31), as a paradigm for the clarity with which the signs of the end time disclose what is taking place to the discerning person. Although Luke called the reference to the fig tree a "parable," he was not using that form in its technical literary sense. It is an analogy from nature. When people see the signs on the earth and in heaven, what is on the verge of occurring will be as clear to them as it is when the winter-dormant fig tree sprouts young leaves.

Jesus' assertion about the eternal durability and dependability of his teaching (vv. 32f.) contains a confusing reference to "this generation" that "will not pass away until all things have taken place." Puzzling as that is, it may be understood as referring to all of the human generation who have opposed God's revealed intent to restore creation to goodness under God's rule (cf. 11:29–32, 50–51), that opposition reaching climactic expression in the rejection by "this generation" of the Son of man (cf. 17:24–25). Another option would be to understand the phrase as referring to the inception of the signs of the end time. Once the end of the ages approaches, its fulfillment will be swift.

Jesus' end-time discourse concludes as he admonished his hearers (vv. 34–36) to studiously avoid all debilitating distractions so that they might exercise vigilant alertness. Trust and assurance that God will bring devine promises to fulfillment and devine plans for the restoration and redemption of all of the creation to completion requires disciples to adopt a consistent quality and style of living that reflect confident, expectant anticipation. When the end time dawns, only such as these who are knowing and ready for it will be ready to be known by the One who is to appear.

A sermon on this discourse might explore the following:

Times of waiting have such a different quality depending on what is anticipated. "Wait until your Daddy gets home and hears what you have been doing!" sets the tone for tense times of terror. What a contrast to the interval that a child impatiently endures waiting for the parade to start. Then the first distant sounds of horns and drums and sirens are heard coming from around the corner.

Adults, too, know the contrast in the quality of waiting. Having arrived at the airport ahead of time, now straining for the first glimpse of grandchildren hurrying into the terminal, fourteen months older than the last visit, has a profoundly different caliber than the defendant's wait for the jury to bring in the obvious and inevitable guilty verdict, or than the anxious interval of waiting for the reports from the oncology laboratory.

The manifestations of turmoil in heaven, on earth and among the peoples of the world, indicate the impact of God's restored control over the powers and forces of God-opposed chaos and the reimposition of divine order similar to that which occurred at creation. Such cosmological upheaval introduces the returning advent of the end-time agent of God, the Son of man, the ascended and exalted Lord Jesus (see Acts 1:11; 7:55–56).

The signs announcing the arrival of the end time, Jesus predicted, will spawn a period of penetrating perception for all humanity. But what a difference in the quality of the waiting! Those who have been, until then, oblivious and obdurate will frantically and despairingly recognize their judgment drawing near (v. 26). Obediently expectant disciples will exhilaratingly discern the approach of redemption fully completed and implemented.

Tragedy and Triumph: Passion and Resurrection

Luke 22:1–24:53

Luke's narrative of the public ministry of Jesus moves with dramatic intensity toward its climactic conclusion in this final segment to his Gospel. Of course this does not terminate the tale. He resumed his narration of the work of the Spirit of God in the life of the Easter community in the second volume of his work, the Acts of the Apostles.

Even then the story was not over. Luke believed that the story still was unfolding in the lives of believers who were hearing or reading his narrative account, and he wanted his community of faith to share his belief. They did, and so do we, which is why both of the volumes that comprised his work continue to be read as Holy Scripture and pondered as authoritative and normative for the believing community of Christians today.

Still, for the Jesus miraculously conceived and born in the Bethlehem manger, the period of his public activity as the primary proclaimer and inaugurator of the restoration of the royal rule of God over creation now moves rapidly to culmination. The scene shifts from the confines of the Temple to the wider setting of the city of Jerusalem. Jesus is in the right locale for his exodus/departure (cf. 9:31). Scriptures have foretold what, of necessity, will happen to him (cf. 18:31–33). The religious leaders have firmed their intent to execute him (cf. 19:47; 20:14–15; 22:2). His ministry repeatedly has been the occasion "for the falling and the rising of many in Israel . . . a sign that will be opposed" (2:34). The time about which Simeon had warned Mary, when "a sword will pierce your own soul" (2:35), was rapidly approaching.

A TIME OF PREPARATIONS (22:1–13)

It is the time of the sacrifice of the Passover/Paschal lamb whose blood protects from divine wrath and gives life. Preparation for the Passover with Jesus in Jerusalem developed in two directions: a) Judas resolves to betray, and b) Peter and John prepare for the celebrative meal.

(a) *Judas agrees to betray Jesus.* The disciple Judas plotted to betray Jesus to his "exodus/departure" in Jerusalem (cf. 9:31). By bracketing his brief account of Judas' defection to the rule of Satan with references to the time of the Passover (vv. 1, 7), Luke invites his hearers to ponder the irony of Judas setting Jesus up for arrest and execution in the season of Exodus remembrance and celebration. Prompted by Satan, Judas joined in the conspiracy with the Temple authorities and religious leaders who were resolved to destroy Jesus. Luke further indicated that events were now rushing rapidly and inexorably toward their tragic conclusion by introducing mention of "the officers of the temple police" (v. 4), the enforcers the religious leaders would use to put into effect their plan for killing Jesus (see v. 52).

Satan had been no match for Jesus at the beginning of his public ministry (4:13) nor for those whom Jesus had commissioned and empowered to be extensions of his ministry (10:18). Now, however, in Judas, Satan found a segment of God's fallen but restored creation that was prepared to repudiate and even to oppose God's claim to rule. Judas did not demand either political or religious power (see the temptations of Jesus, 4:1–12). All he required was enough to purchase a piece of land (cf. Acts 1:18). All that he wanted was one small corner of the world over which he could exercise control. He could have asked for so much more, and Satan still would have considered it a bargain.

By satanic design, Judas' intent and the murderous purposes of the religious leaders converged. The religious leaders charged with upholding and promoting obedience to the revealed will of God had surrendered themselves to their intent to destroy Jesus. Instead of defending him and remonstrating with Judas' purpose, they were delighted at his proposal and paid him to ensure that he would follow through with the betrayal.

Judas accepted money from them in return for scheming with them to turn Jesus over for arrest, trial, and condemnation. (We recall that Luke had portrayed Jesus as frequently cautioning his disciples against a preoccupying concern about money.) Because of the religious leaders' apprehension at the possibility of a violent and rebellious reaction by the crowd (Luke had carefully prepared his hearers for this, cf. 19:48; 20:6, 19, 26, 45–46), Judas agreed to find a private occasion, "when no crowd was present" (v. 6), to deliver Jesus over to them.

(b) *Peter and John prepare for the Passover meal.* Meanwhile Jesus had sent two other of his disciples, Peter and John, to make preparation for their celebration of Passover. He frequently sent a pair of followers ahead to make advance preparation (see 10:1; 19:29; cf. 9:52, and the frequent mention of pairs of believers in Acts).

Luke emphasized the precision with which Jesus foretold in detail what the disciples would encounter as they made the necessary preparations. That lent additional force to the claim for veracity with which Luke expected his hearers to receive the predictions that Jesus would make in his final discourse to the disciples while they were at the table. What a pity that Peter, who was entrusted with making preparations for the feast, did not devote equal attention to preparing himself to endure with constancy the traumatic experiences that lay just ahead (see vv. 54–62).

A sermon on the passage might expand on the following:

It is sobering to reflect on the difficulty of dependable discernment. After all, Jesus, the beloved and well-pleasing Son of God (3:22), full of the Holy Spirit (4:1, 14), after having spent an entire night in searching communication with God (6:12), singled out twelve from the larger group of his disciples to be his intimate companions and friends—and one of them plotted to betray him for money, and another out of terror was to deny him when the chips were down. It was Judas and Peter who did those things, but it could have been any one of them.

That reflection is sobering because it is precisely that "iffy" with all of us. Why did Jesus call us? When we not only evade but even betray because we think we can strike a better deal, whose fault is it? God, who made us like that? Jesus, who should have seen through us more cogently? Who will be held accountable? To whom will we have to give account? And on what will the outcome depend?

THE LAST SUPPER (22:14–23)

Luke's report of the story of the Last Supper Jesus shared with his disciples contains some features that are unique from the versions of the other evangelists. It has four parts, of which the first three are closely interdependent:

- Jesus' celebration of the Passover meal (vv. 15–18)
- Jesus' reinterpretation of that meal with reference to his impending fate (vv. 19–20)
- Jesus' disclosure of his imminent betrayal (vv. 21–23)

The fourth part, Jesus' farewell discourse, is more loosely structured. We will consider it in the next section.

(*a*) *The Passover meal.* Jesus' strong yearning to celebrate this Passover feast with his disciples (v. 15) was especially intense in anticipation of his passion. Because of the sign of the cross looming over the feast, this was the final Passover that the earthly Jesus would celebrate with the apostles before his passion (vv. 16, 18). (That sign had shadowed their fellowship since just before the trip from Galilee to Jerusalem was begun [cf. 9:22, 31, 44; etc.] but now its proximity was so pronounced!)

There is a deeper level of meaning to his remarks. The climactic conclusion to the public ministry for which God had sent and empowered Jesus, and its victorious vindication in his resurrection, all of which will occur before the eight-day interval of this Passover celebration will have been completed, lends a particularly poignant profundity to Jesus' yearning.

Jesus capitalized on the end-of-the-ages significance with which religious Judaism had already invested the Passover celebration to focus on the full realization of the royal rule of God his own ministry had inaugurated. At the end of time, Passover feast and messianic banquet converge. The deliverance from bondage in Egypt and the reconstitution of a people dedicated to the covenant service of God, which God had initiated with the first Passover, is now, in the restoration of God's royal realm in the ministry and, especially, the fate of Jesus, being inordinately advanced toward fulfillment.

Our recognition of the shift of focus between verse 18 and verse 19 helps us to clarify the otherwise confusing double reference to the "cup" (vv. 17, 20) on either side of the breaking of the bread in the course of the meal. Multiple cups were employed in the Passover celebration. Joseph Fitzmyer provides a helpful summary overview of the components of a Passover *Seder,* the ceremonial feast (Joseph A. Fitzmyer, S. J., *The Gospel According to Luke,* [Garden City, N.Y.: Doubleday & Co., 1985], II, 1390). The second cup to which Jesus assigned a new meaning connected with his own execution (v. 20) is probably the concluding cup of the Passover meal, the "cup of blessing" (cf. 1 Cor. 10:16).

(*b*) *Jesus recasts the meaning of the meal.* The festive meal–and the approaching events involving Jesus that it anticipated and interpreted– transformed the Passover celebration for the fellowship of believers. From now on, Jesus' crucifixion and resurrection give primary meaning to the ritual meal (vv. 19–21).

The special bread used for the Passover meal, known as the "bread of affliction," remained just that for Jesus in that his body was the locus of his impending suffering (cf. v. 15). In another sense it was the "bread of affliction" for Judas in that Jesus' body, delivered over by betrayal to Jesus' enemies, was the locus of the prophetic condemnation for Judas' treachery (cf. vv. 21–22). For the other apostles present, and for all of the followers of Jesus who come to the table of the Lord since, it is transformed into a "bread of blessing," (though the Judas option always remains), a "remembrance, a making present" of Jesus' vicarious self-offering on our behalf.

So is it also with the cup (v. 20). In the Passover celebration, the blood of the sacrificed lamb protected the firstborn sons of Israel, who were the first line of succession, the heirs of the promise given to Abraham. It effected saving deliverance in order that God's covenant people might be restored and reconstituted as a people set apart and holy unto God. For the disciples with Jesus, the cup announced that the blood of the sacrificed first and only Son of God, the blood of true Israel, was to be poured out in covenant renewal, the ratification of a "new covenant" (cf. Jer. 31:31–34), in order that God might found the Israel of the end time, the church.

(c) *Jesus announces that he is being betrayed.* Luke bracketed his account of the Last Supper with references to Judas' decision to betray Jesus to the Temple authorities (vv. 21–22, cf. vv. 3–6). To betray Jesus is to betray oneself into subservience to Satan and those forces supporting Satan's hostile resistance to the reassertion of God's right to rule.

Judas camouflaged his infidelity by entering into religious table-fellowship for this Passover celebration with the other apostles with whom he had already broken fellowship, and with Jesus whose lordship he had renounced. How painfully ironic to have him participating in a meal the meaning of which from now on derives from events that were set in motion by his treachery. It is a penetrating parable for the despicable duplicity of all of those members of the religious community, especially the leaders, who, while still claiming to serve God, maliciously and murderously oppose God's will.

Preaching possibilities on this passage include:

1. Considering our solidarity with the betrayer. God maintains a tension between divine control and human double-dealing. Jesus' unjust death will not thwart God's purposes, but neither does that excuse the betrayer nor relieve him of his appalling accountability (v. 22).

Accountability for it is not restricted just to those present at that Last Supper or to those promoting the events soon to follow. It encompasses all double-minded Christians who again and again gather at the table of the Lord with hedged, compromised, and equivocated loyalties. It is not sufficient to look around and wonder which of the others around the table may have viciously betrayed the trust of Jesus (v. 23). "Woe to the betrayer" must evoke painfully precise and thorough self-examination.

2. *God is yet open to Judas.* Luke's decision to locate Jesus' announcement and warning about his betrayer until the end of the meal, after the bread and the cup of participatory communion and fellowship have been shared, nudges our reflection in yet another direction. It can be heard as a dramatic, narrative proclamation of the scope of forgiving grace. The one who has resolved to set Jesus up, so that he may be seized by those enemies with murderous intent, also received the bread of Christ's body, "given for you"; this one also was embraced in the "new covenant in (Jesus') blood." Even at this eleventh hour, Judas still, "in remembrance of Jesus," may remember, may recall, may make present, may make memorial before God, may repent, may abort what he has resolved to do, may assume again the role of faithful disciple, may be "with Jesus" (v. 21) in a far more profound manner than that measured by physical proximity.

When Judas chose to persist in perfidy (cf. vv. 47–48), he not only breached the Abrahamic covenant God had renewed and ratified through Moses, he proleptically violated the "new covenant" yet to be ratified by the blood of Jesus on the cross. He personified St. Paul's later observation that "whoever . . . eats the bread or drinks the cup of the Lord in an unworthy manner will be answerable for the body and blood of the Lord" (1 Cor. 11:27). (Paul was not concerned here with impious desecration of the eucharistic elements. He meant that such a person has solidarity with and shares in the guilt of those who viciously and unjustly crucified Jesus.)

3. *Indignation can disguise a bent toward betrayal.* The disciples' divertive desire to unmask the traitor in their midst segues into a report of their dispute over which of them has earned the right to be regarded as the greatest (cf. vv. 24ff.). This is the second time Luke has used the sequence of announcement about betrayal followed by the disciples' bickering about rank and status within their fellowship. The sequence also appeared just prior to the start of the extended journey to Jerusalem, a trip they had made under the constantly looming specter of the cross (9:44–45 and 46–48).

After all that has taken place in that interval, after all of Jesus' efforts to prepare them for his fate and their function, after all that he had taught them about the demands of the royal rule of God and the nature of true discipleship, they still have not gotten it. They are hardly better prepared now to endure the events just ahead, much less serve the unfolding disclosure of God's eternal rule, than they were back then. God had told them, "Listen to him!" (9:35). They have not done that very well. The initial question is not, "How is it going in your community of faith?" The initial question is, "How is it going with you?"

FAREWELL DISCOURSE (22:24–38)

A "farewell discourse" is a device authors frequently use in heroic literature. As the strong leader approached the time of succession or dying, he delivered final remarks to his followers and adherents that reviewed significant events in his time of leadership. He usually also gave advice for what the followers must do if they were to continue to progress and prosper, and/or warned of what would happen if the followers veered from the direction in which he had been leading them. The speeches of Moses (Deut. 32 and 33) and of Joshua (Josh. 23 and 24) are good examples of the use of this literary device.

In this section Luke organized a series of sayings from Jesus into a kind of "farewell address" at the conclusion of the final meal. (A more extended example of the use of this literary device in a narrative about Jesus at the last meal may be found in John 13–17.) Luke structured the address around four loosely related topics: (a) *true greatness* (vv. 24–27), (b) *anticipated delegation of authority* (vv. 28–30), (c) *prediction of Peter's denial* (vv. 31–34), (d) *two swords* (vv. 35–38).

(*a*) *True greatness.* Luke has been forthright in indicating in his narrative that the disciples simply could not even begin to fathom the passion of Jesus and its significance (cf. 9:44–45; 18:31–34). By following Jesus' reference to Judas's betrayal with mention of the disciples' squabble about their relative status, Luke implied that with such concerns they, too, were betraying Jesus, although perhaps not in so blatant and violent a way as did Judas. This transition verse provided the occasion for introducing Jesus' farewell discourse.

The same sequence—Jesus' announcement of his betrayal followed by an argument as to which of the disciples was the greatest—had been used by Luke earlier (9:44–48). The prior occasion was in the introductory prelude to the ten-chapter-long period of special instruction to the disciples as Jesus and they journeyed together to Jerusalem where he was to be betrayed and executed.

After all of that, the apostles have not made much progress in perception. They still do not get it, and will not be able to understand until they have been illumined (cf. 24:45) and empowered by the Spirit (cf. 24:49; Acts 2:1ff.) and committed to the commission to testify and witness (cf. 24:47–48; Acts 1:8). Even then, their fidelity, perception, and progress would be erratic, as the narrative in Acts and the subsequent history of the church documents.

Jesus contrasted the political values and structures of this age, which had already been supplanted in his relationship to his disciples. That new relationship embodied values, functions, and roles appropriate to the realm of divine dominion. The assumption and exercise of authority for the primary purpose of enhancing one's prestige and reputation is characteristic of a profane, pagan view of what constitutes true greatness. If, however, authority is delegated primarily to advance the reestablishment of God's sovereignty, then the employment of such authority is controlled by the compulsion to extend God's royal rule.

In what does authority consist among a fellowship that has been brought together to serve the royal rule of God? Obviously it rests most deservingly on those who selflessly serve with the greatest consistency, integrity, and sacrifice. Witness the model of Jesus' behavior in their midst throughout his public ministry, but especially as they had just experienced his serving them (as if he were the waiter!—cf. 12:37) in the Passover celebration. Humility and self-effacing service rather than assertive self-commendation are always the more appropriate attitudes when the community of faith gathers in table-fellowship. That should be particularly apparent when the church celebrates the Lord's Supper. Any concern about being thought of as the greatest which is not driven by a willing subservience that honors and serves others is Satanic deflection, a form of denial and of betrayal.

(b) *Jesus delegates authority to the disciples.* From concern over authority assumed for defective and even demonic motives, Jesus turns their attention to the authority with which Jesus is entrusting them (vv. 28–30). It is nothing less than a share in the authority God has assigned to Jesus. The Twelve had already been set apart, empowered and commissioned by Jesus to be extensions of his ministry (9:1–6; cf. 10:1–20). That assignment was still in effect and would remain so up to and including the interval during which God would complete the reassertion of divine rule over the entire creation at the end time.

Jesus' authority is kingly authority. The disciples' function at the end time is more royal than juridical. (It was similar to the role of the "judges" as described in the book of Judges). The "twelve tribes of Israel" is not to be understood in the restricted sense of empirical, ethnic Israel but rather with reference to the Israel that is reconstituted by the new covenant ratified in the blood of Jesus, that is, the church. (Luke will portray the disciples as allowing themselves to be distracted from the clear instructions of the risen but not yet ascended Christ by taking this description of their activity too literally—Acts 1:21–26.)

This section on the delegation and exercise of kingdom authority does not contradict or stand in qualifying tension with the preceding verses 24–27. Table-fellowship at the banquet of the royal Messiah in the end time sets the tone for the "judging" function conferred by Jesus. Even that fearful royal activity is to be carried out by disciples who knew themselves to be like the youngest and the least (cf. 9:46–48), who were called to unassuming service in the realm of God.

(c) **Prediction of Peter's denial.** Jesus predicted Peter's defection (vv. 31–34) as a specific instance of capitulation during that fearful interval when all of the disciples would be put to the test. Satan had not only found "an opportune time" (cf. 4:13) for subverting Judas (v. 3), Satan would be trying each of the followers of Jesus during the tumultuous events that lay ahead to see if any of them would evidence a similar vulnerability to that which Satan had found in Judas.

Jesus assured his disciples that at least one of them, Simon Peter, would succumb. Even then Jesus would not abandon him. He would rehabilitate him for pastoral responsibilities in the community of faith.

Peter's attempt to protest the limitless scope and intensity of his loyalty to Jesus was but another way of belatedly asserting that his vaunted stability in the face of adversity proved that he deserved "to be regarded as the greatest" (v. 24). We often tend to view Peter's defection as simply human weakness collapsing before raw terror, whereas Judas' treachery was saturated with the demonic. From the perspective of the grace of God, the only difference between Peter and Judas is the phrase "when once you have turned back" (v. 32). Peter was to repent; Judas did not.

Even in the context of this stern warning against cowardly mendacity, Jesus would continue to uphold Peter as "one who serves." He was absolutely convinced that Peter would capitulate to his own terror. But Jesus did not scold or berate him. Instead, he assured Peter and the rest of his followers of his prayers for strength and steadfastness.

Although Peter would fail him, Jesus compassionately served Peter in his frailty by entrusting to him a critical assignment once he recovered from his defection. He was to assume again the role of leader in the Christian community and, through his warnings, admonitions, and prayers, become a source of service and support to other Christians, in a manner similar to what Christ was doing for him right then. He would, through his ministry as "one who serves," finally become the church's great leader. (Cf. Luke's description of Peter's subsequent leadership role in the extension of his narrative in Acts.) On the other side of denial, Peter will prove to be one of "the greatest," not by self-willed character correction but because Jesus has acknowledged him and prayed for him. Although he denied Jesus, Jesus would not deny him.

(d) **Jesus warns them to prepare for hostility.** The final section to Jesus' farewell address (vv. 35–38) registered another instance of the disciples' misperception of what Jesus was telling them. In view of the looming crisis as events were rapidly rushing to the point of Jesus' arrest and trial on false charges, the disciples were to make different preparation from that which Jesus had at one time commended.

When Jesus had sent the disciples out on mission previously, he had urged them to flaunt and celebrate their vulnerability so that their complete dependence on God would be displayed (10:4–8; cf. 9:3–5). Their proclamation was validated when God met their needs through the hospitality they were offered spontaneously by those with whom they stayed in each place.

Now, however, the times are radically transformed. Now, instead of anticipating hospitality, they must expect hostility. They must prepare to fend for themselves. The threatening character of the times is such that extreme measures are called for to be prepared to meet and withstand the onslaught. Their preparations needed to be thorough and complete! That is what Jesus' "get a sword" saying (v. 36) meant. But the disciples, taking it literally, informed him that in anticipation of an armed confrontation they already had supplied themselves with two swords that were hidden away until they were needed. In his frustration at their imperception, Jesus, in essence, replied, "Enough of that! Forget it!"

ARREST ON THE MOUNT OF OLIVES (22:39–53)

The account of Jesus' period of prayer with his disciples on the Mount of Olives serves in Luke's narrative as a counterpart at the conclusion of his period of ministry in Jerusalem to the time of trial and temptation in the wilderness preceding the inauguration of his public ministry (cf. 4:1–13). As had been the case before, once again Jesus prevailed, though the disciples fared less well.

Luke tempered the harsh presentation of the disciples he found in Mark's version in three ways:

1) Jesus' followers continued in their relationship of disciple to rabbi (they "followed him"—v. 39. Luke dropped Mark's subsequent assertion of the disciples' total defection—cf. Mark 14:50).
2) Jesus reprimanded the disciples only once instead of Mark's threefold reprimand.
3) Whereas in Mark the sleeping of the disciples stood for their willful refusal to accept the necessity of Jesus' suffering or to have a part in it, Luke qualified their act of sleeping by adding

the phrase "because of grief" (v. 45), which attested that they slept because of their dread of being bereft of him.

Jesus urged the disciples to fervent prayer (vv. 40, 46), not that they might share in his spiritual struggle, but that they might themselves be strengthened to endure being "sifted like wheat" by Satan (22:31). They were to petition for protection from compromising their own commitment to the purposes of God.

Even though Jesus had warned them, the disciples underestimated both the proximity and the scope of the time of trial and temptation that was descending on them. After he had exhorted them to follow his example and pray for readiness to conform steadfastly to the will of God in response to impending intense temptation, they instead went to sleep "because of grief" (v. 45). It was a missed opportunity for them to prepare through prayer for the threatening events. That the disciples required such petitionary preparation had already been indicated by Judas' defection (22:3–6, 21) and would be reiterated by Peter's terrified collapse (vv. 54ff.).

The primary focus of the narrative scene is on Jesus at prayer. For Luke's presentation it is the culmination of a series of references to Jesus' dependence on prayer (cf. 3:21; 5:16; 6:12; 9:18, 28; 11:1). The prayer he offered (v. 42) clearly established that Jesus' execution was not simply an instance of colossal human injustice. His death was integral to God's strategic plan to restore and save. Jesus is faithfully submissive to that plan. Even his physical attitude signaled humble submission. (The usual posture for prayer was standing, cf. 18:10–14.)

"The cup" of Jesus' suffering was the cup of God's wrath (cf. Ps. 75:8; Isa. 51:17; Jer. 25:15; 49:12; Hab. 2:15–16). But it was full of that wrath of God that we, not Jesus, deserve. Only when we know that can we know it, at the same time, as the cup of the new covenant (cf. 22:20), the cup that has become for us through the death of Jesus the "cup of blessing" (cf. 1 Cor. 10:16).

Even as Jesus was exhorting the disciples to make prayerful preparation for approaching temptation, Judas, the one from among them who had already capitulated and gone over to the enemies of Jesus, was leading the hostile horde to where Jesus was standing. The religious leaders had refrained from arresting Jesus when he was teaching in the Temple because they feared that a negative reaction from the crowd of people who admired Jesus and were listening eagerly to his teaching might spark an uprising that would bring the destructive retribution of Imperial Rome upon the city. His arrest had to occur somewhere when he was away from the crowd (cf. 19:47–48; 20:19; 22:6)—for instance, where Judas knew that he habitually spent the night. Judas showed them where that was.

The authority that empowered the religious authorities to arrest Jesus was not an authority delegated by God—not an authority legitimately derived from the religious heritage they claimed to serve. It was the same "power of darkness" (v. 53) Jesus had repudiated (cf. 4:5–7) but which they have embraced. Those who were serving the ends of Darkness came in the dark of night to do their dark deed.

Sermon initiatives emerging from this section include:

1. This is our story. We listen to these stories poorly if all that we see in them are accounts of events in the interval leading up to Jesus' execution, which perplexingly differ in detail from similar versions in the other biblical Gospel narratives, the resolution of which has eluded the scholarly community. The stories should evoke from us such reflections as:

- When have we sorely underestimated the extreme urgency of a brief but critical interlude when our obtuseness diverted us from making careful preparation to deal with the challenge?
- How frequently have we literally or figuratively gone to sleep, for whatever reason, when the moment cried for our focused and perceptive attention?
- When have we abandoned and even turned hostile toward commitments whose maintenance we once regarded as fundamental to our being and integrity?
- Can we recall occasions when we have sought to conceal our treacherous duplicity with phony gestures of intimate affection and trust?

If we feel discomfort as we consider those questions primarily with reference to our relationships with other people, how much more ought we to be troubled by the realization that, like the disciples, we do the same to our Lord Jesus and to God? That sets the mood for us to participate in these stories.

The violent, aggressive reaction of the unnamed disciple (v. 50) illustrates both how caught off guard Jesus' followers were at this turn of events—which unthinkably was being facilitated by one of their close fellowship—and also how little they had understood Jesus' enigmatic advice about necessary provisions (22:36b, 38). Jesus' response is one of unexpected, stern, compassionate concern. Jesus is capable even here of applying the restorative power of God's royal rule to human hate and hurt.

Even here he is willing "to give light to those who sit in darkness and in the shadow of death" (1:79).

They came for his hurt. At least one of them experienced, instead, his healing help. (One wonders if, later, that slave became a Christian?) More of them could have experienced that same healing help right there if they had wanted it—even Judas!

On the Mount of Olives, Jesus set the example for all true piety to emulate. The stakes have been raised, since that earlier time of temptation in the wilderness (4:1ff.). It had nothing to do with gaining something desirable, but rather with escaping something horrendous. With his prayer Jesus died to himself in order that he might live to God. It is the conclusion consistent with that steadfast, faithful endurance in the face of trial he had first manifested just prior to the beginning of his public ministry.

2. *A canonical interpolation.* We need to note that many English translations put verses 43–44 in brackets or even in a footnote. Since they are not in a number of the earliest manuscripts, it is likely that they were not part of Luke's original text but were added by an early Christian copyist. They have the effect of conforming Luke's version to those of Matthew and Mark, which graphically portrayed Jesus immersed in intense spiritual anguish.

Unlike Mark, Luke had not mentioned angels ministering to Jesus in his account of Jesus' earlier temptation in the wilderness. That an early copyist expanded this account to include an angel appearing to Jesus in order to strengthen him illustrated vividly the conviction of the early church that the kind of prayer Jesus had commended to the disciples was effective. The detail that Jesus sweat copiously intensifies our sense of the immense volitional effort it required for Jesus to make the act of submission he had just offered.

Even though the Evangelist may not have written those two verses, they are a part of the canon and are thereby commended to our prayerful reflection by the church. How easily we rationalize when our intentions are at cross purposes to behavior consistent with the plainly revealed will of God for human living. How proud we are on those rare occasions when we give way to God's intent. How foreign to us is that deep intense struggle that permeates one's being when faced with the fundamental option to choose for or against God, knowing that it really does have life and death implications.

It is even more shattering if we, like Jesus, are brought to realize that to opt for life is to choose death, and to opt for death is to choose life. If that ever happens to us, we, too, will know that sweating profusely as if hemorrhaging, and desperately needing angelic succor, are proper to the crisis.

When it happens, we are transformed. From then on, like Jacob of old, we limp from that encounter into whatever future we have by our choice embraced.

3. *Judas is not the only betrayer.* Luke will not allow us to forget that the one who identified Jesus for arrest by the religious authorities was "one of the Twelve." He was one of the disciples singled out by Jesus to belong to the intimate innermost circle of religious fellowship. He, too, had been empowered to continue and to extend the ministry and the proclamation of the royal reign of God Jesus had inaugurated.

It is not atheists or those on the fringes of the church who are God's worst enemies. It is those at the center, those who have known themselves to be loved by God and who have loved God, and who, for whatever reason, allow themselves to be distracted from single-minded, devoted service to God, who provide "the power of darkness" with "an opportune time" (v. 53; cf. 4:13).

Even more outrageously, Judas intended to betray Jesus with a kiss (vv. 47–48). Betrayal is bad enough. To intend to use as the sign of treachery that act which expresses intimacy, affection, and trust, as if nothing were wrong, was doubly despicable.

The hostile crowd was coming to kill Jesus, not to see Jesus, or to hear Jesus, or to know Jesus. They thought that they needed Judas to show them which one was Jesus and where he could be found. What they really needed was someone finally to show them *who* Jesus was, who he *actually* was. That is precisely what Judas, at one time, had been empowered to do. Now, however, the powerful presence within him was satanic (v. 53, cf. vv. 3–6). He knew which one was Jesus. He had forgotten who Jesus was. Other than Jesus' steadfast fidelity to God's purposes in all of this, the healing of the high priest's servant is the one glimmer of grace in a scene otherwise filled with painful pathos.

INTERROGATED BY THE JEWISH COUNCIL (22:54–71)

Although Jesus was arrested and detained at the high priest's house on Thursday evening (v. 54), his actual examination before the Jewish religious authorities did not take place until the next morning (v. 66). In the interval, two tangential events that have proved animating for Christian reflection occurred: Peter's triple denial (vv. 54b–62) and the harassment of Jesus by those who were assigned to guard him (vv. 63–65).

(a) *Peter denies knowing Jesus.* Peter certainly was culpable. He had been given advanced warning that he would be required publicly to acknowledge allegiance to Jesus. He had been urged to prepare himself and solicit supernatural strengthening through prayer. We have only to recall the indispensable role Peter was to play as leader of earliest Jerusalem Christianity, as Luke portrayed him in the continuation of his narrative in the Acts of the Apostles, to realize that Luke was not interested in this anecdote because it demeaned Peter.

The scene played itself out just as Jesus had predicted (vv. 31–34). No, he absolutely was not associated with Jesus, did not even know him (v. 57—reflecting Jesus' exact words in v. 34). No, he certainly did not belong to the group of followers of Jesus (v. 58). No, he was not willing even to acknowledge regional affiliation with Jesus (vv. 59–60).

The threefold assertion by those gathered around the fire was, ironically, more accurate than they realized. That Peter was "one of those with Jesus" went beyond recognition of a factual association. He was "with Jesus" in the sense that he had experienced that basic transformation which God's reasserted right to rule, proclaimed by Jesus in his teaching and made present in his person, effected.

When Peter rejected their pondering assertion, he not only falsely contradicted their recognition of his being intimately associated with Jesus, he also repudiated that liberating deliverance which unequivocating devotion to the reign of God enjoyed. In the high priest's courtyard, Satan sifted Peter's commitment like wheat (cf. v. 31) and proved it to be, mostly, chaff. Peter was tested and tempted (cf. vv. 40, 46)—and Peter failed.

Then the rooster crowed. The recollection of Jesus' forthright prediction froze his mind. The pathos of the look that the captured Jesus directed toward him seared his soul. Peter could not even come to terms with his failing in agonized anonymity. Those people who were gathered around the fire thought that they knew Peter for his having been associated with Jesus. Jesus knew him for his foretold capitulation, and for the phony bravado with which he had tried earlier to promote himself as "the greatest" (cf. 22:24).

In Jesus' gaze Peter saw himself for who he was—not unlike Judas in his vulnerable undependability—and weeping, he began to repent. Peter was tested and tempted, and, through the arrested Jesus' compassionate judging, Peter was freed from Satan's constraint and prevailed. *That* was what differentiated Peter from Judas. It transformed Peter into the champion and leader of the cause of Christ and his church (Acts 1:13, 15; and often in Acts) while unrepentant Judas went to gross destruction (Acts 1:18–20).

A sermon on Peter's denial might explore the following:

Before we come down on Peter too hard, we need to probe our awareness of the fragility of our faith with candor. Nationwide surveys repeatedly report the high incidence of religious conviction claimed by residents of our country. Even the number discovered of those willing to associate themselves with the cause of Christ and the Christian enterprise evokes astonished reactions from ecclesiastical bureaucrats entrusted with tallying church membership. One cannot help but wonder about the fragility of such affirmations and how rapidly and radically the statistics would decline if the chips were ever to be down again in a crass, vicious, physical way, as they clearly were for Peter.

We need not cast our nets so broadly, however. It suffices for us to recall the rapidity with which our own loyalty lessens, even vanishes when, for reasons that have nothing to do with physical constraint and pain, much less with possible life-threatening consequences, the integrity of our commitment is put to the test.

All of the disciples had *followed Jesus* to the Mount of Olives (v. 39); only Peter *followed Jesus* to detention and trial, and even then only at a tentative, terrified "distance" (v. 54b). Earlier Peter had brashly bragged of his unqualified readiness to accompany Jesus "to prison and to death" (v. 33). He did get as far as the courtyard of the high priest's house, but then his courage—that is, his willingness to trust God utterly—failed. But Jesus restored God's dominion even there!

(*b*) ***Jesus was harassed by his captors.*** Verses 63–65 relate the first of several instances during the interval before his death when Jesus had to suffer the humiliation of being mocked (cf. 23:11, 36–37, 39). Look at the extraordinary way that Luke has set it up! The juxtaposition of the scene where his captors mocked Jesus for presuming to have prophetic capabilities directly following the narration of Peter's denial heightens the absurdity of their ignorant sarcasm. Peter could have provided dramatically moving testimony at that moment to the authenticity of Jesus' prophetic powers.

Even more ironically, their act of mocking Jesus gave the lie to their caustic sarcasm for it fulfilled a prophetic apprehension that Jesus had anticipated (cf. 18:32). Recollection of Jesus' nonretaliatory demeanor in the face of such humiliation during his passion served as a treasured model for Christians as they later faced similar abuse (cf. 1 Peter 2:23).

(*c*) ***The Jewish Council examines Jesus.*** The religious leaders who had plotted, authorized, and accomplished Jesus' arrest were the first to examine him to discover possible grounds for prosecution (vv. 66–71). Betrayal, arrest, denial, mocking mistreatment—these all were works of the power of darkness, appropriately accomplished in the night (cf. v. 53). Arrogant, hostile, and unjust interrogation also is a work of the hour of darkness power, even when pursued in the daylight.

Their first probe jabbed at Jesus' putative messiahship (v. 67). Jesus would not play their game. He had repeatedly experienced the unwillingness of the belligerent Jewish leaders to listen to him perceptively or to respond forthrightly when he questioned them. If they thought that the notion of his being the Messiah was outrageous and preposterous and exposed him to their power, what would they think of his ultimate destiny? Jesus combined elements from Daniel 7:13 and Psalm 110:1 to identify the goal of the exalted authority and power of the royal rule of God toward which God was moving him through all of this (v. 69).

The council was not through yet. They would not hear or believe what Jesus had just said. Next they wanted to inquire about his pretensions to divine sonship (v. 70). Actually "the Son of God" by itself was not all that extravagant or provocative. "Children of God" was a frequently used term in scriptures to refer to the faithful of Israel. But combine it with the figure of awaited Messiah, and with the motif of exalted Son of man in the privileged position of power and authority at the right hand of God, and that is some volatile image!

With his response, ("You say that I am"—v. 70b), Jesus indicted them in their stiffnecked, hardhearted imperception. "You say" is emphatic. *They* had called Jesus *Son of God.* If their locution had any substance for them, what were they going to do about it? If they knew and believed what they were asking concerning Jesus' identity, they would cease interrogating him. They would instead release him, offer submission to him, follow after him, and praise God.

As has frequently occurred earlier in Luke's narrative, when people presumed to judge Jesus they, inevitably, are judged in their judging. When the religious leaders interrogated Jesus, they asked precisely the right questions: Are you the Messiah? Are you the Son of God empowered with the authority of God's royal rule? Those were the central, crucial questions Luke wanted his community to affirm without reservations. They still are that central and that crucial for us.

Jesus' responses scored his inquisitors because, although they had asked the right questions, they were not really interested in the substance of his responses. They considered their questions to have nailed Jesus' liable delusions. It never occurred to them that affirmations to their questions were the only appropriate response.

If they really knew who it was they were investigating, they would have to acknowledge exactly the identities about which they skeptically were inquiring. But then they would no longer be in control. Instead they would be under the control of the one they were resolved to kill.

The power of darkness under whose control the Jewish religious authorities were carrying out their program against Jesus prevented them from hearing or making positive response on at least two counts: 1) although they believed that Messiah would come sometime, they simply could not entertain that time being now; 2) of the variety of speculations about the role and function of the awaited Messiah, none of them conformed to the activity of Jesus they had observed and heard reported, especially his apparently disdaining dismissal of the elaborate cult structure over which they presided and from which they derived their power. Still, their resistance, far from thwarting God's purposes which were being fulfilled in Jesus, would serve to advance events toward his vindication and exaltation. The outcome of all of this would not accomplish their ends but instead would serve and fulfill God's ends.

THE TRIAL OF JESUS (23:1–25)

In Luke's account of Jesus' trial, the number "three" is a recurring accent. (That number had also figured prominently in Luke's relating of the denial of Peter—cf. 22:34, 54–62.) The Jewish authorities made three accusations against Jesus before Pilate (v. 2), Pilate pronounced Jesus innocent three times (vv. 4, 14, 22—in the next section the penitent criminal and the centurion join Pilate for a threefold witness to Jesus' innocence—vv. 41, 47), Pilate proposed three times to release Jesus (vv. 16, 20, 22), and three times the Jewish leaders joined by a throng of people renounced Jesus and demanded that Pilate authorize his execution (vv. 18, 21, 23). Luke's use of threefold repetition emphasizes the deliberateness with which events moved toward their inevitable conclusion. Jesus was sent to the place of the Skull not by accident but with studied intentionality.

(a) *Jewish authorities offer Herod three counterfeit accusations against Jesus.* The three charges the Jewish religious leaders brought against Jesus did not grow out of their interrogation of Jesus as Luke had described it (cf. 22:66–71) and were patently false.

First, Jesus, from infancy, had been raised in accord with the recognized religious requirements. He regularly refuted accusations during his public ministry that he ignored Mosaic mandates, frequently reinterpreting the Torah as more demanding than his detractors realized. By fabricating such a false accusation they, not Jesus, were "perverting the nation."

Second, they charged Jesus with rebellious activity in advocating resistance to Roman taxation. Yet Luke had prepared his readers to know that accusation to be a blatant lie with his carefully drawn account of how they actually had failed in their attempt to lure Jesus into an injudiciously seditious comment about paying taxes to Caesar earlier (cf. 20:21–26). Again, they, not Jesus, verged on the brink of supporting treason as they insisted (vv. 18–19) that a proven lethal insurrectionist be restored to freedom among them in lieu of Pilate's releasing the innocent Jesus.

Third, they fraudulently represented Jesus to be a proven politicized royal messianic pretender. Luke had just portrayed Jesus as carefully evading their attempts to bully him into compromising himself in this regard during their interrogation (cf. 22:66–71).

Nevertheless, by ascribing to Jesus royal as well as messianic pretensions, they heightened the aura of potential political threat, a threat Pilate could not afford to ignore. It immediately caught Pilate's attention (v. 3). Still, Jesus' ambiguous response to Pilate's query about his political ambitions (v. 3b) sounded to Pilate like a denial. (The religious leaders earlier had taken a similar ambiguous response from Jesus to be affirmative—cf. 22:70b–71.) He would not have dared to adopt the position implied by his statement in v. 4 if he had understood Jesus' answer to be a blatant affirmation of royal ambitions.

Jesus' accusers summarized their allegations against Jesus (v. 5) by branding him an agitator of the people. The way in which they did it sought to exploit any prejudices Pilate might still entertain against Galileans (cf. 13:1) to enlist him in their program to kill Jesus. It was certainly true that the authoritative clarity with which Jesus taught about God and God's purposes for creation and humanity evoked appreciative astonishment and stimulated vigorous loyalties that may well have appeared to anyone observing from a distance as potentially volatile agitation. Still, that did not begin to stack up with the anti-Roman political agitation already perpetrated by their preferred alternate, Barabbas.

(*b*) *Pilate referred Jesus to Herod's jurisdiction.* The Jewish leaders' devious intent in reminding Pilate of Jesus' Galilean associations backfired. Instead of provoking Pilate to pronounce immediate lethal condemnation, it suggested to him a way by which he might be able to avoid having to act in the matter. Since Galilee was Herod's responsibility, Jesus was *Herod's* problem (vv. 5–7). (Frustrated in their push for a swift judgment and not willing to leave anything to chance, the religious leaders had to troop along with those escorting Jesus to Herod to ensure that Herod might not treat the matter indifferently and, out of disinterest, simply let Jesus go—v. 10).

There is an historical irony behind the incident. Pilate sent Jesus, who had been reported to him as claiming to be "the king of the Jews," to Herod Antipas, whom Rome had refused to designate "the king of the Jews" (as Rome had designated Herod the Great before him). That in itself should have been sufficient to bias Herod against Jesus. But we recall that

Luke had mentioned earlier in his Gospel that Herod had been intrigued by reports about Jesus (9:9) and, at one time, had resolved to execute him (13:31–33).

Apparently Herod's animosity toward Jesus had diminished. Certainly he had moderated his earlier murderous intent. Verse 8 mentions no less than three times (*another* triplet!) Herod's eagerness at the chance to see Jesus.

Luke used the term "to see" ironically. Herod did not want to "see" Jesus in the sense of perceptive reflection and recognition of his real identity and God-empowered purpose. Herod simply did not want to miss the chance to see firsthand a demonstration of flamboyant, bizarre, magical behavior—to "see a sign"—about which he had heard reports (v. 8). The sign that he could not see was the fact that Jesus, the royal Messiah who as Son of God would be seated at God's right hand to judge all creation, must submit to this humiliating procedure.

Where shepherds had seen their Savior, Messiah, and Lord in the baby in the manger and had been moved to praise and glorify God (2:11–12, 20), Herod only saw in the mature Jesus a ridiculous, ludicrous pretender and was moved to degrading mockery (v. 11). Perhaps Herod, for all of his contempt of Jesus, was not unmindful of the tremendous popularity Jesus had attracted in Galilee as well as in Jerusalem. At any rate he evaded having to make final disposition of the matter and sent Jesus back to Pilate for formal judgment. It was inexcusably incongruous that a shared disdain for the captive Jesus and a common reluctance to be the one to decide his fate should become the catalyst that spurred Herod and Pilate to reorder their own relationship on a more congenial level (v. 12).

(*c*) *Remanded back to Pilate, Jesus is sentenced to be executed.* Luke saturated the final scene before Pilate where Jesus received condemnation (vv. 13–25) with irony and incongruity. Pilate, who was being called on to pass judgment on Jesus, served as his advocate, pleading his innocence with the adamantly homicidal crowd, and even pleading Herod's failure to sentence Jesus (v. 15) as corroborating witness to Jesus' guiltlessness. The name of the incarcerated insurrectionist whom "the chief priests, the leaders and the people" loudly preferred to have loose among them meant "son of the father"; the one whose destruction they demanded had been correctly named by them "Son of God" (22:70).

Luke and his copyists provided helpful clarifications. Verse 19 is Luke's parenthetic identification of Barabbas, with an explanation for why he had been imprisoned. A later copyist supplied an explanation for why the crowd suddenly demanded the release of another prisoner in response to Pilate's offer to release Jesus (v. 17). Contemporary translators of Luke's Gospel sometimes are overzealous. The NRSV's "have him flogged"

(v. 16) is more severe than the Greek word, which only indicates a light lashing intended as official remonstrance and warning.

Pilate was in a delicate and potentially volatile position. Condemning Jesus to execution without clear cause violated Roman justice, but flaunting the autonomy of Roman power and control before this incensed crowd could well provoke insurrection and riot. (Pilate had been the instigator, earlier, of a Jerusalem uprising because of his insensitivity to Jewish religious feelings.) So Pilate elected the expedient. He chose to pervert Roman justice in order to mollify the mob. He released a proven insurrectionist and murderer, and delivered over for execution one whom he had just pronounced innocent three times.

Preaching on this passage might begin with the following:

A kaleidoscopic array of characters surrounds Jesus and relate in various ways to him and to the events swirling about him as Luke unfolds the scenes of the Passion drama. The Evangelist exploited those varied postures to invite his readers/hearers to put themselves in each of those roles and to explore thereby the ambiguities, the ambivalences, even the hostilities in their own attitudes toward Jesus. This characteristic of Luke's narrative style is particularly evident in the Lukan account of Jesus' trial. We have not read it carefully enough until we have become participants in the story and tried on each role to test the limits and expose the reservations that mar our trusting devotion to Jesus.

Political expediency, jaded curiosity, satanically motivated mob psychology, grossly insensitive and sarcastic buffoonery—all were attitudes and inclinations represented by those clustered around Jesus during the course of his trial. Those attitudes and inclinations prevented them from seeing who Jesus was and what God was doing through him, and from responding to his presence in faith and adoration. Similar attitudes can impede our spiritual perception, too.

Even the adamant hostility of the religious establishment must be tried on for fit—the rigidly inflexible attitudes and aggressively defensive actions of sincerely religious people who are preoccupied with preserving the heritage of the tradition. They can lose view of the dynamic of the faith, and that makes them liable to resist and even to oppose the Jesus who would make all things new.

THE CRUCIFIXION (23:26–56)

Luke now arrives at the culminating crisis of his Gospel's account of the life and career of Jesus Messiah, the righteous Son of God. As Jesus' ministry progressed, the resistance, opposition, and hostility evoked by his unequivocal fidelity to the divine mandate to announce and inaugurate the restoration of the royal reign of God increased and hardened.

For all of the winsome authority with which Jesus proclaimed and taught, for all of the astonishing success he had in graphically demonstrating the reassertion of God's renewing rule through his mighty works, for all of the crescendo of popularity with which the people received him as he approached Jerusalem, his enemies have prevailed. Their plans to destroy him, having found a welcome though unexpected assist from Judas' treacherous defection, have crystallized.

The charade of orchestrating Jesus' examination and condemnation, first by themselves, then before a smirking Herod, and, finally, by the disinclined Pilate was accomplished. Having reluctantly released the rebel Barabbas, Pilate handed Jesus over to the chief priests, the leaders, and the people who escorted Jesus to the place of his execution, appropriately called "the Skull." The crowd of people surely included many of those who had shrieked for Jesus' execution, demanding that Barabbas be released instead.

(*a*) *Jesus delivers a prophetic oracle on the way to his execution.* As the procession began the trip to the crucifixion site, Luke introduced a singular saint who continues to tantalize the imaginations of pious Christians. Under coercion from those taking Jesus to be executed, Simon of Cyrene bore the cross (probably only the horizontal cross piece) behind Jesus (v. 26). Because of the task Jesus' captors forced on him, Simon serves as the proleptic model for the posture and performance of all followers of Jesus. He shouldered the cross and took up his position behind Jesus where all disciples who follow Jesus belong (cf. 9:23; 14:27).

A group of women in the throng took up the cultically correct ritual mourning in anticipation of Jesus' death. He admonished them with a prophetic warning that they should save their wailing for the indescribable desolation and grief soon to fall upon the Jewish people, and especially Jerusalem (vv. 28–31).

Jesus concluded the oracle with a proverbial saying that seems to mean: If Jesus, though innocent (full of the life of God), must endure that which looms now immediately before him, imagine what Jerusalem, which has compromised itself before God so often and in so many ways (so that through infidelity it has already become dead and dry), will have to endure. Luke's readers would recall the rapid Roman retribution for the recent Jewish revolt and the devastating destruction of the city of Jerusalem, which had occurred just ten or so years before.

(*b*) *Ridicule, remorse, and grief surround the cross.* Once Jesus was elevated and suspended on the cross, he was thrice reviled. The leaders, unable to restrain their shabby triumphalism, cruelly ridiculed him. The soldiers who had been detailed there to lend an aura of official acquiescence and civil order joined in with their taunts. Even one of the criminals who had been crucified with him derided and scorned him in his extremity. (Luke indulged a fondness for triple repetition in his version of the passion narrative—cf. the discussion of this feature in the previous section.) By the conclusion of this section, Luke has portrayed Jesus as deprived of his freedom (v. 26), his few remaining possessions (v. 34b), his dignity (vv. 35b–39), and his life (v. 46).

Accumulated before the cross was also a wide array of people who sympathetically suffered with Jesus and on Jesus' behalf. The ritually wailing and weeping women on the way (v. 27); the other contrite criminal from his cross (vv. 40–42), the awed centurion who was so impressed that only he articulated the just and correct verdict Rome should have pronounced on the charges against Jesus (v. 47); the receded cluster of those who had been associated with Jesus during his ministry (v. 49); the pious Arimatheite member of the Sanhedrin, in strikingly low profile until the very end, who dissented from that council's deadly decision and rashly risked rebuke by petitioning Pilate for permission to remove Jesus' body (vv. 50–52)—all provided a compassionate contrast to those who were there out of enmity and malice toward Jesus.

Their grief was reflected and confirmed by both cosmos and cultic place (vv. 44–45). Those startling phenomena made it unambiguously evident to the rest of the assembled throng, whether hostile toward Jesus or impassively curious, that God was not pleased (v. 48).

(c) *Reprise of the temptation of Jesus.* Jesus' public ministry was preluded with a temptation experience (cf. 4:1–13). It now concludes with another temptation scene, only this time the adversaries are far less persuasive.

The primary perpetrators of the unjust execution of Jesus vindictively intensified his suffering with their disdainful, sarcastic mocking. The religious leaders' sarcasm: "If he is the Messiah of God, his chosen one . . ." (v. 35), and the soldiers' harassment in echo of the sardonic inscribed crime: "If you are the King of the Jews . . ." (vv. 36–37) evoked a similar reaction from one of the criminals crucified with Jesus: "Are you not the Messiah . . . ?" (v. 39).

It was a renewal of the temptations, only this time through the derisive, contemptuous comments of those hostile to Jesus. Jesus will have none of it. He will not use his spirit-endowed power to serve himself, not even for self-preservation before the crisis of the cross, but only to serve God.

"He saved others" (v. 35)—only they did not really believe it, or they would be demanding his release. What they meant was, "*Supposedly* he saved others; it has been reported that he saved others."

The ironic error in those expressions of derision is profound. The reason why the Jewish religious authorities and the Roman civil authorities executed Jesus was exactly the reason why Luke and his community confessed Jesus to be the Christ of God. Because he is "King of the Jews," the Messiah of God, Jesus must not save himself by countering the will of God and evading the proffered cup of suffering.

It is in obedience to the will of God that he chose not to save himself and, thereby, continues to offer to save others—first, his executioners, the very ones who were mocking, humiliating, and murdering him (v. 34a); next, the repentant criminal (v. 43); and hordes of others ever since (cf. the Acts of the Apostles, etc.). There, on the cross, Jesus continued his mission "to seek out and to save the lost" (cf. 19:10).

Luke used the anecdote of the two contrasting criminals crucified with Christ (vv. 39–43) to illustrate dramatically the astonishing irony. The second, contrite, criminal recognized the spiritual validity to the charge under which Jesus was being executed as a politically dangerous, phony pretender. The radical peril of the criminal's situation underscored the urgent need for faithful response to the kingdom's summons. He admitted his own guilt and the justice in his fate in contrast to his recognition of Jesus' innocence and the injustice of his suffering and crucifixion. His request to Jesus was that Jesus think of him in the future when, at the end of time on the Day of the Lord, he would assume his royal role. It was a confession of Jesus' messiahship, and voiced trust and dependence on that messiahship, and on the God for whom Jesus was messianic agent.

With that confession, Jesus did exactly what the first, mocking criminal had demanded. Jesus, the spirit-empowered royal agent of the reign of God, is not impotent. There, on the cross, the Messiah of God continued to "save others" (v. 43, cf. vv. 35, 39). His enemies have not prevailed—*none* of them. Submission to the reign of God is a present option, not simply a future hope. Jesus' response to the confessing criminal promised immediate inclusion and eternal participation in Jesus' royal rule. As had been true throughout his ministry, Jesus mediated forgiveness for the penitent outcast. With the two criminals on their crosses, Jesus had again occasioned the "falling and the rising of (many) in Israel" (cf. 2:34); again he has given "light to those who sit . . . in the shadow of death" (cf. 1:79).

(*d*) *Jesus' death and burial, and the reactions evoked.* Luke's depiction of the death of Jesus is both brief and powerful. Dark portents of calamity in cosmos and cult presaged the moment of expiration. The entire creation reflected the fact that the sinister powers of darkness were at work (cf. 22:53). Though it drove dread chill through the onlookers (v. 48), with a final exclamation of confident conviction and reliance on God, Jesus serenely died. Uttering words from Psalm 31:5, he expired trustingly (v. 46), consistent to the end in that commitment and surrender to the will of God he had voiced on the Mount of Olives (cf. 22:42).

Luke recorded three different reactions to Jesus' death. In the person of the centurion, a representative of the might of Rome testified to Jesus' innocence of any capital offense and was moved thereby to praise the God Jesus served (v. 47). His perception motivated him to join the ever-expanding company that began when the shepherds saw the babe and returned "glorifying and praising God" (cf. 2:20).

The crowds—curious, indifferent, caustic, concerned—were stunned by the intensity of it all. Whatever else was occurring, this was not like all of the other executions that habitually were carried out in this somber place. A phenomenon of creation-wide import had transpired and they sensed their culpability (v. 48).

Of special interest to Luke and to Luke's intended audience was the response of the group of those who had been associated with Jesus (v. 49). They stood off "at a distance." The returns for them were not all in yet. The potential for denial was still there (cf. 22:54). Luke made specific mention of the women in anticipation of the special role they shortly were to play. Of supreme significance was the fact that they simply were there, witnessing Jesus' death, for thereby they were singularly qualified to testify as eyewitnesses to the veracity of that aspect of the church's Easter proclamation.

Luke's account of the burial of Jesus is affirmation of an act of considerable courage by one who belonged to a group from which Jesus and his followers had no reason to expect anything but antipathy. Joseph of Arimathea personified Luke's persuasion that a different posture concerning Jesus by a Jewish religious leader before Pilate was possible. His petition having been granted, Joseph reverently wrapped and respectfully deposited the corpse in a hitherto unused tomb.

The Galilean women followers of Jesus observed the interment, thereby qualifying them to verify later that the body of Jesus actually had been buried. As agonizing as the entire series of episodes had been for them, the awesome import of it all still had not penetrated their awareness. In an almost offhand remark to "business as usual," Luke noted their obedient observance of the ordinary Sabbath restrictions. But *the curtain of the Temple had been torn in two* (v. 45)!

A review of Luke's dependence on First Testament themes can provide a broadened context for homiletically exploring this passage:

Luke shared the conviction of many early Christians that details of the events surrounding Jesus' death fulfilled anticipations that were in the

Jewish scriptures. Through allusions and by his use of "bible language" (intentionally shaping his writing style to reflect the biblical idiom), he urged his readers/hearers to make those connections, too. An illuminating exercise, which will disclose Luke's artful interweaving of scripture traditions, is to look up quotations and likely allusions in this section to passages in the First Testament: v. 27—Zech. 12:10–14; v. 28—Jer. 9:17–22; v. 29—Isa. 54:1; v. 30—Hos. 10:8; v. 31—Isa. 11:1; vv. 32 (cf. 22:37), 34a, 43—Isa. 53:12; v. 34b—Ps. 22:18; v. 46—Ps. 31:5–6.

David Tiede (*Luke,* [Minneapolis: Augsburg Publishing House, 1988], pp. 412–413) helpfully directs our attention to the section describing the "torture and murder of the righteous one" in Wisdom of Solomon 2–5 (a book in the OT Apocrypha) as a passage that may well have informed Luke as he shaped his version of the execution of Jesus. To extend the exercise, additional OT references to investigate may be secured from commentaries on the Gospel of Luke.

"THE SON OF MAN HAS BEEN RAISED!" (24:1–53)

The final chapter in Luke's narrative of the life and ministry of Jesus recounts two traditions about the discovery of the empty tomb, the eucharistically modified account of the experiences of two followers from Emmaus, the appearance of Jesus among his followers, his further instructions to them, and his departure. Luke presented this series of occurrences as having all taken place within the space of a single day—the Day of Resurrection (cf. vv. 1, 13, 33, 36, 44, 50–51).

The events related in this chapter form the climax to his Gospel, the first part of his two-volume literary effort, and, in addition, serve as transition to the continuation of the story in the second part, the Acts of the Apostles. Themes prominent in the telling of events in chapter 24—the return of the disciples to Jerusalem, the wait for empowering, their illumination to comprehend the scriptures, their qualifications as witnesses, the anticipatory reference to the mission they will be charged to carry out, Jesus' ascension into heaven—all are recalled and reiterated by Luke in the first two chapters of Acts in order to weld together the two parts of his narrative work.

It is likely that members of Luke's community already knew multiple stories about appearances of the resurrected Jesus. Early Christians told and retold them frequently. Those stories illumined central facets of the faith they professed and the gospel message they taught and preached. In the early years of the church's formation and growth, there were eyewitnesses who could confirm the death of Jesus (cf. 23:49) and his burial (cf. 23:55). But *no one* had seen the actual resurrection event. Still, those who had seen his body placed in the tomb could relate how, three days later, his body was gone from the stone grave site where they had seen it placed.

An even larger group of the earliest Christians could relate their eye-witness experiences when the risen Jesus appeared to them, talked to them, ate with them, and gave them specific directions for what they were to do in the interval ahead. (Paul reported in 1 Cor. 15:5–8 that the pool of firsthand witnesses to post-resurrection appearance experiences eventually rose to include over five hundred Christians.)

These appearance reports were important confirmation traditions that supported the church's teachings. Accounts of post-resurrection appearances by Jesus corroborated by stories that the tomb really was empty substantiated the proclamation of the community of faith that Jesus was not dead, for God had raised him from the dead and elevated him to a position of honor and authority in God's presence.

The Empty Tomb (24:1–12)

Luke made careful preparation in his narrative for the inclusion of the account of the discovery of the empty tomb at this juncture. During his telling of Jesus' crucifixion, as he described the knot of Jesus' followers who witnessed his death from a distance, he specifically noted that the group included "the women who had followed him from Galilee" (23:49). As Joseph of Arimathea completed his compassionate yet precarious service on Jesus' behalf, Luke noted that same group of women followed and witnessed the burial of the corpse.

(a) *The women are reassured by two divine attendants.* Luke indicated the importance with which he regarded the episode, first, by relating the story of the women's discovery of the empty tomb as the initial scene in his narration of Jesus' resurrection and, second, by finding occasion twice later to allude to it. The reason why Peter rushed to the tomb (v. 12) was because he was as dubious and skeptical as the rest about their report, and he wanted to test its veracity firsthand. In the succeeding episode, the two disappointed disciples from Emmaus specifically referred to both occurrences, the women's experience and report, and Peter's astonished verification (vv. 22–24).

The women brought their preparations to the grave only to be startled at finding the tomb open. That they were unable to find Jesus' body served as counterweight for any potential misunderstanding the stories of post-resurrection appearances might evoke to the effect that what appeared to disciples both within and without Jerusalem was a spectral apparition (cf. v. 37).

Luke described the two men whom they did encounter (v. 4) in such a way as to repeat a motif encountered earlier, in his account of Jesus' transfiguration. There Jesus, dressed in dazzling attire, and two supernatural figures spoke together of his "exodus" that was to happen in Jerusalem (cf. 9:29–30). Only later (v. 23) do we learn what is implicit here, namely, that they were angels.

These divine messengers asserted and thereby gave anticipatory, supernatural confirmation to what would be central to the affirmation of the community of the Easter faith, "He is not here, but has risen" (v. 5c). What did the women make of that? Did they remember what Jesus had told them (cf. 9:22; 13:32–33)? They should have made the connection before, even without hearing the angels' stunning statement. That they had not, however, was indicated 1) by their transparent intent to complete the process of preparation of the corpse for interment, and 2) their intense surprise at the open, empty tomb, for which the angels chided them (v. 5b).

(b) Will the women grasp the radical revision to reality that the messengers' message requires? Did the women make the connection after they saw the empty tomb and heard the angels' announcement? That is the central issue with which Luke wants us to struggle, not only in response to this episode but with the entire chapter. There is a motif of rebuke, admonition, and correction woven throughout the events of chapter 24 (cf. vv. 5, 25, 38, 44, 46). Even if the events leading up to and including what happened on the Place of the Skull were so overwhelming as to defy the perspective of faith, have the women gotten it right since then, after having heard the angels' word? Will the rest of the disciples get it right after hearing their report? After seeing the resurrected Jesus? After touching him? After sitting at table-fellowship with him? After being illumined by him? After listening to his instructions and charge?

Luke located the women in the vanguard of the community of the Easter faith. They belonged to the inner circle of the disciples. They had exercised concern and initiative for tending to his needs both in life (cf. 8:1ff.) as well as when he was dead. They had heard his instruction to his disciples concerning his betrayal, death, and resurrection.

The story is about more than sensory experience—what the women saw or did not see, what they found or did not find. It has to do with seeing with perception, with remembering, with putting things together in the broader context, with making the appropriate connections. It has to do with believing.

Did the messengers' words jolt the women to recall what Jesus had told them previously and make the connection? They remembered (v. 8); they made the connection. In Mark's version, although the women were instructed to tell the disciples, they raced from the tomb in sheer panic and did not tell anyone for fear (cf. Mark 16:8). However, Luke described them as assuming the posture of faithful witnesses and testifying to others about what they knew to be true. They took the initiative and reported their experience to the apostles without even being told.

The critical issue now becomes, what do the others make of their testimony? None of them remembered Jesus' words, either. That was why, instead of standing before the tomb to welcome their resurrected Lord, disciples were returning home, or were huddled in fearful uncertainty and grieving misery in Jerusalem. Peter, impelled by curiosity, raced to the tomb and found it empty (v. 12)—but did not yet remember. So he returned amazed, but not yet faithful. Not only did the other "soon-to-be-apostles" fail to make the connection, they dismissed the women's report as fiction. That testified not to a chauvinistic, Semitic paternalism toward women, but to the demonic darkness in control that had blinded them and all the others to the purposes of God as disclosed in scripture.

Preaching on this passage might explore the following:

What stimulated the dejected disciples to begin to look at the entire situation in a new light? Luke hints that the cumulative effect of faithful testimony can begin to turn the tide. The women's report, reinforced by Peter's experience of an appearance by the resurrected Lord (puzzlingly not related but only alluded to by Luke), prodded them to expressions of the beginning glimmers of belief. This was further supported by the description brought by the two Emmaus disciples of their illuminating experience with the resurrected Jesus when they were together at the table (v. 34).

It surely took a lot to convince them, finally, of the realization of the Easter hope. What does it take to make us believe? Luke has already told us in the words of Jesus that if we do not believe Moses and the prophets we will not make the connection, not even if someone were raised from the dead (cf. vv. 25–27; comp. 16:31).

The disciples remembered and made the connection only after their minds were opened and their hearts empowered to perceive and believe the astounding truth (vv. 32, 44–47, 49). How have we remembered? In what ways has God illumined our minds and empowered our hearts to perceive and, making the connection, to believe? How would God use our testimony to excite perception in others?

Walking to Emmaus (24:13–35)

In his rendering of the Emmaus tradition, Luke masterfully recasts a story well known to early Christians, and he places it at a climactic moment in his narrative. It is a dramatically moving story that has nurtured sincere pious reflection for countless Christians. The account progresses from sorrowful imperception, through joyful recognition, to eager, urgent proclamation.

Such insightful illumination is not a human accomplishment but depends entirely on the active intervention of God. (Note the passive verbs representing the direct activity of God in both v. 16 and v. 31.) Nevertheless, those who attend faithfully to the scriptural testimony concerning God's will and purposes as God has previously made them known will be advantageously positioned so that the divine revelation concerning Jesus will have the most positive impact.

(*a*) *The structure of the account.* The story artfully employs the narrative framework of a double sequence of events related in reverse order:

> A. The disciples departed from Jerusalem (vv. 13–14),
>   B. Jesus appeared and joined them (v. 15),
>   C. God prevented their recognizing Jesus (v. 16),
>   D. Interval of dialogue and interaction (vv. 17–30),
>   C'. God caused their perceptive recognition (v. 31),
>   B'. Jesus vanished (v. 32),
> A'. The disciples returned to Jerusalem (v. 33).

During the interval at the center of the story, indicated as "D" in the outline, as Jesus accompanied the Emmaus disciples he listened to their imperceptive misreading of recent events (vv. 17–24), admonished and reproved them (vv. 25–26), and instructed them (v. 27)—all of which took place "on the road" (vv. 32, 35). It echoed that extended interval on the road from Galilee to Jerusalem prior to the Passion (9:51–19:28, cf. esp. 9:57: "along the road," 10:38; 14:25; 17:11; etc.), during which Jesus had devoted himself to similar activity with the larger group of his disciples who had not comprehended any better than had the Emmaus pair.

In both cases, physical proximity to Jesus and auditory reception of his teaching were insufficient to evoke recognition, comprehension, and acceptance. It took openness and an interval of being together (v. 29), culminating in religious table-fellowship with the risen Lord who was the table host (vv. 30, 35), for it all to fall into place for them. When it did happen, they had to tell others right away, no matter what (v. 33)—no matter how inconvenient (it was late in the evening by then) or taxing the effort (they had already made the trip once that day), no matter how incredibly astonishing and startling the content of their report (v. 35).

(*b*) *Disciples above all must see with perception.* That the dejected disciples traveling back home to Emmaus were unprepared to be encountered by the resurrected Jesus offered Luke the opportunity to introduce the motif of perceptive discernment so central to this story—and to his entire Gospel narrative. It was not only, or even primarily, that the Jesus who had been raised from the dead was so radically transformed as to be unrecognizable. The story dramatized the point that if one has not listened "to Moses and all the prophets" one is unprepared to perceive. Because of that spiritual inattention, many underestimated the extent to which Jesus during the course of his earthly ministry was the embodiment of all that God had disclosed through scriptures. For such as them, even someone raised from the dead is obscure and enigmatic (cf. 16:31). Seeing the resurrected Jesus with clarity involves more than visual acuity. It requires openness, responsiveness, and acquiescence to divine illumination.

Jesus' request to discover what they were discussing (v. 17a) permitted Luke to give an overview of those events that had transpired since Jesus' arrest (vv. 19–24). It reinforced for his hearers recognition of the tremendous importance of those events as components of the church's testimony.

What took place was widely known (v. 18). What those events meant in the context of the purposes of God was not nearly so evident. The dismal demeanor of the two travelers (v. 17b) demonstrated that their perception as to the true significance of those events was lamentably deficient.

The disciples told a lot about themselves as they reported their version of recent events to the stranger who had unexpectedly joined them. Because they had underappreciated the full identity of Jesus and the scope of his role in God's reclamation program for all of creation, the consequence was calamitous. They knew only part of the incredible story of Holy Week. They, like the other disciples, were reluctant to grant credulity to the women's report, even when ratified and explained by "a vision of angels" (v. 23). They did not make the essential connection between the fate of Jesus and the messianic anticipations attested in scripture. (Luke returns to this crucial issue in vv. 44–47.)

(*c*) **Scripture discloses what the "recent events" mean.** Jesus' rebuking response (vv. 25–26) insisted that, to those reading perceptively and with belief, scripture plainly predicted the fate of the Messiah of God that he had just endured. Rather than having particular texts in mind, Luke indicates here that the cumulative disclosure of God's will and purposes as revealed throughout Moses and the prophets pointed toward and found fulfillment in Jesus.

What God had promised to accomplish for creation can be recognized as attained in the resurrected Messiah. It forms an *inclusio* with the narrative with which Luke initiated his account of Jesus' public ministry when he read from "the prophet Isaiah" (4:16–21), then announced, "Today this scripture has been fulfilled in your hearing." With mention of Jesus' insistence on the necessity of all this (v. 26), Luke nudged his hearers to recall repeated predictions of the passion Jesus had given to the disciples during the course of his public ministry (9:22, 44; 13:33–34; 17:25; 18:31–33; 20:13–14; 22:22, 37).

(*d*) *Jesus hosts the meal in their house at their table.* Although Jesus had taken the initiative in joining them as they traveled the road toward Emmaus, he would not intrude uninvited into their home. They had to take the initiative to offer hospitality as piety required and invite him to stay with them, share the shelter of their house, and join with them in the religious fellowship of a meal around their table. Eucharistic echoes of the Last Supper reverberate (cf. 9:16; 22:14ff.; especially v. 19) as Jesus and the two Emmaus disciples were at table.

It was the two disciples' house and their food, but paradoxically it is Jesus who hosts. With the breaking of bread God cleared their vision and they knew who he was. Those two disciples saw Jesus more perceptively and completely—even though "he vanished from their sight"—than they had ever seen him from their association with him either before his execution or during the extended walk they had just made together with him to their village.

The breaking of bread occasioned a revelatory recollection. The connection between what God had promised through Moses and all the prophets and what God had delivered through Jesus became clear. It produced within them reflective recognition of how extensively and intensively Jesus had illumined their spiritual understanding of scripture while they had traveled the road together. That scriptural testimony disclosed the purposes of God embodied in the person of the Messiah. Jesus is the Messiah who perfectly interprets the will of God revealed in scripture.

A sermon on the passage might develop from the following:

The two Emmaus disciples serve as a paradigm for the entire church. Like them, believers ever since, by reverently receiving word and sacrament, have encountered, experienced, and recognized who Jesus is and what God has accomplished and is accomplishing with him. Like them, members of the community of faith need to recover the central convictions of trusting Christian belief and be transformed, in the remembering and in the eucharistic celebration, to have their eyes opened, to be renewed and supported, to be given to each other as the Body of Christ, to be taken, blessed, broken, and given to the world as Christ's presence in it and for it.

In the conclusion to the story of the walk to Emmaus, there occurred what always should occur as a consequence of spiritual perception and insight into the accomplishment of God's royal will. The two disciples, now single-mindedly focused on their recognition of the resurrected Jesus to the suppression of every other concern, responded faithfully to the urgency of the opportune moment and went back to Jerusalem to announce such good news to the others.

They were greeted with similar testimony of awakened recognition and glad realization called forth by Simon's report of the appearance of the resurrected Christ he had experienced. Their combined testimony met the minimum requirements under Jewish law to establish veracity. (Luke's community must have known the story of Jesus' appearance to Peter— cf. 1 Cor. 15:5. Why Luke only referred to that tradition without relating this important incident is a mystery.) So the reports of the two appearances reciprocally supported and reinforced each other.

It is striking to note that, at first, the two Emmaus disciples testified to their conviction concerning the resurrected Messiah only to others of Jesus' disciples. They announced the Easter proclamation to those whom they believed to be still as despondently hopeless as they themselves had been when they first downheartedly left Jerusalem for Emmaus. Only later, after they will have received "power from on high" (v. 49) will they give their testimony expression before nonbelievers (vv. 47–48; cf. Acts 1:8).

Appearance and Ascension (24:36–53)

In the concluding segment to the first half of his two-volume work, Luke summarized and reiterated important observations already made in the story. He also anticipated the continuation of the narrative in the second volume. This section outlines the necessary theological perspective in terms of which the Acts narrative makes sense.

Prior to his heaven-bound departure, Jesus showed himself to the Eleven and the others (vv. 36–43), taught and enlightened the disciples' minds for understanding (vv. 44–47), charged them with a missionary mandate (vv. 47–48), instructed them concerning their impending supernatural empowering (v. 49), and blessed them (v. 50), after which he departed from them into heaven (v. 51). The disciples obediently did as he told them (v. 52).

In this final section to Luke's Gospel, his listeners hear significant elements that will be repeated in Luke's resumption of the narrative in the Acts of the Apostles. Examples include: Jesus appeared to the disciple-apostles and taught them (Acts 1:1–3, 6–7), gave to them instructions with reference to the approach of their divinely promised empowering with the Holy Spirit (Acts 1:4–5, 8a), commissioned them (Acts 1:8b), and was taken up from them into heaven (Acts 1:9). The disciple-apostles did what he said (Acts

1:12), received the promised baptism of the Holy Spirit (Acts 2:1–4), and immediately embarked on their mission (Acts 2:4b–12, 14–36, etc.).

(*a*) *Jesus instructs the disciples prior to his ascension.* The appearance of the resurrected Jesus to the Eleven together with the broader circle of disciples in Jerusalem (vv. 36–43) reinforced and confirmed the reports of similar, related occurrences (vv. 10, 12, 34–35). It also qualified those present to function as witnesses to the accuracy of the Easter message and the presence of the royal rule of God it so dramatically proclaimed.

Jesus' sudden, inexplicable appearance in their midst severely rattled those gathered there, who misinterpreted its significance (vv. 37–38). Unprepared as they were to grant credulity to the reports of others, they were equally unready to trust their own direct and immediate experience, assuming instead that they were being afflicted with a spectral apparition.

Jesus' invitation to the disciples for tactile confirmation of his physical reality (perhaps by implication to note the visible presence of crucifixion wounds) and his act of consuming the fish served to demonstrate the corporeal continuity of the resurrected Jesus with the crucified and buried Jesus. Luke held that in narrative tension with the assertion in the prior story when the disciples on the road to Emmaus did not recognize him, which attested to the apparent discontinuity between the crucified Jesus and the resurrected Jesus.

Even as all of the firsthand evidence accumulated, it was still insufficient to move them to affirming joyous faith. Table-fellowship with the risen Jesus and enlightened insight into the scriptural testimony confirming Jesus' messianic fulfillment of the saving purposes of God drove them to conviction. (Both components were pivotal in the previous story of the faith awakening of the Emmaus disciples, although the sequence is reversed.)

These transforming experiences are available to all, even if the corporeal appearances of the risen, ascended, and exalted Jesus have ceased for the interim. Spiritual perception at the eucharistic meal correlates to cognitive perception of the full sense of scripture. Opened eyes and opened minds communing with Jesus are what it takes to see clearly and to comprehend with discernment.

(*b*) *Jesus opens the disciples' minds to comprehend the testimony of scripture.* The central portion (vv. 44–49) of this concluding segment to his Gospel was especially significant for Luke—and for Luke's listeners, then and now. Jesus gave his disciples perceptive access to that scriptural testimony not only for their own expanded comprehension but also as the primary authoritative corroboration to their announcement concerning Jesus the Messiah that they will be making before others (v. 48).

"Everything written about me in the law . . ." (v. 44), "thus it is written . . ." (v. 46)—the scriptures testify that all that has occurred to Jesus conformed to the revealed will of God. Luke has now insisted three times in this final chapter on the divinely established necessity of Jesus' suffering and resurrection (v. 46; cf. vv. 7, 26). Far from thwarting God's purposes for restoring creation, the passion of Jesus had been anticipated from the beginning and was integral to the accomplishment of those purposes. The will of God revealed in scripture ("the law of Moses, the prophets, and the psalms") is most clearly and profoundly comprehended when read and interpreted in the light of Jesus' passion and resurrection.

Jesus charged his followers to continue his proclamation of the restoration of the royal reign of God, and to effectively extend its control. This was the mandate that shaped Jesus' ministry (cf. 4:18–19) and that will shape the work of the church (cf. Acts of the Apostles, especially 1:8). This commissioning of the disciples plays off and expands the earlier commissioning of the Twelve (cf. 9:1–6) and of the Seventy (10:1–12).

The disciple-apostles have the content of the message they are being commissioned to carry to the entire inhabited world (v. 47b). They have been schooled by Jesus to situate the specific events of Jesus' own life and ministry including, especially, his passion and resurrection in the broader scope of the saving purposes of God stretching all the way back through the salvation-history of Israel to the dawn of creation as attested in scripture. They have the supporting and verifying testimony of their own direct firsthand experiences with the risen Jesus. All that they lack is reception of the outpouring of that supernatural dynamism that will effectively empower their witnessing proclamation.

As Jesus had received "power from on high" (v. 49) prior to launching his public ministry (cf. 3:21–22), so the disciples must be empowered prior to beginning their mission in the service of the royal rule of God. For that supernatural power they must wait, for without it they have nothing to say that will matter. It will come to them in Jerusalem. Jerusalem was the goal of Jesus' extended journey during his public ministry, the place of his pain-filled "departure" (literally "exodus") (cf. 9:31) where human antipathy and resistance to God's reclamation of creation for divine rule reached its apogee in the crucifixion of Jesus, the locus of his triumphant restoration, and vindication from death and the grave. Jerusalem is to become the point of inauguration of the proclamation by the community of the Easter faith, which ultimately will extend the heralding of the rule of God to every nation.

Jerusalem thereby also will be the first audience the infant church will summon to repentance, and to which the church will proclaim God's forgiveness in the name of Jesus—precisely to those who just recently were shrieking "Crucify him!" (cf. 23:21, 23). So great is God's mercy, so re-creating is God's love.

(c) *Jesus' assumption into heaven.* The abbreviated report of the ascension (v. 51) marks the conclusion of the physical appearances of the resurrected but not yet heavenly glorified Jesus (cf. v. 26). He will continue to appear to followers, but not as a corporeal presence (Acts 7:55; 9:3–6; 1 Cor. 15:5–8; Rev. 1:13). Those latter experiences, while essentially different, still were effective for giving validating testimony. Repeatedly Jesus will be immediately known and experienced by the believing community in the breaking of bread, through scripture that tells of him, and through the power from on high that Jesus, in accord with God's promise, is sending upon them.

A Lukan reprise of the ascension scene may be found recorded in Acts 1:9–11. Luke described it there as occurring after an extended forty-day period rather than as in Luke 24 on the day of the resurrection. The interval carries the symbolic number "forty," which occurred frequently in the biblical narrative as a prelude to the launching of a significant new stage in salvation history. (It functions much in the same way as forty years in the desert prior to Israel's conquest of Canaan, Jesus' forty days in the wilderness prior to the beginning of his public ministry, etc.)

As Jesus was being taken from them, the disciples—all of whom have now seen their risen Lord, been enlightened and taught by him, received his charge and instructions to wait for divine empowering—all join in that swelling great chorus of joyful worship of God that began with the angels and the shepherds (cf. 2:14, 20). Worship in the curtain-torn temple after the events and experiences of Easter surely have a different quality and tone than worshipers had ever experienced before.

BIBLIOGRAPHY

A wealth of commentaries is available on the Gospel of Luke. Very thorough and detailed analysis of each verse, together with dependable if sometimes pedantic interpretation, may be found in Joseph A. Fitzmyer, *The Gospel According to Luke,* The Anchor Bible, 2 vols., Garden City, N.Y.: Doubleday & Co., 1981, 1985.

Commentaries that are slanted more toward congregational teaching and homiletic appropriation but that have less descriptive information than Fitzmyer include:

David L. Tiede, *Luke,* Augsburg Commentary, Minneapolis: Augsburg Publishing Co., 1988.

Fred B. Craddock, *Luke,* Interpretation, Louisville, Ky.: John Knox Press, 1990.

Frederick W. Danker, *Jesus and the New Age,* Philadelphia: Fortress Press, 1988.

Eduard Schweizer, *The Good News according to Luke,* Atlanta: John Knox Press, 1984.

Some interesting theological studies illumining major themes or aspects of the Gospel of Luke include:

Charles H. Talbert, *Reading Luke,* New York: Crossroad, 1982.

Raymond E. Brown, *The Birth of the Messiah,* Garden City, N.Y.: Doubleday & Co., 1977.

Charles E. Carlston, *The Parables of the Triple Tradition,* Philadelphia: Fortress Press, 1975.

Douglas R. A. Hare, *The Son of Man Tradition,* Minneapolis: Fortress Press, 1990.

Luke T. Johnson, *Sharing Possessions,* Philadelphia: Fortress Press, 1981.

Jacob Jervell, *Luke and the People of God,* Minneapolis: Augsburg Publishing House, 1972.

David P. Moessner, *Lord of the Banquet,* Philadelphia: Fortress Press, 1989.

Robert F. O'Toole, *The Unity of Luke's Theology,* Wilmington, Del.: Michael Glazier, 1984.

Norman Perrin, *The Resurrection according to Matthew, Mark, and Luke,* Philadelphia: Fortress Press, 1977.

Joseph B. Tyson, *The Death of Jesus in Luke-Acts,* Columbia, S.C.: University of South Carolina Press, 1986.

Collections of stimulating essays may be found in *Political Issues in Luke-Acts,* ed. Richard J. Cassidy and Philip J. Scharper, Maryknoll, N.Y.: Orbis Books, 1983; and in *Luke-Acts: New Perspectives from the Society of Biblical Literature Seminar,* ed. C. H. Talbert, New York: Crossroad, 1984.